Regional Trade and Economic Integration

Analytical Insights and Policy Options

Regional Trade and Economic Integration

Analytical Insights and Policy Options

Ram Upendra Das
*Research and Information System
for Developing Countries, India*

Piyadasa Edirisuriya
Monash University, Australia

Anoop Swarup
Shobhit University, India

 **World Scientific**

NEW JERSEY · LONDON · SINGAPORE · BEIJING · SHANGHAI · HONG KONG · TAIPEI · CHENNAI

Published by

World Scientific Publishing Co. Pte. Ltd.

5 Toh Tuck Link, Singapore 596224

USA office: 27 Warren Street, Suite 401-402, Hackensack, NJ 07601

UK office: 57 Shelton Street, Covent Garden, London WC2H 9HE

British Library Cataloguing-in-Publication Data
A catalogue record for this book is available from the British Library.

REGIONAL TRADE AND ECONOMIC INTEGRATION
Analytical Insights and Policy Options

ISBN-13 978-981-4374-60-6
ISBN-10 981-4374-60-1

In-house Editors: Sandhya Venkatesh/Divya Srikanth

Typeset by Stallion Press
Email: enquiries@stallionpress.com

Printed in Singapore by B & Jo Enterprise Pte Ltd

To Our Teachers and Our Families

Contents

Preface   xiii
Acknowledgments   xvii

Chapter 1: Introduction   1

1.1. India's Trade Policy Reforms   2
1.2. Rationale   5
1.3. Scope   5

Chapter 2: Regional Economic Agreements of India: Status,   7
                Potential, and Some Experiences

2.1. Experience Gained from Implementation   7
    2.1.1. India–Bhutan Free Trade Agreement   7
    2.1.2. India–Nepal Trade Treaty   8
    2.1.3. India–Sri Lanka Free Trade Agreement   8
    2.1.4. South Asian Free Trade Area Agreement   9
    2.1.5. India–Afghanistan Preferential Trade Agreement   12
    2.1.6. India–Thailand Early Harvest Scheme and FTA   14
    2.1.7. India–Singapore Comprehensive Economic   15
        Cooperation Agreement
    2.1.8. India–ASEAN FTA   18
    2.1.9. India–Malaysia CECA   21
    2.1.10. India–New Zealand CECA   23
    2.1.11. India–Indonesia CECA   24
    2.1.12. Asia Pacific Trade Agreement — The erstwhile 26
        Bangkok Agreement
    2.1.13. Global System of Trade Preferences   27
    2.1.14. East Asia Summit   29

Annex 2.1   31
Annex 2.2   57
Annex 2.3   58

Chapter 3:   The Economics of Regional Integration and   63
                 Analytical Insights from Negotiations

3.1. Economic Rationale of Regional Integration   63
      3.1.1.   Adjustment cost versus efficiency concerns   63
      3.1.2.   Linkages between trade in goods and trade   66
               in services
      3.1.3.   Trade-Investment linkages   67
      3.1.4.   Importance of regional economic integration   67
               for scale expansion
      3.1.5.   Trade creation and diversion   68
      3.1.6.   Trade diversion not necessarily bad   69
      3.1.7.   Rules of origin: Developmental outcomes   69
      3.1.8.   Some empirical estimates   70
      3.1.9.   Tests of stationarity   74
      3.1.10. Levin–Lin–Chu test   75
      3.1.11. Im–Pesaran–Shin test   76
      3.1.12. Hadri test   77
3.2. Analytical Insights from Negotiations   80
      3.2.1.   "Substantially all trade"   80
      3.2.2.   Sensitive list   81
               3.2.2.1. Safeguarding the sensitivities of the   81
                        agriculture sector: Lessons from RTAs
                        of the ASEAN countries and some
                        developed countries
               3.2.2.2. Treatment of agriculture sector in   91
                        agreements of the developed countries
               3.2.2.3. Summary   93
      3.2.3.   Rules of Origin   94
               3.2.3.1. The rationale   94
               3.2.3.2. Modalities   95
               3.2.3.3. Change in tariff heading versus change   96
                        in tariff subheading

3.2.3.4. Rules of Origin as a development policy 98
tool
3.2.3.5. Enhancing the feasibility of welfare-inducing 99
FTA
3.2.4. Trade in services 100
3.2.4.1. Uniqueness of services 100
3.2.4.2. Major characteristics of services 100
3.2.4.3. Theories of trade in services 101
3.2.4.4. Relevance of services trade integration 104
in SAARC
3.2.5. Investment cooperation 105
Annex 3.1 107
Annex 3.2 111

Chapter 4: Empirical Estimation of Economic and Welfare 145
Gains

4.1. Computable General Equilibrium Modeling Estimates 145
(GTAP Simulations)
4.2. Effects of Tariff Reduction and Trade Facilitation 146
4.2.1. Simulation results 146
4.2.1.1. GDP and welfare gains 146
4.2.1.2. Trade gains 147
4.2.1.3. Saving, investment, and net foreign 148
capital inflows
4.2.1.4. Intra-FTA imports and prospects for 149
exports to the world
4.3. Bilateral FTA 150
4.3.1. India–Thailand FTA 150
4.3.1.1. The model and assumptions 150
4.3.1.2. Impact not captured by the model 153
4.3.1.3. Potential areas of trade expansion 156
4.3.2. India–Malaysia FTA 161
4.3.2.1. Bilateral exports projection 161
4.3.2.2. Computable General Equilibrium simulations 162
4.3.2.3. Gains from the EAS process 164

Annex 4.1   168

Chapter 5: Policy Implementation Issues in Regional   171
           Trading Arrangements

5.1. Circumvention   171
   5.1.1. Objective to check unfair trade practices   171
           5.1.1.1. Antidumping Duty (AD):   171
                    Price-discrimination
           5.1.1.2. Countervailing duty: Foreign export   173
                    subsidy
   5.1.2. Circumvention of rules: Case studies   173
           5.1.2.1. Tariff-rate quota   173
   5.1.3. Are rules necessarily bad?   177
5.2. Improving Implementation   177
   5.2.1. Harmonization of codes, valuation, and procedures   177
   5.2.2. E-implementation   183

Chapter 6: Issues for Further Negotiations   185

6.1. Non-tariff Barriers   185
6.2. Major Categories of Non-tariff Measures and Related   190
   Policies
   6.2.1. Quantitative restrictions and similar specific   190
           limitations
   6.2.2. Non-tariff charges and related policies affecting   191
           imports
   6.2.3. Government participation in trade, restrictive   191
           practices, and more general government policies
   6.2.4. Custom procedures and administrative practices   193
   6.2.5. Technical barriers to trade   193
6.3. Trade in Services   193
   6.3.1. GATS framework   194
   6.3.2. Approaches to trade in services liberalization   195
           6.3.2.1. Economic Needs Tests   195
           6.3.2.2. Negotiating modalities   195

6.3.2.3. Approaches to interrelated services sectors 196
6.3.2.4. Transparency in domestic regulation 196
6.3.3. Rules of origin for services 196
6.4. Investment Cooperation 200
6.4.1. Investment and services inter-linkages in 206
Regional Trading Agreements
6.5. Trade Facilitation 209

Chapter 7: Conclusion 215

Bibliography 217

Index 229

Preface

*"Who that recalls the attention of mankind to any part of learning which time
has left behind may be truly said to advance our age"*

Samuel Johnson

*Regional Trade and Economic Integration: Analytical Insights and Policy
Options* acquaints reader to the terms and concepts necessary for academicians, policy makers, businessmen, and students in the emerging borderless
world of new economic engagements. The book covers a wide and rich
array of topics that, though being contemporary, do not lose sight of the
basic principles in this very fast, interconnected, and ever changing world
of sociopolitical and geopolitical landscape with economic implications.

This book show cases the enormous effort that has gone into collecting and analyzing a substantial number of Regional Trade Agreements
(RTAs) among nations. In particular, the book presents the recent emergence of China and India as economic powers and the trend of trade and
economic engagement within the Asia Pacific region that has become a
significant area of interest even to the general public. As international
trade has been increasing among the countries in the region, many have
decided to explore possibilities to introduce free trade by negotiating Free
Trade Agreements (FTAs), due to its many advantages. This book
comprehensively covers the existing economic cooperation arrangements
in the region as well as those that are at various stages of study and
negotiations.

Understanding the nature of free trade requires a conceptual framework as well as perspective — drawn from historical and recent advances
in the area of international trade — including those from the economic
agreements in India and the Asian region. The organization and coverage of the book is innovative in a number of ways.

The introductory chapter lays the foundation for the book by examining the rationale and scope of India's trade policy reforms, including its trade and economic agreements. The second chapter expands upon the economic agreements of India and Asia in terms of their status of implementation and negotiations in a synoptic way.

The third chapter tries to explain the trends in the proliferation of RTAs as documented in the previous chapters. This chapter presents a more comprehensive analytical basis for RTAs, often not captured in the existing literature on the subject. In doing so, it brings about certain new analytical insights from trade negotiations.

Traversing a wide canvas of conceptual issues underlying RTAs, this research enters into the domain of empirical estimation of economic and welfare gains potentially emanating from RTAs and accruing to trade and economic partners in the fourth chapter. The Computable General Equilibrium (CGE) Modeling estimates with the help of GTAP simulations form the core of such empirical analysis. However, some of the well-known limitations of CGE estimations given in the book also supplement the empirics by taking recourse to various other methodologies.

Extending the analysis of RTAs in terms of its conceptual and empirical basis, the book finds it necessary to examine issues related to policy implementation. The fifth chapter fulfills this necessity by focusing on various policy implementation issues in RTAs, including unfair trade practices; circumvention of rules of origin; customs codes, valuation, and procedures; and e-implementation.

The sixth chapter further looks at issues on which negotiations are much more difficult due to lack of objectivity that prevails in different countries' trade and economic regimes. These include non-tariff barriers, restrictive practices, custom administrative practices, technical barriers to trade, rules of origin for services, and investment cooperation. Apart from illustrations for better understanding and case studies for ease of reference, the book also provides topics suitable for students to ensure coverage from an academic perspective.

In this era of globalization, the book sheds light on the very complex and myriad world of free trade and regional economic engagements and allows the reader to discover new perspectives and insights in order to improve business and trading options for better profitability and policy analysis. This book is not only meant as an asset for graduate students, but has also been written with policy makers, experts, academicians, researchers, and the curious readers in mind. We are sure that this book will emerge as an invaluable source of analysis and reference for professionals and amateurs alike, and a veritable resource for posterity.

Dr. Ram Upendra Das
Dr. Piyadasa Edirisuriya
Dr. Anoop Swarup

countries brought about by India's former Prime Minister Mr. A. B. Vajpayee and present Prime Minister Dr. Manmohan Singh. This shift has and shall remain crucial for broader economic integration efforts both toward the *Eastern* and the *Western* arcs.

Dr. Ram Upendra Das
Dr. Piyadasa Edirisuriya
Dr. Anoop Swarup
17 December 2011
New Delhi

CHAPTER 1

Introduction

The global trends in economic growth across countries have traversed different economic regimes over the past decades. In the more recent decades, the globalization process has entailed decisive policy changes throughout the world. It has resulted in trade openness and greater emphasis on foreign direct investment and stabilization policies for redefining the role of the state, among other changes. Observations reveal that there have been positive growth outcomes in both the developing and developed worlds. However, it has also been noticed that while the developing world has been unable to reap the full benefits in terms of economic growth across countries, the developed world has shown signs of sluggish growth in country-specific contexts. More recently, the subprime debt–related global financial crisis has complicated the issue further (see Chandrasekhar and Ghosh, 2010; Griffith-Jones et al., 2010; Sen, 2008; Stiglitz et al., 2006).

Another major global trend has been in the realms of trade interactions among countries. Along with the advent of WTO, in contrast to previous decades, the last decade has witnessed the growth of Regional Trading Arrangements (RTAs) at an unprecedented pace (see Figure 1.1). By January 2005, around 312 RTAs were notified to GATT/WTO (Crawford and Fiorentino, 2005). As of June 15, 2006, about 197 RTAs were in force (WTO, 2006). It is important to highlight that there has been a major increase in the number of RTAs since 1995. A rather well-known fact is that around two-thirds of the global trade is conducted on a preferential basis than the MFN basis.

Such a scenario raises the issue of the impact of increasing regionalism on the growth prospects of various economies. In the wake of the recent global financial meltdown, there has been an increased emphasis on RTAs, as observed in the case of India.

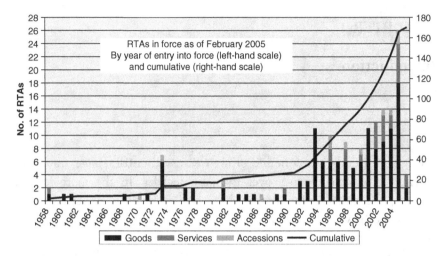

Figure 1.1. Notified RTAs to the GATT/WTO (1948–2005) by entry into force. *Source:* Crawford and Fiorentino (2005).

Furthermore, an attempt has been made to analyze the conceptual and empirical basis of RTAs, with special reference to a developing country such as India.

1.1. India's Trade Policy Reforms

As summarized in Box 1, the Indian trade policy strategy considers trade as not an end in itself but a means to economic growth and national development. "The primary purpose is not the mere earning of foreign exchange, but the stimulation of greater economic activity." Any Free Trade Agreement (FTA) between India and a partner country needs to be viewed with such a consideration. In addition, trade-related activities need to be viewed in a comprehensive manner by forging economic co-operation links with other countries that can help at various levels of developmental pursuits such as employment generation, innovation, and infrastructural improvements.

In recent times, India has engaged actively in regional economic integration processes at various levels of bilateral, sub-regional, and regional cooperation. India has a treaty of trade with Nepal and an FTA with

Box 1: India's Trade Policy Strategy

Context

For India to become a major player in world trade, an all-encompassing, comprehensive view needs to be taken for the overall development of the country's foreign trade. While increase in exports is of vital importance, we have also to facilitate those imports which are required to stimulate our economy. Coherence and consistency among trade and other economic policies is important for maximizing the contribution of such policies to development. Thus, while incorporating the existing practice of enunciating an annual Exim Policy, it is necessary to go much beyond and take an integrated approach to the developmental requirements of India's foreign trade. This is the context of the new Foreign Trade Policy.

Objectives

Trade is not an end in itself, but a means to economic growth and national development. The primary purpose is not the mere earning of foreign exchange, but the stimulation of greater economic activity. The Foreign Trade Policy is rooted in this belief and built around two major objectives. These are:

(i) To double our percentage share of global merchandize trade within the next five years; and
(ii) To act as an effective instrument of economic growth by giving a thrust to employment generation.

Strategy

These objectives are proposed to be achieved by adopting, among others, the following strategies:

(i) Unshackling of controls and creating an atmosphere of trust and transparency to unleash the innate entrepreneurship of our businessmen, industrialists, and traders.
(ii) Simplifying procedures and bringing down transaction costs.
(iii) Neutralizing incidence of all levies and duties on inputs which are used in export products, based on the fundamental principle that duties and levies should not be exported.
(iv) Facilitating development of India as a global hub for manufacturing, trading, and services.

(*Continued*)

Box 1: (*Continued*)

(v)   Identifying and nurturing special focus on areas which would generate additional employment opportunities, particularly, in semi-urban and rural areas, and developing a series of "Initiatives" for each of these.

(vi)   Facilitating technological and infrastructural upgradation of all the sectors of the Indian economy, especially, through import of capital goods and equipment, thereby increasing value addition and productivity, while attaining internationally accepted standards of quality.

(vii) Upgrading our infrastructural network, both physical and virtual, related to the entire Foreign Trade chain, to international standards.

(viii) Activating our Embassies as key players in our export strategy and linking our Commercial Wings abroad through an electronic platform for real-time trade intelligence and enquiry dissemination.

Source: Department of Commerce, Preamble. In *Foreign Trade Policy: 2004–2009*, Ministry of Commerce and Industry, Government of India.

Bhutan. Both the experiences have been successful in generating bilateral trade flows on a preferential basis. India also signed and implemented an FTA with Sri Lanka, which has also emerged as a success story. India is also actively participating in the South Asian Free Trade Area (SAFTA) agreement.

More recently, India has implemented an Early Harvest Scheme (EHS) with Thailand under the Framework Agreement. Presently, negotiations for the India–Thailand FTA are underway. A Comprehensive Economic Cooperation Agreement (CECA) has also been implemented between India and Singapore, which includes agreements for promoting trade in goods and services as well as investment.

The India–ASEAN FTA and BIMSTEC FTA are also at different stages of implementation and negotiations, and efforts are on to build upon various initiatives leading toward an Asian Economic Community. Studies and negotiations are underway for examining the feasibility of bilateral economic cooperation initiatives viz., India–China, India–Japan, India–South Korea, India–Malaysia, etc. India is also focusing on cooperation to augment trade and investment with GCC, Central Asian Republics, Africa, MERCOSUR, etc. Economic partnership agreements with developed regions like the EU and the US are also being contemplated upon.

These measures indicate that India is making attempts to tap trade complementarities with various countries and regions in the world by taking advantage of the trade creating effects of regional trading blocs. However, there is not even one study of these economic engagements of India, which takes a comprehensive view of the subject.

1.2. Rationale

In the background of the above scenario, the basic need for undertaking such a study is three-fold: (i) India's familiarity with regional economic engagements makes it possible to synthesize some new insights pertaining to the economics of RTAs and CECAs; (ii) an empirical examination is undertaken to determine the potential economic gains for India and partner countries, across various agreements; and (iii) on the basis of the above two, inferences are drawn to evolve policy options for India, in future, alongside a broader regional cooperation architecture in Asia.

1.3. Scope

The scope of the book would cover most of the existing economic co-operation arrangements of India and those that are at various stages of study and negotiations. It will also draw upon some of the relevant aspects of major trade and economic engagements of other Asian countries.

CHAPTER 2

Regional Economic Agreements of India: Status, Potential, and Some Experiences

In this chapter, a brief overview of India's regional economic agreements, ranging from a Preferential Trade Agreement (PTA) to Comprehensive Economic Cooperation Agreement (CECA), is presented. Depending upon their status of study, their economic potential and/or experience is highlighted, in order to set the context for subsequent chapters.

2.1. Experience Gained from Implementation

2.1.1. India–Bhutan Free Trade Agreement

The bilateral Trade Agreement between India and Bhutan provides free trade and commerce. Commercial transactions are carried out in Indian Rupees and Bhutanese Ngultrum. India provides unhindered transit facilities to landlocked Bhutan, in order to facilitate its trade with other countries. Bilateral trade and economic relations continue to run smoothly. India is Bhutan's largest trade partner. In 2008, exports from India constituted 73.8% of Bhutan's total imports. Bhutan's exports to India in 2008 constituted 99.4% of its total exports.

Petroleum products, cereals, motor vehicles and their spare parts, iron and steel products, machineries and mechanical appliances, chemical products, edible oil, wood charcoal, and coal are India's main exports to Bhutan. Besides, electricity, calcium carbide, gypsum, ferro-silicon, particle-board, and Portland cement are the main imports from Bhutan. Indian vehicles dominate the automobile market and have captured more than 80% of the market. Government of India (GOI) funded projects have also contributed to increasing imports from India (MEA, 2004, 2009; Mehta and Narayanan, 2006; and MoC, 2004, 2008).

2.1.2. India–Nepal Trade Treaty

Indo–Nepal relation, on trade and other related matters, is governed by the bilateral Treaties of Trade and Transit and Agreement for Cooperation to Control Unauthorized Trade.

Under the international conventions and with Nepal being a land-locked country, India is obliged to provide only one transit route to facilitate Nepal's trade with third countries. Already, 15 transit routes have been provided through the Indian Territory and more such routes can be added to the list with mutual agreement. In addition, facilities have also been provided for Nepalese trade with Bangladesh by road and rail routes and with Bhutan by road route. Movement of Nepalese goods from one part of Nepal to another through the Indian Territory is also permitted. On the request of Government of Nepal, an additional transit route was opened during 1997 through Phulbari–Banglaband to facilitate movement of Nepalese goods to and through Bangladesh over a shorter distance.

India gave permission for the duty-free entry of goods of Nepalese origin in order to provide a special privilege to that country. This led to a large-scale duty-free import into India of items using substantial inputs of third-country origin with minimal value addition in Nepal, causing losses to the Indian industry. Accordingly, as provided in the Treaty, the process of negotiations was initiated for making modifications in the Treaty and its Protocols, in order to address the problems faced by the Indian industry. The India–Nepal Treaty of Trade was reviewed and modified on March 2, 2002, for the restoration of the concept of value addition on imports from Nepal and thus making the value-addition criteria more transparent (see Mehta and Narayanan, 2006). This has tackled the problem of trade deflection and contributed to bilateral trade in recent years.

2.1.3. India–Sri Lanka Free Trade Agreement

Sri Lanka has traditionally been an important export market for India and is the second largest importer of Indian goods in the region after Bangladesh.

Both India and Sri Lanka signed a Free Trade Agreement (FTA) on December 28, 1998, in order to phase out the tariff on a large number of items within an agreed time frame except for those in the negative list.

Since March 2000, trade has grown rapidly, turning Sri Lanka into one of the India's largest trade partners in the SAARC region. India is Sri Lanka's largest trade partner worldwide. India accounts for 16.8% or one-sixth of the total trade turnover of Sri Lanka. Bilateral trade rose to US$3.3 billion in 2007. Exports from India to Sri Lanka amounted to US$2.8 billion, while imports from Sri Lanka stood at US$516.5 million. India is the biggest source of Sri Lankan imports and the third largest destination for Sri Lankan exports. In 2008, total trade stood at US$2.8 billion.

What is more, with Foreign Direct Investment (FDI) approvals of over US$500 million, India is also the fourth largest investor in Sri Lanka. The Indian Oil Corporation (running 170 petrol pumps as well as managing the Trincomalee Oil Tank Farm), Taj Hotels, L&T, Ambujas, Tatas, and Ashok Leyland are among the prominent Indian companies operating in Sri Lanka. Bharti Airtel is another Indian company venturing into Sri Lanka as the fourth mobile operator (MEA, 2009). It points to the dynamics of trade-investment linkages in the region since the implementation of the FTA.

2.1.4. *South Asian Free Trade Area Agreement*

The SAARC region comprises Afghanistan, Bangladesh, Bhutan, Maldives, Nepal, Pakistan, and Sri Lanka. It is considered as a major step forward in making a transition from SAARC Preferential Trading Arrangement (SAPTA) to a South Asian Free Trade Area (SAFTA) Treaty, which was signed in January 2004. India has recently extended duty-free, quota-free scheme for the Least Developed Countries (LDCs). A particular Mechanism for Compensation of Revenue Loss (MCRL) to LDCs has also been agreed upon. The Rules of Origin (ROO) formulation includes Change in Tariff Heading (CTH) at four-digit Harmonized System (HS), along with domestic value content of 40% for non-LDCs (LDCs) and 30% for LDCs. Product-Specific Rules (PSRs) for 191 tariff lines on technical grounds where both inputs and outputs are on the same four-digit HS level have also been agreed.

It may be further highlighted that, while some of the apprehensions concerning SAFTA's success are genuine, several of them are based on unfounded reasons. The South Asian region, with its geographical contiguity and cultural, social, and historical ties, has good potential for emerging as a strong, efficient, and dynamic region in an economically integrated setting. However, there is no economic cooperation in the region due to the lack of awareness of the potential for cooperation and costs of non-cooperation. A detailed quantitative assessment of costs of non-cooperation in the SAARC region has revealed that some SAARC members imported many items at higher unit values than those imported from within the SAARC region. That is why these countries lose enormous amount of scarce foreign currency resources.

In the context of SAFTA, it is widely believed that trade diversion would outweigh the trade creation effects and hence, SAFTA could be welfare-reducing. However, it may be argued that trade diversion effects need not always have negative connotations. It is often believed that trade diversion in some products could itself lead to trade creation in other products over a period of time.

Having highlighted the potential of the region in generating trade, it is prudent to point out that trade generation is not merely a function of tariff reduction alone, as envisaged primarily by the SAFTA Treaty. Tariff liberalization, though not a sufficient condition, could only be an enabling condition for enhancing trade flows. In the absence of measures that strengthen trade-investment linkages, the economic impact and even impact on higher trade flows of SAFTA would remain limited. It would also be limited if non-tariff barriers are not addressed adequately as argued.

In the context of SAFTA, one of the arguments often forwarded is its limited product coverage. While one must take cognizance of such an issue, the implementation of SAFTA needs to be viewed in a positive perspective. The more important issue is not the product coverage but the enhancement of the trade capability of the SAARC countries. For this, mechanisms to forge trade-investment linkages would be crucial. Setting in place policy mechanisms toward this objective would help augment the level of export supply capabilities and also contribute to export diversification in case of sectoral targeting. This can be executed by spurring intra-SAARC investments as well as attracting extra-SAARC investments into the region.

One of the major limitations of SAFTA is that the terms of its scope are restricted to cover trade in goods only. Most often, the inter-linkages between trade in goods and services and the concomitant need for investment forging them are not given adequate consideration. It can be argued that trade in goods cannot be stepped up, unless institutional mechanisms exist for facilitating trade in services. Similarly, trade in services in a sector is often dependent upon trade in goods pertaining to the specific service sector. Thus, the region needs to recognize the two-way linkages with the trade in goods and services; otherwise, SAFTA's impact on trade in goods may remain limited.

Over the past decade, services have emerged as the engine of growth in the SAARC economies. The service sector is also emerging as an important source of employment. Some SAARC countries have also begun to exploit the potential of services in trade. However, the trade potential of services remains to be exploited by the region. Recognizing this, the SAARC Heads of State or Government at their 13th SAARC Summit (Dhaka, November 12–13, 2005) had called for a study to see how services could be integrated into the SAFTA process. At their 14th Summit (New Delhi, April 3–4, 2007) also, the Leaders stressed that to realize its full potential, SAFTA should integrate trade in services, and called for finalization of an Agreement in the services sector at the earliest. Accordingly, the Study on Potential for Trade in Services under SAFTA Agreement was launched within the framework of the SAARC, Network of Researchers on Global Financial and Economic Issues with Research and Information System for Developing Countries (RIS) along with New Delhi as the Coordinator, on the basis of national studies prepared by each national focal points with the support of the Asian Development Bank.

Upon the adoption of RIS Regional Study Trade in Services and as per the recommendation of the SAFTA Committee of Experts (COE) the Third Meeting of SAFTA Ministerial Council held in New Delhi on March 3, 2008, decided as follows: "The Meeting appreciated the fact that the Regional Study on Potential of Trade in Services under SAFTA Agreement has since been concluded. It commended the Research and

Information System for Developing Countries (RIS), New Delhi, and the National Focal Points for their hard work in finalizing the Study."

"The Meeting endorsed the recommendations of the Third Meeting of SAFTA COE and decided that RIS be requested to draft the text of Draft SAARC Framework Agreement on Trade in Services (SAFAS) by June 30, 2008." Subsequently, a Draft SAFAS (Das, 2008) was submitted to the SAARC Secretariat, which was signed by the SAARC members at the Thimpu Summit (2010) after deliberations (see Annex 2.1 on SATIS).

In sum, the preceding insights underscore the imperatives of strengthening trade-investment linkages for moving beyond SAFTA and to reap the full potential of regional economic integration in the region in trade in services. Against this backdrop, countries in the region need to understand the dynamics of mutual economic interdependence in the context of economics of neighborhood. This, apart from yielding economic benefits, has the potential to create peaceful coexistence via regional economic cooperation.

2.1.5. India–Afghanistan Preferential Trade Agreement

The Agreement for Preferential Trade Agreement between India and Afghanistan was entered on March 6, 2003, and it was made effective by issuance of customs notification for tariff concession and rules of origin on May 13, 2003.

Afghanistan provided a 100% concession of duty for eight tariff items imported from India. India, on the other hand, provided concession of basic customs duty varying from 50% to 100% of applied rate of customs duty for 25 tariff items on goods imported from Afghanistan.

The extension of concession was subject to fulfillment of conditions of Rules of Origin as agreed between the governments. In other words, the benefit of concessional customs duty on import into India will be granted to the notified products only when they meet the conditions of Rules of Origin and goods that are exported directly from Afghanistan.

The Agreement also reiterate the Article III of GATT, 1994, of National Treatment to provide no less favorable treatment to domestic products in respect of internal taxation and all other domestic laws and regulation that affect their sale, purchase, transportation, distribution, or use. However, the fact is that the Indian states, in their zeal for revenue collection and with total disregard to India's commitment to World Forum, levy the taxes. An example of such taxation is the sales tax by Delhi Government that discriminates sugar and fabrics as imported and levies sales tax on them, while these items are exempted from sales tax when produced domestically.

The Agreement provides for termination of the agreement after serving six months notice. The Agreement also authorizes the governments to apply their domestic legislations to restrict import in cases where prices are influenced by unfair trade practices, including subsidies or dumping. Hence, even after allowing duty preference, India still can impose safeguard duty or anti-dumping duty wherever circumstances so warrant.

Rules of Origin

The concession of basic customs duty on import into India is available only when goods conform to the Rules of Origin notified on this behalf. The Indian importer has to make a declaration to the customs authorities at the time of clearance of consignment that the products are produced or manufactured in Afghanistan and such products are eligible for preferential treatment under the India–Afghanistan Agreement. Further, with respect to consignment under import, the importer has also to furnish to customs authorities the Certificate of Origin issued by authorities nominated by the Afghanistan Government. For the purpose of export from India, the Export Inspection Council is the sole agency to issue the Certificate of Origin.

The benefit of concessional duty on import is available only when the products have been wholly produced or manufactured in Afghanistan. The examples of wholly produced or obtained goods are raw or mineral products extracted from soil, water, or seabed of Afghanistan; vegetable products harvested; animals born and raised there; and waste and scrap resulting from manufacturing operation conducted there.

The benefit can also be extended to goods even when they have not been wholly produced in Afghanistan but have undergone sufficient manufacturing to achieve specified value addition and emergence of a new product. At present, items that are products in raw form and have not undergone any manufacturing process are eligible for concessional duty; however, a provision does exist to include some manufactured products in future to ensure continuity of concession.

Under this provision, benefit of concessional duty on import can also be granted on products that are not wholly produced or obtained in Afghanistan. The benefits are:

- Value of the inputs, such as product, or parts of products produced in countries other than Afghanistan and used in finally exported products that do not exceed 50% of the FOB value of export;
- Final process of manufacturing is performed in Afghanistan;
- A different new product, at four-digit tariff level, emerges out of inputs used for that final product. Even after emergence of new tariff heading at four-digit levels, the benefit of concessional duty can be granted only if sufficient working or processing was involved therein. The example of insufficient working is the simple assembly of parts of products to complete the product.

However, some relaxation has also been provided with respect to value addition, and it has been dealt as cumulative Rules of Origin (ROO). This relaxation is when goods exported from India have been used as inputs for the manufacture of goods that have finally been imported from Afghanistan. In this case, it will be sufficient for granting concessional duty benefit that is provided on the total value addition in both the country i.e. India and Afghanistan, which is 40% minimum and also on value addition on the country that exports the product at 30% minimum.

2.1.6. India–Thailand Early Harvest Scheme and FTA

During the State visit of the Thai Prime Minister to India in November 2001, it was agreed that India and Thailand would explore together the possibility of establishing a bilateral FTA with a view of intensifying trade and economic relations between the two countries. It was also decided that a Joint Working Group (JWG) at the Government level be set up to undertake feasibility study on an FTA. The JWG has, in its Fourth meeting in Thailand on December 22–23, 2002, finalized its Report (Das *et al.*, 2002).

The study has concluded that there exists immense potential for enhancing cooperation in trade and other areas such as services and investment and also the proposed FTA was feasible and mutually beneficial.

The framework agreement to establish the Thailand–India Free Trade Agreement (TIFTA) was signed on October 9, 2003. Trade negotiations to move closer to full liberalization are still continuing and are expected to be concluded by 2010. To accelerate the realization of benefits, both countries agreed to implement an Early Harvest Scheme (EHS) covering trade in goods for 84 products. The TIFTA–EHS covered a three-year period between September 1, 2004, and August 31, 2006, and has now ended.

The 84 items (HS code six-digit level) under the TIFTA–EHS included fruits (fresh mangosteens, mangoes, durian, rambutans, longans); fishery products (salmon, sardines, mackerel); electrical appliances (window/wall air-conditioners, color TVs, ball-bearings); precious metal and jewellery; polycarbonates etc. Tariffs on these goods were cut by 50% on September 1, 2004, 75% on September 1, 2005, and eliminated entirely on September 1, 2006.

It has been found that both the countries have benefited due to the EHS. Thailand is certainly benefiting more than India with respect to TIFTA–EHS, as total exports to India have increased much more than the total imports from India. Now that the EHS has ended, Thailand should support a continuation and extension and propose to merge it into the broader Thailand–India FTA for the benefits of both countries. Authorities, however, should be very careful in listing the products to be included in the agreement, by examining the trade impacts on the country's economy, efficiency, and welfare.

2.1.7. India–Singapore Comprehensive Economic Cooperation Agreement

After long-drawn negotiations, the CECA with Singapore was concluded in 2005. The India–Singapore CECA was signed on June 29, 2005, during Prime Minister Lee Hsien Loong's state visit to India. This landmark agreement is India's first ever CECA. It is also Singapore's first comprehensive bilateral economic agreement with a major developing country. The agreement encompasses trade in goods and services, investment protection, and other features like the Mutual Recognition Agreements (MRAs) that will eliminate duplicative testing and certification of products in specific sectors. The CECA process has also encompassed a review of the existing Avoidance of Double Taxation Agreement between India and Singapore. The India–Singapore CECA became effective from August 1, 2005.

The India–Singapore CECA entered into Phase-2 on December 20, 2007, when both sides agreed to further revise the tariff rates as agreed under the CECA signed in June 2005. According to the provisions of the revised CECA, India will further reduce tariffs on 539 items under the existing agreement. Out of this, tariff reduction for 307 items would be completed in five steps between January 2008 and December 2011. Tariff reduction for another 97 products would be completed in 9 steps between January 2008 and December 2015. For the remaining 135 items, tariff reduction of only 5% would be completed between January 2008 and December 2015. In this manner, after the implementation of the proposed tariff liberalization program, 93% value of India's total imports from Singapore would be the subject of tariff reduction process.

The existing potential of economic cooperation has remained hugely underutilized as the bilateral trade, investment, and business linkages have increased after the signing of the CECA. By 2009, Singapore emerged as the second largest source of FDI for India, with US$85 billion, accounting for 9% of total cumulative FDI inflows since 2000.

In addition to the increase in the bilateral trade, the CECA has also offered opportunities to the Indian companies for their market expansion in Southeast Asia. Being a regional economic hub, many Indian companies have extended their market operations to Singapore. Now almost 2800 Indian companies such as TATA, Mahindra, Godrej, Satyam Computers, and NIIT are functioning in Singapore, and the presence of Indian companies in Singapore has been growing at the rate of 10% per year.

The total FDI from Singapore to India also increased after the signing of the CECA, from US$893 million in September 2005 to US$2.127 billion in June 2007. Singapore is the sixth largest investor in India. However, Singapore's investment in India has remained much below the existing potential, since many sectors for investment such as ports, urban infrastructure, biotechnology, food processing, animation, entertainment, and tourism have not been explored fully. Given the expertise of Singapore in developing Special Economic Zones (SEZs) in China and Vietnam, the former could also be considered as a source of investment for establishing SEZs in India. The Singapore Business Federation (SBF), the apex business chamber, has also recommended huge possibilities for investment in the development of SEZs in India, especially in West Bengal. However, the lack of consensus among Indian political parties and continued protests over the setting up of SEZs have desisted Singaporean investors from investing in SEZs.

There are some other issues in the CECA which require immediate attention from both sides, such as the issue of movement of Indian professionals to Singapore. As a part of the CECA 2005, both governments had signed MRAs in goods and services along with the mutual recognition to the degrees and technical qualifications of each other's institutions. Both sides agreed to liberalize the visa regime on 127 categories of professionals. However, after two years of the signing of CECA, the movement of Indian professionals to Singapore has not gained momentum yet and Singapore has not shown enough willingness to recognize the technical and professional degrees of second-grade Indian institutes. Even India has not taken required initiative in this regard. In order to reap the benefits from the MRAs, both sides have to consider this issue seriously. Apart from government-level dialogue, the beginning of discussions between Indian professional bodies, such as the Institute of Charted Accountants of India and the Medical Council of India, and their respective counterparts in Singapore could also play an active role to sort out this issue at the earliest.

Moreover, a lot of effort is needed in the case of mutual recognition of the service sectors in both countries, particularly the recognition of banking services. Since Indian banks such as SBI and ICICI have not yet received the Qualified Full Banking (QFB) license in Singapore, the Singapore banks have also not been extended the QFB license in India.

An assessment of the CECA after two-and-a-half years shows that the bilateral trade that has gone up is not only due to the signing of CECA but also due to the lower tariffs that existed in Singapore before the signing of the CECA. As Singapore was already an open economy, the liberalization program in goods under the CECA was not the main area of India's interest. India's focus was, rather, on the tariff liberalization in services. However, due to the lack of required initiatives at the implementation level, the existing complementarities in the services sector could not be tapped fully. Therefore, now when India–Singapore CECA has entered into phase-2 and talks to establish CECA with EU, Malaysia, and Japan are in the pipeline, the appraisal of India–Singapore CECA conveys a message that only signing of an agreement is not enough. To extract all possible advantages from such agreements, close monitoring at the implementation level is needed.

2.1.8. India–ASEAN FTA

India's focus on a strengthened and multi-faceted relationship with the Association of South East Asian Nations (ASEAN) is an outcome of the significant changes in the world's political and economic scenario since the early 1990s and India's own march toward economic liberalization. India's search for economic space has resulted in her *"Look East"* Policy. ASEAN's economic, political, and strategic importance in the larger Asia-Pacific region and its potential to become a major partner of India in trade and investment is a significant factor in this context. India became a Sectoral Dialogue Partner of ASEAN in 1992 and Full Dialogue Partner in 1996. The political level mechanisms for ASEAN–India dialogue consist of the annual ASEAN–India Summit and an annual Foreign Ministers Meeting.

These political-level interactions are further strengthened through the Senior Officials' Meeting and also specialized working groups in the various functional areas: Science and Technology, Health, Trade, and Investment, and Transport and Infrastructure (GOI, Ministry of External Affairs, 2009).

Six years of obstacle-ridden negotiations between India and the 10-member ASEAN have finally culminated in giving shape to an FTA that the trade ministers of all these countries are comfortable with. The deal was formally inked in 2009. The government is confident that the overall benefits will outweigh any possible negative impact in some sectors, but some segments of Indian industry as well as farmers, especially plantation owners, are wary about the FTAs meaning in terms of import competition.

The FTA will provide the Indian trade and industry with access to a large and vibrant market in a region that is increasingly prosperous (Annex 2.2). This market is bound to expand further as the ASEAN trading bloc is already having FTAs with countries like China, Japan, South Korea, Australia, and New Zealand.

The FTA will result in import tariffs on substantially all trade among the signatory nations being reduced to nil in a phased manner through different lists with tariff reduction schedules of varying time-frames. The FTA also has a negative or exclusion list with around 489 items at HS six-digit level. This would benefit India, in particular, in sectors like oil cake, wheat, chemicals, synthetic textiles, steel, some types of auto components, and engineering goods. Plantation sectors such as natural rubber, tobacco, coconut, cashew kernel, areca nut, mango, orange, apple, and grape, along with main agricultural and marine products, are in the negative list on which no tariff concessions are committed. To protect the domestic growers, even after 10 years since the implementation of the FTA, India would be able to apply 45% tariff. Similarly, the tariffs could be 37.5% and 45%, respectively, on crude palm oil and refined palm oil even after 10 years, on which tariffs in India are at zero percent.

The recent debate on the India–ASEAN FTA is not on its desirability but its modalities. The debate has highlighted the need for striking a balance between addressing domestic economic concerns and the imperatives of international economic engagements. The domestic stakeholders need to view the India–ASEAN FTA in a broader long-term perspective. It is possible to argue that regional economic cooperation initiatives provide for an avenue to tackle efficiency concerns without losing sight of the requirements of a level-playing field for domestic economic entities. This is possible with the help of various mechanisms that an FTA entails. Efficiency concerns are addressed under a liberalized trade regime of an FTA, both through the pressures of improving export competitiveness with the availability of enhanced market access as well as through import-competition.

The very fact that trade liberalization is calibrated both in terms of its product-coverage and time-frame, ensures that the level-playing field is intact. Calibration of tariff liberalization both in terms of defining trade coverage as "substantial trade" and phased tariff liberalization schedules, thus, needs to be understood as a safeguard-modality. Safeguards are available on various other dimensions as well, including trade remedial measures like anti-dumping and countervailing duties, ROO stipulations, tariff-rate quotas, and negative list.

It is against this background that the India–ASEAN FTA needs to be approached. It is true that ASEAN has evolved as a source of very competitive supplies in recent years. However, with these safeguards in place, there may be very few instances where any other special measures are needed. On the other hand, India can source competitive inputs from ASEAN to improve its own manufacturing productivities. It may be reminded that ASEAN should be viewed also as an export destination of our products that have become equally competitive. In fact, there is ample evidence to argue that with relatively smaller neighbors, India must embark upon the path of unilateral concessions due to its inherent economic strength and export competitiveness. Considering that, on an average, the per-capita gross domestic product (GDP) of ASEAN as a grouping is almost double than that of India is a fact of significance from the demand side. Further, except the newer members of the ASEAN, the rest of ASEAN-6 has per-capita GDP greater than India. This simple observation points to the fact that a more intensive economic interaction with the ASEAN resulting in a greater market access for the Indian products would mean an opportunity for scale expansion.

In the second round, this would mean reaping the economies of scale and enhancing the export competitiveness of Indian exports, not only targeted to the ASEAN market but also to the global market. It is in this sense that a long-term view, which takes cognizance of the dynamic trade gains, needs to be adopted while analyzing the economic engagements with the ASEAN.

Taking these into account, the imperatives of ASEAN to formulate an FTA with India need a special mention. With India's per-capita income spread over a large populace and GDP rising at an unprecedented pace, it is ASEAN's turn to take a serious note of India's recent economic dynamism. ASEAN must acknowledge that the magnitude and direction of developmental challenges that India faces are second to none.

Prior to this, India had already displayed flexibility in agreeing to somewhat diluted ROO provisions (CTSH plus 35% local content) as a sign of acknowledgment of ASEAN's flexibility in accepting India's formulation of the twin-criteria along with detailed minimal operations. One way of further building safeguards in this respect is to have a sizeable number of PSRs of origin at HS six-digit level.

Going by the above scenario, India as a nation must not retract from international economic commitments. Domestic stakeholders must treat ASEAN as an opportunity, given the multifarious ways in which internal economic interests can be safeguarded. This can come about only when ASEAN as an economic grouping is viewed in a holistic manner and in a dynamic setting. In addition, the India–ASEAN agreement on trade in services and investment needs to be concluded for India to tap the ASEAN's services market and for ASEAN to integrate the Indian investment space.

2.1.9. India–Malaysia CECA

During the visit of Honorable Excellency Dato' Seri Abdullah Haji Ahmad Badawi, Prime Minister of Malaysia, to India and his meeting with Honorable Excellency Dr. Manmohan Singh, Prime Minister of India, on December 20, 2004, it was decided that a Joint Study Group (JSG) be set up to explore the feasibility of a comprehensive economic cooperation between the two countries. Subsequently, the Minister of Commerce and Industry, Government of India, and the Minister of International Trade and Industry, Malaysia, in their meeting on January 17, 2005, emphasized the desirability of a CECA.

The analysis of the JSG Report (2007) suggests that the bilateral trade volume between the two countries has remained low. Equally significant is the observation that the relative mutual importance in each other's trade is also low. Nevertheless, in the recent years, trade growth has been high, although trade flows have been highly volatile. It is also noticed that both bilateral exports and imports are characterized by high concentration and thinly spread shares across wide range of sectors.

The projection-estimates of India's exports to Malaysia are in the range of US$1 billion to US$5 billion by 2012. The estimates of exports from Malaysia to India would be in the range of US$3 billion to US$11 billion by 2012. The economic gains of the proposed CECA have been estimated using a multi-sector Computable General Equilibrium (CGE) model. The estimations were made for four scenarios, that is, (1) 50% import tariff reduction; (2) 50% import tariff reduction and trade facilitation; (3) 100% import tariff reduction; and (4) 100% import tariff reduction and trade facilitation.

Under the Scenario 1 with 50% import tariff liberalization; the change in value of GDP comes out as 0.55% per annum. It increases to 1.25% with the adoption of trade facilitation measures (Scenario 2). The figures increase to 1.16% and 2.6% in Scenarios 3 and 4, respectively. The gains can be considered as significant. The overall welfare gains range from US$662 million (Scenario 1) to US$2.24 billion (Scenario 4). While 79.3% of Malaysia's imports from India are subject to zero duty, about 78.7% of India's imports from Malaysia are subjected to duties of up to 5%. In both cases, the imports are limited to a narrow range of products. The study highlights that in a dynamic setting it is imperative that the range of products traded expands. As a consequence, increasing the range and volume of products would attract different levels of tariff (India–Malaysia JSG Report, 2007).

India and Malaysia are important destinations for FDI. Both countries have adopted proactive investment policies and measures to attract FDI inflows. Both countries are also becoming increasingly significant sources of outward investment. Although two-way investment flows between India and Malaysia are limited, the continuous investment flows and increase in bilateral trade in recent years indicate that there is potential for increased investment flows between the two countries. Based on the Central Bank of Malaysia (BNM) data, Indian investments into Malaysia during the period 2000–2006 totaled US$45.5 million, which is equivalent to approximately 0.06% of total investments into Malaysia. These investments were mainly in the construction and other services sectors, in particular, the utilities and transportation sub-sectors. Malaysia's investments into India from 2000 to 2006 amounted to US$110 million, most of it being in highway construction projects, hotels, and tourism and transportation industry. The study shows that there is potential in two-way investment flows in a number of sectors in both countries. These include power, roads, ports, telecommunications and civil aviation, IT sector, services like education, tourism, R&D, design and prototyping, and regional distribution centers, among others.

The inclusion of services in the CECA will benefit both countries. The sectors of mutual interest include medical, healthcare and diagnostics; advertising; audio-visual (including film making, production, and related services); education; computers, IT, and telecommunications; financial; tourism and travel, transport; architectural, construction, and engineering; distribution; human resource development; and accounting and taxation services (India–Malaysia JSG Report, 2007).

2.1.10. *India–New Zealand CECA*

In April 2007, the Indian and New Zealand Ministers agreed to undertake a joint study into the feasibility of negotiating a CECA or an FTA. The economic gains of the proposed India–New Zealand FTA were also estimated under a more liberal scenario of 100% tariff liberalization accompanied with trade facilitating measures in place, using a multi-sector CGE model.

The welfare gains can be considered modest but significant in the context of India–New Zealand FTA. The overall welfare gains range from US$2.5 billion for New Zealand (2.4% of GDP) to US$12.6 billion (1.4% of GDP) for India. The simulations suggest that the asymmetric gains emanate more from the trade facilitation measures rather than tariff liberalization, as exports do not show substantive increases. Given that the trade facilitation infrastructure and associated mechanisms in the case of India are much less developed, the gains accrue more to India than New Zealand. In this context, one of the assumptions made was that any improvements in trade facilitation infrastructure due to the sheer bilateral import volume that augments technical change would facilitate trade vis-à-vis the rest of the world as well. This was adopted uniformly for both India and New Zealand in the modeling simulation. Due to rather well-known inherent limitations of the CGE modeling, bilateral trade projections were also made with the help of time-series modeling. While India's exports to New Zealand are projected to increase in the range of US$231 million (2015) to US$345 million (2020), New Zealand's exports to India are projected to increase in the range of US$298 million (2015) to US$435 million (2020) in a dynamic setting. The asymmetric mutual exports gains can be explained in terms of New Zealand getting a relatively larger market access in India (JSG Report, 2009a).

2.1.11. *India–Indonesia CECA*

India and Indonesia are dynamic market economies and have undertaken wide-ranging economic reforms. Recognizing that the present economic linkages between the two are important yet below their potential, both the governments agreed to undertake a joint study for exploring the feasibility of a bilateral CECA and they set up a JSG in 2005. The study assesses the potential economic impact both in terms of trade and welfare gains arising out of the reduction of tariff barriers that could occur under the proposed CECA.

The different empirical estimates made by the JSG indicate that trade can increase manifold between the two countries. Detailed CGE modeling estimates and other methodologies of export projection suggest impressive trade and welfare gains that can result from trade liberalization under the FTA of the proposed CECA. In a partial-equilibrium framework, the projection-estimates of India's exports to Indonesia are in the range from US$1.7 billion to US$7.8 billion by the year 2020. The estimates of exports from Indonesia to India would range from US$3.4 billion to US$9.7 billion by 2020. In order to complement these estimated trade gains, welfare gains of the proposed FTA in goods have been estimated using a multi-sector CGE model. According to this model, the welfare gains accruing to India could be to the tune of 1.0% of GDP and to Indonesia to the extent of 1.4% of GDP under the scenario of full tariff liberalization along with setting in place trade facilitating infrastructure (Das, 2009). These estimates were complemented with some other estimates identifying potential products having comparative advantages, trade complementarities, intra-industry trade, etc., which could be the focus of bilateral trade expansion. Overall, the analysis of the various dimensions of trade in goods between India and Indonesia suggest that there is ample potential for bilateral trade expansion in a mutually beneficial manner for which adequate institutional mechanisms need to be put in place. These aspects build a strong case for setting in place an FTA in goods under the proposed bilateral CECA. The proposed CECA also aims at setting in place trade facilitation architecture by focusing on greater cooperation on customs facilitation, standards, mutual recognition agreements, sanitary and phytosanitary (SPS) measures, and trade remedial measures.

The JSG noted that while India and Indonesia are destinations of FDI inflows, both countries have also emerged as sources of outward investment in different sectors. The JSG further concludes that the proposed CECA would enable the establishment of more liberal investment conditions in a cooperative framework to support increased investment flows between the two countries alongside stronger investment facilitation and protection provisions. Some of the sectors amenable for investment from Indonesia into India include hybrid seeds, processed food, electrical and nonelectrical machinery, chemicals, infrastructure, hotel, hospitality and tourism, among others, whereas Indian investment into Indonesia could be tapped in areas such as food processing, textile fibre, plastics, wood products, agri-biotech, pharmaceuticals, light engineering, audio-visual, telecommunications, and IT and education, among others.

According to the study, the CECA is also expected to enable additional market access for service providers in both countries, across a broad range of service sectors and in all modes of service delivery. In respect of trade in services, the JSG has identified possible services sector for enhanced cooperation between India and Indonesia and these include IT, telecommunications, financial, audio-visual, education, health, tourism and travel, construction, professional services, and transportation. The proposed bilateral CECA needs to include sectors of export interest of both the countries covering all the four modes in a GATS-consistent and GATS-plus framework. To this end, the study concludes that it is important to develop rules and disciplines on trade in services based on GATS provisions and improving on them, further wherever possible including disciplines on domestic regulation. It further suggests facilitating increased dialogue between the regulatory bodies of the two countries for possible MRAs. The CECA should include a separate chapter on the movement of natural persons designed to facilitate the movement of business people between the two countries (India–Indonesia JSG Report, 2009a).

2.1.12. Asia Pacific Trade Agreement — The erstwhile Bangkok Agreement

The Bangkok Agreement is an initiative under the Economic and Social Commission for Asia and the Pacific (ESCAP) for trade expansion through exchange of tariff concessions among developing country members of the ESCAP region. This agreement was signed on July 31, 1975. Seven countries, namely Bangladesh, India, Lao PDR, Republic of Korea, Sri Lanka, the Philippines, and Thailand met at Bangkok and agreed to a list of products for mutual tariff reduction. This agreement was ratified by five of the seven countries. Thailand and the Philippines, due to their ASEAN commitments, did not ratify. Lao PDR is not an effective participating member since it has not issued Customs Notification on the tariff concessions granted to other participating States. Thus, this agreement remains operational between four countries, namely Bangladesh, India, Republic of Korea, and Sri Lanka. The GATT Council approved the Bangkok Agreement in March 1978.

The developing countries and associate members of ESCAP are eligible to accede to the Agreement. The applicant country may accede to the Agreement if at least two-thirds of the participating states recommend its accession. Papua New Guinea acceded to the Agreement in December 1993, but has not yet ratified the Agreement.

China's accession to the Agreement was accepted at the Sixteenth Session of the Standing Committee of the Bangkok Agreement in April 2000 and subsequently, that country deposited the Instrument of Accession to the Bangkok Agreement with the ESCAP Secretariat.

Three Rounds of Trade Negotiations have taken place till date. The First Round was in 1975, when the agreement was signed and the Second Round commenced in 1988 and was completed in 1990. Up to the Second Round, India's general concessions are on 106 items correspond to 188 tariff lines (six-digit HS). The 12 items on which special concessions have been provided to Bangladesh correspond to 33 tariff lines.

As part of China's accession procedures, it granted tariff concessions to India with an average of 13.5% on 217 tariff lines. India, on the other hand, has granted concessions on 106 items corresponding to 188 tariff lines (six-digit HS) under the Bangkok Agreement to other member countries. Bilateral negotiations with China were concluded in February 2003 and these concessions have been implemented with effect from January 1, 2004.

The Third Round of Negotiations under the Bangkok Agreement was launched in October 2001 and concluded in July 2004. The exchange of concessions during the Third Round of Negotiations can be summarized in the following manner:

"No concessions were exchanged with Sri Lanka as India has already entered into a bilateral Free Trade Agreement with Sri Lanka. As Bangladesh is the only Least Developed Country (LDC) member in the Bangkok Agreement, we agreed to extend unilateral tariff preferences to Bangladesh on 25 items based on the principle of non-reciprocity. India gave concessions to China on 311 items (six-digit HS) and received concessions from China on 589 items (eight-digit HS)." India also gave concessions to Republic of Korea on 88 items (six-digit HS) and received concessions from Republic of Korea on 138 items (eight-digit HS).

Since the Bangkok Agreement was signed in 1975, it was felt that the text of the Agreement needed amendments by taking into account the recent economic developments that have taken place. The text was revisited and slightly modified. It now has a Ministerial Council as the apex body, which would decide policy issues relating to the Agreement. The revised text of the Bangkok Agreement renamed as "Asia Pacific Trade Agreement (APTA)," has been signed in the First Session of the Ministerial Council held in Beijing on November 2, 2005. As per the decisions taken in the Ministerial Council, the concessions exchanged under the Third Round of negotiations of Bangkok Agreement was implemented from July 1, 2006.

2.1.13. *Global System of Trade Preferences*

The road to the Global System of Trade Preferences (GSTP) began in Mexico City in 1976, when the Group of 77 first articulated the establishment of a global system of trade preferences among developing countries. In Arusha and Caracas, the Group formulated the principles that underpin the GSTP today. Following a decision taken in New York in 1982, work on a framework agreement proceeded in Geneva. Ministerial meetings in New Delhi in 1985 and in Brasilia in 1986 prompted the elaboration of the text of an agreement and the beginning of the First Round of negotiations. Finally, in Belgrade in 1988, developing countries that participated in the negotiations adopted the text of the Agreement on the Global System of Trade Preferences among developing countries. The following year, the Agreement entered into force.

In June 2004 in Brazil, Ministers of GSTP participants adopted the Sao Paulo Declaration, launching the Third Round of negotiations. Today, representatives of Participants in Geneva are engaged in negotiations to further, promote, and expand trade ties among developing countries in Africa, Asia, and Latin America, for the benefit of global trade. Through trade, GSTP Participants aspire to increase their participation in the global economy and identify complementarities among their economies to open the tremendous potential for trade cooperation envisaged when they adopted the Agreement in 1988.

A total of 43 countries are parties ("Participants") to the Agreement. In 2005, Burkina Faso, Burundi, Haiti, Madagascar, Mauritania, Rwanda, Suriname, Uganda, and Uruguay applied for accession to the Agreement. Every three years, Participants may modify or withdraw their concessions, subject to consultations and negotiations. They may also take safeguard measures to ward-off serious injury or threat thereof to their domestic industries or to address serious balance-of-payments difficulties. Products in the schedules of concessions are eligible for preferential treatment, if they satisfy the rules of origin under the Agreement. The Agreement has provisions for consultations and settlement of disputes.

The coverage of the GSTP extends to arrangements in the area of tariffs, para-tariff, non-tariff measures, direct trade measures, including medium- and long-term contracts and sectoral agreements. One of the basic principles of the Agreement is to be negotiated step by step, improved upon, and extended in successive stages.

So far only two Rounds of negotiations have been concluded under GSTP. The number of products covered for tariff concessions is very limited and so was the number of countries that participated in negotiations.

As per the decision taken in the Special Ministerial Session, a Negotiating Committee has been constituted to carry forward the Third Round of negotiations. The Committee has constituted two Negotiating Groups viz. the Negotiating Group on Rule Making to review the Rules of Origin and related issues and the Negotiating Group on Market Access for market access negotiations. The Negotiating Groups commenced negotiations in November 2004. India is participating in these negotiations.

2.1.14. *East Asia Summit*

India is actively participating in the East Asia Summit (EAS) process. The EAS is a forum held annually by leaders of 16 countries in the East Asian region. EAS meetings are held after annual ASEAN leaders' meetings. The first summit was held in Kuala Lumpur on December 14, 2005. The economic, strategic, and business perspectives on the relevance of Asian economic integration in the EAS framework need to be understood. Specific issues concerning integration of trade and investment regimes, and monetary and financial cooperation, among other issues, against the background of emergence of Asia as the new locomotive and an emerging centre of gravity of the world economy, become important.

China and India are together contributing an overwhelming proportion of the global incremental output now. The Asian economies have also developed profound synergies that have helped in expanding the intra-regional trade in Asia to more than 55%. The new Asian dynamism and the emergence of the Asian middle classes as a center of final demand, and the synergies, make regional economic integration in Asia a viable strategy besides enabling Asia to exercise its influence in global economic governance commensurate with its rapidly growing economic weight.

In this context, the evolution of the EAS as an annual forum for dialogue on regional issues bringing together ASEAN10 and their six dialogue partners, viz. Japan, China, India, Korea, Australia, and New Zealand, needs to be appreciated. The EAS has launched a Track-II feasibility study of a Comprehensive Economic Partnership Arrangement of East Asia (CEPEA) bringing together the 16 member countries of EAS emphasizing on economic cooperation as a key pillar of the regional arrangement (see also Annex 2.3). The exemplary progress made by the regional economic think-tank called Economic Research Institute of ASEAN and East Asia (ERIA) created within the framework of the EAS is a major development (for further details see Das, 2009b; and Kumar, 2007).

The preceding brief on India's economic cooperation initiatives and RTA engagements suggests that, although being a late entrant, India has embarked upon a multitude of initiatives to harness the dynamics of trade in goods and services cooperation with investment integration with countries of importance. It would be thus crucial to understand the conceptual underpinnings of such initiatives that are often missed out from analysis. This has been undertaken in the next chapter.

SAARC

Annex 2.1

SAARC Agreement On Trade In Services (SATIS)

Preamble

The Governments of the South Asian Association for Regional Cooperation (SAARC) Member States comprising the Islamic Republic of Afghanistan, People's Republic of Bangladesh, the Kingdom of Bhutan, the Republic of India, the Republic of Maldives, Nepal, the Islamic Republic of Pakistan and the Democratic Socialist Republic of Sri Lanka hereinafter referred to individually as "Contracting State" and collectively as "Contracting States";

Being committed to strengthen SAARC economic cooperation to maximise the realization of the region's potential for trade and development for the benefit of their people, in a spirit of mutual accommodation, with full respect for the principles of sovereign equality, independence and territorial integrity of all States;

Recognising that regional trading arrangements both in goods and services in SAARC shall act as avenues for achieving objectives of economic development and growth in the region by expanding intraregional investment and production opportunities;

Noting that the Agreement on South Asian Free Trade Area (SAFTA) provides for trade liberalization on a preferential basis in trade in goods;

Being convinced of the increasing role that the services sector is playing in the economies and trade of the Contracting States; and immense potential to augment intra-regional trade in services in a mutually beneficial manner; and also

Recognizing further that Least Developed countries in the region need to be accorded special and differential treatment commensurate with their development needs;

Have agreed as follows:

Article I

Definitions

For the purposes of this Agreement:

1. a juridical person is:

    1.1 **owned** by persons of a Contracting State if more than 50% of the equity interest in it is beneficially owned by persons of that Contracting State;

    1.2 **controlled** by persons of a Contracting State if such persons have the power to name a majority of its directors or otherwise to legally direct its actions;

    1.3 **affiliated** with another person when it controls, or is controlled by, that other person, or when it and the other person are both controlled by the same person;

2. **a service supplied in the exercise of governmental authority** means any service which is supplied neither on a commercial basis nor in competition with one or more service suppliers;

3. **aircraft repair and maintenance services** mean such activities when undertaken on an aircraft or a part thereof while it is withdrawn from service and do not include so-called line maintenance;

4. **commercial presence** means any type of business or professional establishment, including through:

    4.1 the constitution, acquisition or maintenance of a juridical person, or

    4.2 the creation or maintenance of a branch or a representative office,

    within the territory of a Contracting State for the purpose of supplying a service;

5. **computer reservation system (CRS) services** mean services provided by computerized systems that contain information about air carriers' schedules, availability, fares and fare rules, through which reservations can be made or tickets may be issued;

6. **direct taxes** comprise all taxes on total income, on total capital or on elements of income or of capital, including taxes on gains from the alienation of property, taxes on estates, inheritances and gifts, and taxes on the total amounts of wages or salaries paid by enterprises, as well as taxes on capital appreciation;

7. **juridical person** means any legal entity duly constituted or otherwise organized under applicable law, whether for profit or otherwise, and whether privately-owned or governmentally-owned, including any corporation, trust, partnership, joint venture, sole proprietorship or association.

8. **juridical person of the other Contracting States** means a juridical person which is either:

   8.1 constituted or otherwise organized under the law of the other Contracting States, and is engaged in substantive business operations in the territory of the other Contracting States,

   8.2 in the case of the supply of a service through commercial presence, owned or controlled by:

      8.2.1 natural persons of the other Contracting States; or

      8.2.2 juridical persons of the other Contracting States, identified under paragraph 8.1.

9. **measure** means any measure by a Contracting State, whether in the form of a law, regulation, rule, procedure, decision, administrative action, or any other form;

10. **measures by Contracting States** means measures taken by:

    10.1 central, regional, or local governments and authorities; and

    10.2 non-governmental bodies in the exercise of powers delegated by central, regional or local governments or authorities;

11. **measures by Contracting States affecting trade in services** include measures in respect of:

    11.1 the purchase, payment or use of a service;

11.2   the access to and use of, in connection with the supply of a service, services which are required by the Contracting States to be offered to the public generally;

11.3   the presence, including commercial presence, of persons of a Contracting State for the supply of a service in the territory of the other Contracting State;

12. **monopoly supplier of a service** means any person, public or private, which in the relevant market of the territory of a contracting state is authorized or established formally or in effect by that Contracting State as the sole supplier of that service;

13. **natural person of a Contracting State** means a natural person who resides in the territory of the contracting State or elsewhere and who under the law of that contracting state is a national of that Contracting State.

14. **person** means either a natural person or a juridical person;

15. **sector** of a service means:

   (i)   with reference to a specific commitment, one or more, or all, subsectors of that service, as specified in a Schedule of the Contracting States.

   (ii)   otherwise, the whole of that service sector, including all of its subsectors;

16. **services** includes any service in any sector except services supplied in the exercise of governmental authority;

17. **selling and marketing of air transport services** mean opportunities for the air carrier concerned to sell and market freely its air transport services including all aspects of marketing such as market research, advertising and distribution. These activities do not include the pricing of air transport services nor the applicable conditions;

18. **service consumer** means any person that receives or uses a service;

19. **service of the other Contracting States** means a service which is supplied:

   19.1   from or in the territory of the other Contracting States, or in the case of maritime transport, by a vessel registered under the laws of the other Contracting States, or by a person of the other Contracting States which supplies the service through the operation of a vessel and /or its use in whole or in part; or

19.2 in the case of the supply of a service through commercial presence or through the presence of natural persons, by a service supplier of the other Contracting States;

20. **service supplier** means any person that supplies a service[1];

21. **supply of a service** includes the production, distribution, marketing, sale and delivery of a service; and

22. **trade in services** is defined as the supply of a service:

22.1 from the territory of a contracting state into the territory of the other Contracting State (**cross-border**);

22.2 in the territory of a Contracting State to the service consumer of the other Contracting State (**consumption abroad**);

22.3 by a service supplier of a Contracting State, through commercial presence in the territory of the other Contracting State (**commercial presence**);

22.4 by a service supplier of a Contracting State, through presence of natural persons of a Contracting State in the territory of the other Contracting State (**presence of natural persons**)

Article 2

Objectives, Principles and Guidelines

1. The objectives of this Agreement are to promote and enhance trade in services among the Contracting States in a mutually beneficial and equitable manner by establishing a framework for liberalising and promoting trade in services within the region in accordance with Article V of General Agreement on Trade in Services.

---

[1] Where the service is not supplied directly by a juridical person but through other forms of commercial presence such as a branch or a representative office, the service supplier (i.e. the juridical person) shall, nonetheless, through such presence be accorded the treatment provided for service suppliers under this Agreement. Such treatment shall be extended to the presence through which the service is supplied and need not be extended to any other parts of the supplier located outside the territory where the service is supplied.

2. Negotiations for schedule of specific commitments shall take place keeping in view the national policy objectives, the level of development and the size of economies of Contracting States both overall and in individual sectors.

3. In light of the priority accorded to services by all Contracting States, the Agreement shall progressively cover liberalization of trade in services with broad-based and deeper coverage of majority of services sectors/sub-sectors with a view to fulfilling the objectives of Article V of GATS.

4. A positive list approach shall be followed. Negotiations for specific commitments for progressive liberalization would be based on "request-and-offer" approach.

Article 3

Scope

1. This Agreement applies to measures by Contracting States as defined in Article 1.10 and measures by the contracting States affecting trade in services as defined in Article 1.11.

2. This Agreement shall not apply to:
    (a) government procurement;
    (b) services supplied in the exercise of governmental authority; and
    (c) transportation and non-transportation air services, including domestic and international services, whether scheduled or nonscheduled, and related services in support of air services[2] other than:
        (i) aircraft repair and maintenance services
        (ii) the selling and marketing of air transport services, and
        (iii) computerized reservation system services.

3. The supply of services which are not technically or technologically feasible when this Agreement comes into force shall, when they become feasible, also be considered for possible incorporation during the review process under Article-10.

4. This Agreement shall not apply to measures affecting natural persons seeking access to the employment market of a Contracting State, nor

shall it apply to measures regarding citizenship, residence or employ- ment on a permanent basis.

5. Nothing in this Agreement shall prevent a Contracting State from applying measures to regulate the entry of natural persons of the other Contracting State into, or their temporary stay in, its territory, includ- ing those measures necessary to protect the integrity of, and to ensure the orderly movement of natural persons across its borders, provided that such measures are not applied in such a manner as to nullify or impair the benefits accruing to the other Contracting State under the terms of a specific commitment undertaken under this Agreement.[3]

Article 4

MFN Treatment

1. subject to the provisions of Article 22.b, commitments undertaken under Article 8 of this Agreement shall be extended to all Con- tracting States on a most favoured nation basis.
2. If, after this Agreement enters into force, a contracting State enters into any agreement on trade in services with a non-Contracting State, it shall give consideration to a request by the other Contracting State for the incorporation herein of treatment no less favourable than that provided under the aforesaid agreement. Any such incorporation should maintain the overall balance of commitments undertaken by each Contracting State under this Agreement.

Article 5

National Treatment

1. In the sectors inscribed in its Schedule, and subject to any conditions and qualifications set out therein, each Contracting State shall

---

[3] The Contracting States understand that ground handling services are part of related services in support of air services. The sole fact of requiring visa for natural persons of cer- tain Contracting State and not for those of other Contracting States shall not be regarded as nullifying or impairing benefits under a specific commitment.

accord to services and service suppliers of any other Contracting State, in respect of all measures affecting the supply of services, treatment no less favourable than that it accords to its own like services and service suppliers.[4]

2. A Contracting State may meet the requirement of paragraph 1 by according to services and service suppliers of the other Contracting State, either formally identical treatment or formally different treatment to that it accords to its own like services and service suppliers.

3. Formally identical or formally different treatment shall be considered to be less favourable if it modifies the conditions of competition in favour of services or service suppliers of a Contracting State compared to like services or service suppliers of the other Contracting State.

Article 6

Market Access

1. With respect to market access through the modes of supply defined in paragraph 22 of Article 1, each Contracting State shall accord services and service suppliers of the other contracting State treatment no less favourable than that provided for under the terms, limitations and conditions agreed and specified in its schedule of specific commitments.[5]

2. In sectors where market access commitments are undertaken, the measures which a Contracting State shall not maintain or adopt either on the basis of a regional subdivision or on the basis of its

---

[4] Specific commitments assumed under this Article shall not be construed to require any Contracting State to compensate for any inherent competitive disadvantages which result from the foreign character of the relevant services or service suppliers.

[5] If a Contracting State undertakes a market-access commitment in relation to the supply of a service through the mode of supply referred to in Article 1 (22) and, if the cross-border movement of capital is an essential part of the service itself that Contracting State is thereby committed to allow such movement of capital. If a Contracting State undertakes a market-access commitment in relation to the supply of a service through the mode of supply referred to in Article 1 (22) (iii), it is thereby committed to allow related transfers of capital into its territory.

entire territory, unless otherwise specified in its Schedule of specific commitments, are defined as:

(a) limitations on the number of service suppliers whether in the form of numerical quotas, monopolies, exclusive servicee suppliers or the requirements of an economic needs test;

(b) limitations on the total value of service transactions or assets in the form of numerical quotas or the requirement of an economic needs test;

(c) limitations on the total number of service operations or on the total quantity of service output expressed in terms of designated numerical units in the form of quotas or the requirement of an economic needs test[6];

(d) limitations on the total number of natural persons that may be employed in a particular service sector or that a service supplier may employ and who are necessary for, and directly related to, the supply of a specific service in the form of numerical quotas or the requirement of an economic needs test;

(e) measures which restrict or require specific types of legal entity or joint venture through which a service supplier may supply a service; and

(f) limitations on the participation of foreign capital in terms of maximum percentage limit on foreign shareholding or the total value of individual or aggregate foreign investment.

Article 7

Additional Commitments

The Contracting States may negotiate commitments with respect to measures affecting trade in services not subject to scheduling under Articles 5 or 6, including those regarding qualifications, standards or licensing matters. Such commitments shall be inscribed in a Contracting State's Schedule of specific commitments.

---

[6] This paragraph 2(c) does not cover measures of a Contracting State which limit inputs for the supply of services.

Article 8

Schedule of Specific Commitments

1. Each contracting state shall set out in a schedule the specific commitments it undertakes under Articles 5, 6 and 7 with respect to sectors where such commitments are undertaken, each Schedule shall specify:

    a. terms, limitations and conditions on market access;
    b. conditions and qualifications on national treatment;
    c. undertakings relating to additional commitments;
    d. where appropriate the time-frame for implementation of such commitments; and
    e. the date of entry into force of such commitments

2. Measures inconsistent with both Articles 5 and 6 shall be inscribed in the column relating to Article 6. In this case, the inscription will be considered to provide a condition or qualification to Article 5 as well.

3. The Contracting States' schedules of specific commitments shall be annexed to this Agreement upon completion of the negotiations and shall form an integral part thereof.

Article 9

Modification of Schedules

1. A Contracting State may modify or withdraw any commitment in its Schedule, at any time after three years have elapsed from the date on which that commitment entered into force, in accordance with the provisions of this Article. It shall notify the other Contracting States of its intent to so modify or withdraw a commitment no later than three months before the intended date of implementation of the modification or withdrawal.

2. At the request of the other Contracting States, the modifying Contracting State shall enter into negotiations with a view to reaching agreement on any necessary compensatory adjustment. In such negotiations and agreement, the Contracting State shall endeavour to maintain a general level of mutually advantageous commitments not

less favourable to trade than that provided for in Schedules of specific commitments prior to such negotiations. The contracting States shall endeavour to conclude negotiations on such compensatory adjustment to mutual satisfaction within six months, failing which recourse may be had to the provisions of Article 26 of this Agreement.

3. Compensatory adjustments shall be made on a most-favored-nation basis.

4. The modifying Contracting State may not modify or withdraw its commitment until it has made compensatory adjustment with the requesting country or in accordance with the decision taken following the procedure of Article 26 of this Agreement.

Article 10

Progressive Liberalisation

The Schedules of Specific Commitments annexed to the Agreement shall be reviewed after every three years, or earlier if mandated by SAFTA Ministerial Council (SMC).

Article 11

Domestic Regulations

1. In sectors where specific commitments are undertaken, each Contracting State shall ensure that all measures of general application affecting trade in services are administered in a reasonable, objective, and impartial manner.

2. Each Contracting State shall maintain or institute as soon as practicable judicial, arbitral or administrative tribunals, or procedures which provide, at the request of an affected service supplier of the other Contracting State, for the prompt review of, and where justified, appropriate remedies for, administrative decisions affecting trade in services. Where such procedures are not independent of the agency, entrusted with the administrative decision concerned, the Contracting State shall ensure that the procedures in fact provide for an objective and impartial review.

3. The provisions of paragraph 2 shall not be construed to require a Contracting State to institute such tribunals or procedures where this would be inconsistent with its constitutional structure or the nature of its legal system.

4. Where authorization is required for the supply of a service, on which a specific commitment has been made, the competent authorities of a Contracting State shall, within a reasonable period of time after the submission of an application considered complete under domestic laws and regulations, inform the applicant of the decision concerning the application. At the request of the applicant, the competent authorities of the Contracting State shall provide, without undue delay, information concerning the status of the application.

5. With the objective of ensuring that domestic regulation, including measures relating to qualification requirements and procedures technical standards and licensing requirements, do not constitute unnecessary barriers to trade in services, the Contracting States shall jointly review the results of the negotiations on disciplines on these measures, pursuant to Article VI.4 of the WTO General Agreement on Trade in Services (GATS), with a view to their incorporation into this Agreement. The Contracting States note that such disciplines aim to ensure that such requirements are *inter alia*:

   (a) based on objective and transparent criteria, such as competence and the ability to supply the service;

   (b) not more burdensome than necessary to ensure the quality of the service;

   (c) in the case of licensing procedures, not in themselves a restriction on the supply of the service.

6. Pending the incorporation of disciplines pursuant to paragraph 5, in sectors where a Contracting State has undertaken specific commitments, a Contracting State shall not apply licensing and qualification requirements and technical standards that nullify or impair such specific commitments in a manner which:

   (a) does not comply with the criteria outlined in paragraphs 5(a), 5(b) or 5(c); and

(b)   could not reasonably have been expected of that Contracting State at the time the specific commitments in those sectors were made.

7.   In determining whether a Contracting State is in conformity with the obligation under paragraph 6, account shall be taken of international standards of relevant international organizations[7] applied by that Contracting State.

8.   In sectors where specific commitments regarding professional services are undertaken, each Contracting State shall provide for adequate procedures to verify the competence of professionals of any other Contracting State.

Article 12

Recognition

1.   For the purposes of the fulfillment of its standards or criteria for the authorisation, licensing or certification of services suppliers, a contracting state may recognise the education or experience obtained, requirements met, or licenses or certifications granted in the other Contracting State.

2.   After the entry into force of this Agreement, upon a request being made in writing by a contracting State to any other contracting State(s) in any regulated service sector, the contracting State shall ensure that their respective professional bodies negotiate and conclude, within a reasonable time, in that service sector for mutual recognition of education, or experience obtained, requirements met, or licenses or certifications granted in that service sector, with a view to the achievement of early outcomes. Such recognition, which may be achieved through harmonization or otherwise, may be based upon an agreement or arrangement among the Contracting States. Any delay or failure by these professional bodies to reach and conclude agreement on the details of such

---

[7] The term "relevant international organizations" refers to international bodies whose membership is open to the relevant bodies of all Contracting States.

agreement or arrangements shall not be regarded as a breach of a Contracting State's obligations under this paragraph and shall not be subject to Article 26 relating to dispute settlement in this Agreement. Progress in this regard will be continually reviewed by the Parties in the course of the review of this Agreement pursuant to Article 10.

3. Where a Contracting State recognizes, by agreement or arrangement, the education or experience obtained, requirements met or licenses or certifications granted in the territory of a country that is not a Contracting State to this Agreement, that Contracting State shall accord the other Contracting State, upon request, adequate opportunity to negotiate its accession to such an agreement or arrangement or to negotiate comparable ones with it. Where a Contracting State accords recognition autonomously, it shall afford adequate opportunity for the other Contracting State to demonstrate that the education or experience obtained, requirements met, or licenses or certifications granted in the territory of that other Contracting State should also be recognized.

4. Settlement of disputes arising out of or under the Agreements or Arrangements for mutual recognition concluded by the respective professional, standard-setting, or self-regulatory bodies under the provisions of this Article shall be the responsibility of the entities signing the Agreements or Arrangements for mutual recognition.

5. Wherever appropriate and if possible Members shall endeavour to base recognition on regionally agreed criteria. In appropriate cases, contracting States shall work in cooperation with relevant inter governmental and non-governmental organizations towards the establishment and adoption of common regional standards and criteria for recognition and common regional standards for the practice of relevant services trades and professions.

Article 13

Monopolies and Exclusive Service Suppliers

1. Each contracting State shall ensure that any monopoly supplier of a service in its territory does not, in the supply of the monopoly service in the relevant market, act in a manner inconsistent with that Contracting State's Schedule of specific commitments.

2. Where a Contracting State's monopoly supplier competes, either directly or through an affiliated company, in the supply of a service outside the scope of its monopoly rights and which is subject to that Contracting State's Schedule of specific commitments, the Contracting State shall ensure that such a supplier does not abuse its monopoly position to act in its territory in a manner inconsistent with such commitments.

3. If a Contracting State has reason to believe that a monopoly supplier of a service of the other Contracting State is acting in a manner inconsistent with paragraphs 1 or 2 above, it may request that Contracting State establishing, maintaining or authorizing such supplier to provide specific information concerning the relevant operations in its territory.

4. The provisions of this Article shall also apply to cases of exclusive service suppliers, where a Contracting State, formally or in effect:

   (a) authorizes or establishes a small number of service suppliers; and
   (b) substantially prevents competition among those suppliers in its territory.

Article 14

Business Practices

1. The Contracting States recognize that certain business practices of service suppliers, other than those falling under Article 13, may restrain competition and thereby restrict trade in services.

2. A Contracting State shall, at the request of another Contracting State, enter into consultations with a view to eliminating practices referred to in paragraph 1. The Contracting State addressed shall accord full and sympathetic consideration to such a request and shall co-operate through the supply of publicly available non-confidential information of relevance to the matter in question. The Contracting State addressed shall also provide other information available to the requesting contracting state, subject to its domestic law and to the conclusion of satisfactory agreement concerning the safeguarding of its confidentiality by the requesting Contracting State.

Article 15

Safeguard Measures

1. The Contracting States note the multilateral negotiations pursuant to Article X of the GATS on the question of emergency safeguard measures based on the principle of non-discrimination. Upon the conclusion of such multilateral negotiations, the Contracting States shall conduct a review for the purpose of discussing appropriate amendments to this Agreement so as to incorporate the results of such multilateral negotiations.
2. In the event that the implementation of this Agreement causes substantial adverse impact to a service sector of a Contracting State before the conclusion of the multilateral negotiations referred to in paragraph I of this Article, the affected Contracting State may request for consultations with the other contracting State for the purposes of discussing any measure with respect to the affected service sector. Any measure taken pursuant to this paragraph shall be mutually agreed by the Contracting States concerned. The Contracting States concerned shall take into account the circumstances of the particular case and give sympathetic consideration to the Contracting State seeking to take a measure.

Article 16

Subsidies

1. Except where provided in this Article, this Agreement shall not apply to subsidies or grants provided by a Contracting State, or to any conditions attached to the receipt or continued receipt of such subsidies or grants, whether or not such subsidies or grants are offered exclusively to domestic services, service consumers or service suppliers. If such subsidies or grants significantly affect trade in services committed under this Agreement, any Contracting State may request for consultations which shall be accorded sympathetic consideration.
2. Pursuant to this Agreement, the Contracting States may, on request, provide information on subsidies related to trade in services committed under this Agreement to any requesting Contracting State.

3. The Contracting States shall review the treatment of subsidies when relevant disciplines are developed by the WTO.
4. Provisions of dispute settlement under this Agreement shall not apply to any request made or consultations held under the provisions of this Article or to any dispute that may arise between the Contracting States out of or under the provisions of paragraphs 1&2 of this Article.

Article 17

Payments and Transfers

1. Except under the circumstances envisaged in Article 1g a Contracting State shall not apply restrictions on international transfers and payments for current transactions relating to its specific commitments.
2. Nothing in this Agreement shall affect the rights and obligations of the Contracting States as members of the International Monetary Fund under the Articles of Agreement of the Fund, including the use of exchange actions which are in conformity with the Articles of Agreement, provided that a Contracting State shall not impose restrictions on any capital transactions inconsistently with its specific commitments regarding such transactions, except under Article 18 or at the request of the Fund.

Article 18

Restrictions to Safeguard the Balance of Payments

1. In the event of serious balance of payments and external financial difficulties or threat thereof, a Contracting State may adopt or maintain restrictions on trade in services in respect of which it has obligations under Articles 5 and 6 or has made Additional Commitments including on payments or transfers for transactions relating to such commitments. It is recognized that particular pressures on the balance of payments of a Contracting State in the process of economic development may necessitate the use of restrictions to ensure, *inter alia*, the maintenance of a level of financial

reserves adequate for the implementation of its programme of economic development.

2. The restrictions referred to in paragraph 1 shall:

   (a) not discriminate among the Contracting States;

   (b) be consistent with the Articles of Agreement of the International Monetary Fund;

   (c) avoid unnecessary damage to the commercial, economic, and financial interests of the other Contracting States;

   (d) not exceed those necessary to deal with the circumstances described in paragraph 1;

   (e) be temporary and be phased out progressively as the situation specified in paragraph 1 improves;

3. Any restrictions adopted or maintained under paragraph 1, or any changes therein, shall be promptly notified to the other Contracting States.

4. The Contracting State adopting any restrictions under paragraph 1 shall commence consultations with the other Contracting States in order to review the restrictions adopted by it.

Article 19

Transparency

1. Each Contracting State may publish promptly and, except in emergency situations, at least fourteen days prior to the entry into force of all relevant measures of general application which pertain to or affect the operation of this Agreement. International agreements pertaining to or affecting trade in services to which a Contracting State is a signatory shall also be published.

2. Where publication as referred to in paragraph 1 is not practicable, such information shall be made otherwise publicly available.

3. Each Contracting State shall respond promptly to all requests by the other Contracting State for specific information on any of its measures of general application or international agreements within the meaning of paragraph 1. Each Contracting State shall also establish one or more enquiry points to provide specific information to other

Contracting State, upon request, on all such matters. Enquiry Points need not be depositories of laws and regulations.

Article 20

Disclosure of Confidential Information

Nothing in this Agreement shall require any Contracting State to provide confidential information, the disclosure of which would impede law enforcement, or otherwise be contrary to the public interest, or which would prejudice legitimate commercial interests of particular enterprises, public or private.

Article 21

Areas for Cooperation

With a view to augmenting trade in services among Contracting States, measures outlined below would be focused upon within an agreed timeframe:

(i)   Development of regulatory capacity: The Contracting States would provide for cooperation among respective regulatory bodies of the Contracting States for exchange of experiences and best practices. For facilitating the cooperation, working groups may be formed for specific sectors of interest comprising the relevant national authorities and stakeholders. These working groups could report to the institutional mechanisms for overseeing the implementation of this Agreement as provided in Article 27.

(ii) Cooperation for collection and exchange of statistics and regulations: A Working Group under the SAARCSTAT comprising central bank officials and others concerned would be constituted. They would also develop a compendium of domestic regulations and seek to improve collection of trade statistics in services.

(iii) Cooperation in WTO/GATS Negotiations: Contracting States shall cooperate and coordinate their positions in the GATS negotiations, as far as possible.

Article 22

Special and Differential Treatment for LDCs

In addition to, other provisions of this Agreement, all Contracting States shall provide, wherever possible, special and more favorable treatment to least developed contracting states as stated in the following sub-paragraphs:

a. There shall be appropriate flexibility for Least Developed Contracting States for opening fewer sectors, liberalizing fewer types of transactions, and progressively extending market access in line with their development situation.

b. All Contracting States shall, wherever possible, consider providing special concessions to Least Developed Contracting States while undertaking commitments on a request-offer basis.

c. Technical assistance shall be provided to LDC Contracting States for enhancing their supply capabilities in service sectors and infrastructure development; for research and capacity building programmes; and for catering to the institutional and regulatory needs with a view to strengthening their domestic service capacity, efficiency, and competitiveness. Such technical assistance may be provided bilaterally or through sub-regional/regional projects under Economic Window of SAARC Development Fund as per its Charter and Bye-laws. A detailed plan of action including timeframe for technical assistance in these areas shall be prepared on a priority basis within a reasonable timeframe after entry into force of the Agreement.

Article 23

General Exceptions

1. Subject to the requirement that such measures are not applied in a manner which would constitute a means of arbitrary or unjustifiable discrimination against any Contracting State, or a disguised restriction on trade in services, nothing in this Agreement shall be

construed to prevent the adoption or enforcement by either Contracting State of measures:

(a) necessary to protect public morals or to maintain public order[8]:

(b) necessary to protect human, animal or plant life or health;

(c) necessary to secure compliance with laws or regulations which are not inconsistent with the provisions of this Agreement including those relating to:

(i) the prevention of deceptive and fraudulent practices or to deal with the effects of a default on services contracts;

(ii) the protection of the privacy of individuals in relation to the processing and dissemination of personal data and the protection of confidentiality of individual records and accounts:

(iii) safety;

(d) inconsistent with Article 5, provided that the difference in treatment is aimed at ensuring the equitable or effective[9] imposition or collection of direct taxes in respect of services or service suppliers of other Contracting States.

---

[8] The public order exception may be invoked by a Contracting State, including its legislative, governmental, regulatory, or judicial bodies, only where a genuine and sufficiently serious threat is posed to one of the fundamental interests of society.

[9] Measures that are aimed at ensuring the equitable or effective imposition or collection of direct taxes include measures taken by a Contracting State under its taxation system which:

(i) apply to non-resident service suppliers in recognition of the fact that the tax obligation of non-residents is determined with respect to taxable items sourced or located in the Contracting State's territory; or

(ii) apply to non-residents in order to ensure the imposition or collection of taxes in the Contracting State's territory; or

(iii) apply to non-residents or residents in order to prevent the avoidance or evasion of taxes, including compliance measures; or

(iv) apply to consumers of services supplied in or from the territory of the other Contracting State in order to ensure the imposition or collection of taxes on such consumers derived from sources in the Contracting State's territory; or

Article 24

Security Exceptions

1. Nothing in this Agreement shall be construed:

    (a)   to require a Contracting State to furnish any information, the disclosure of which it considers contrary to its essential security interests; or

    (b)   to prevent a Contracting State from taking any action which it considers necessary for the protection of its essential security interests:

       (i)   relating to the supply of services as carried out directly or indirectly for the purpose of provisioning a military establishment;

       (ii)   relating to fissionable and fusionable materials or the materials from which they are derived;

       (iii) taken in time of war or other emergency in international relations;

       (iv)   relating to protection of critical public infrastructure, including communications, power and water infrastructure from deliberate attempts intended to disable or degrade such infrastructure;

    (c)   to prevent a Contracting State from taking any action in pursuance of its obligations under the United Nations Charter for the maintenance of international peace and security.

2. Each Contracting State shall inform the other Contracting States to the fullest extent possible of measures taken under paragraphs r (b) and (c) and of their termination.

(vi)   determine, allocate, or apportion income, profit, gain, loss, deduction, or credit of resident persons or branches, or between related persons or branches of the same person, in order to safeguard the Contracting State's tax base.

Tax terms or concepts in paragraph 1(d) of this Article and in this footnote are determined according to tax definitions and concepts, or equivalent or similar definitions and concepts, under the domestic law of the Contracting State taking the measure.

Article 25

Denial of Benefits

1. Subject to prior notification and consultation, a Contracting State may deny the benefits of this Agreement:

    (a) to the supply of a service, if it establishes that the service is supplied from or in the territory of a country that is not a Contracting State to this Agreement;

    (b) in the case of the supply of a maritime transport service, if it establishes that the service is supplied:

        (i) by a vessel registered under the laws of a non-Contracting State, and

        (ii) by a person which operates and/or uses the vessel in whole or in part but which is of a non-Contracting State;

2. Contracting State may deny the benefits of this Agreement to a service provider of the other Contracting State where the Contracting State establishes that the service is being provided by an enterprise that is owned or controlled by persons of a non-Contracting State and that has no substantive business operations in the territory of the other Contracting State.

3. In case of special concessions, if any, provided exclusively to LDC Contracting States as per Article 22.b, subject to prior notification and consultation, Contracting State may deny the benefits of those special concessions to a service provider of the LDC Contracting State where the Contracting State establishes that the service is being provided by an enterprise that is owned or controlled by persons of a non-LDC Contracting State and that has no substantive business operations in the territory of that LDC Contracting State.

Article 26

Dispute Settlement and Enforcement

For the purposes of this Agreement the mechanisms available as per Articles 19 and 20 of the Agreement on South Asian Free Trade AIEA (SAFTA) would be applicable and enforced through Article 27 of this Agreement.

Article 27

Institutional Mechanism

The SAFTA Ministerial Council (SMC) constituted under the Article 10 of SAFTA Agreement shall be the highest decision-making body for the purpose of this Agreement and shall be responsible for administration and implementation of this Agreement and all decisions and arrangements made within its legal framework.

The SAFTA Committee of Experts (CoE) shall monitor, review, and facilitate implementation of the provisions of this Agreement and undertake any task assigned to it by the SMC. The SAFTA COE shall submit this report to SMC every six months.

Article 28

Withdrawal

Any Contracting State may withdraw from this Agreement at any time after its entry into force as per Article 21 of the SAFTA Agreement.

Article 29

Entry into Force

This Agreement shall enter into force on completion of formalities, including ratification by all Contracting States and issuance of a notification thereof by the SAARC Secretariat. This Agreement shall be an adjunct to the SAFTA Agreement.

Article 30

Annexes

The following Annexes attached to this Agreement form an integral part of this Agreement:

a. The General Understanding on Principles and Guidelines for the Negotiations — **(Annex-I)**
b. Schedules of Specific Commitments of Contracting States as referred to in Article 8 (3) — **(Annex-II)**.

Article 31

Amendments

This Agreement may be amended by consensus in the SAFTA Ministerial council. Any such amendment will become effective upon the deposit of instruments of acceptance with the secretary General of SAARC by all Contracting States.

Article 32

Depository

This Agreement will be deposited with the Secretary General of SAARC, who will promptly furnish a certified copy thereof to each Contracting State.

IN **WITNESS** WHEREOF the undersigned being duly authorized thereto by their respective Governments have signed this Agreement.

DONE in Thimphu, Bhutan on This Twenty-ninth Day of April Two Thousand Ten In Ten Originals In The English Language, All Texts Being Equally Authentic.

Minister of Foreign Affairs
Islamic Republic of Afghanistan

Minister for Foreign Affairs
People's Republic of Bangladesh

Minister-in-Charge of Foreign
Affairs Kingdom of Bhutan

Minister of External Affairs
Republic of India

Minister of Foreign Affairs
Republic of Maldives

Deputy Prime Minister and
Minister for Foreign Affairs Nepal

Minister for Foreign Affairs
Islamic Republic of Pakistan

Minister of Foreign Affairs
Democratic Socialist Republic of
Sri Lanka

Annex-I

General Understanding on Principles and Guidelines for the Negotiations on Saarc Agreement on Trade in Services (SATIS)

1. This Agreement shall provide real and effective market access to all Contracting States in an equitable manner.
2. Negotiations for schedule of specific commitments shall take place keeping in view the national policy objectives, the level of development and the size of economies of contracting states both overall and in individual sectors.
3. In light of the priority accorded to services by all Contracting States, the Agreement shall progressively cover liberalization of trade in services with broad-based and deeper coverage of majority of services sectors/sub-sectors with a view to fulfilling the objectives of Article V of GATS.
4. A positive list approach shall be followed. Negotiations for specific commitments for progressive liberalization would be based on "request-and-offer" approach.
5. There may be specific texts in mutually agreed areas.
6. MTN/GNS/WI20 (WTO Secretariat's services Sectoral classification List) could be a basis for, but may not be limited to, the sectoral coverage of the sector specific commitments.
7. Initial offers of the WTO-Member Contracting States shall be in addition to their existing levels of multilateral commitments with substantial sectoral and modal improvement over those commitments.
8. Agreement and schedules of specific commitments shall be subject to review periodically.

*****

Annex 2.2: India's Importance in ASEAN's Trade (US$ Million)

Partner Country/Region	2003 Exports	2003 Imports	2003 Total Trade	2004 Exports	2004 Imports	2004 Total Trade	2005 Exports	2005 Imports	2005 Total Trade	2006 Exports	2006 Imports	2006 Total Trade	2007 Exports	2007 Imports	2007 Total Trade
ASEAN	116,831.1	95,701.4	212,532.5	141,931.4	120,059.4	261,990.7	165,457.7	141,888.1	307,345.8	194,325.8	165,319.5	359,645.3	920,203.4	188,490.9	408,624.3
	24.7	*24.4*	*24.4*	*24.9*	*23.9*	*24.4*	*25.3*	*24.3*	*24.9*	*25.0*	*23.6*	*24.3*	*24.9*	*23.2*	*24.1*
Japan	56,570.0	63,160.0	119,730.0	67,200.0	75,890.0	143,090.0	79,610.0	81,290.0	153,900.0	82,540.0	83,330.0	165,870.0	87,620.0	95,170.0	182,790.0
	12.0	*15.9*	*13.8*	*11.8*	*15.1*	*13.4*	*11.1*	*13.9*	*12.5*	*10.6*	*11.9*	*11.2*	*9.9*	*11.7*	*10.8*
USA	75,120.0	49,460.0	124,580.0	85,240.0	56,010.0	141,250.0	93,970.0	60,950.0	154,920.0	109,940.0	69,650.0	179,590.0	109,790.0	73,790.0	183,580.0
	15.9	*12.4*	*14.3*	*15.0*	*11.2*	*13.2*	*14.4*	*10.5*	*12.5*	*14.1*	*9.9*	*12.1*	*12.4*	*9.1*	*10.8*
European Union	65,280.0	44,350.0	109,630.0	78,580.0	56,550.0	135,130.0	83,150.0	60,220.0	143,370.0	100,910.0	68,800.0	169,710.0	109,570.0	82,480.0	192,050.0
	13.8	*11.2*	*12.6*	*13.8*	*11.3*	*12.6*	*12.7*	*10.3*	*11.6*	*13.0*	*9.8*	*11.5*	*12.4*	*10.2*	*11.3*
China	30,930.0	33,730.0	64,660.0	41,510.0	47,620.0	89,130.0	52,600.0	61,200.0	113,800.0	66,100.0	81,370.0	147,470.0	93,190.0	104,220.0	197,410.0
	6.6	*8.5*	*7.4*	*7.3*	*9.5*	*8.3*	*8.1*	*10.5*	*9.2*	*8.5*	*11.6*	*10.0*	*10.5*	*12.8*	*11.6*
Korea	17,330.0	19,310.0	36,640.0	20,910.0	24,120.0	45,030.0	24,940.0	27,390.0	59,260.0	27,830.0	35,100.0	69,930.0	32,730.0	40,890.0	73,550.0
	3.7	*4.9*	*4.2*	*3.7*	*4.8*	*4.2*	*3.8*	*4.7*	*4.2*	*3.6*	*5.0*	*4.3*	*3.7*	*5.0*	*4.3*
Australia	13,460.0	7,520.0	20,980.0	17,980.0	9,630.0	27,610.0	29,300.0	12,010.0	34,310.0	27,400.0	15,250.0	42,650.0	31,750.0	15,850.0	47,600.0
	2.9	*1.9*	*2.4*	*3.2*	*1.9*	*2.6*	*3.4*	*2.1*	*2.8*	*3.5*	*2.2*	*2.9*	*3.6*	*2.0*	*2.8*
India	8,580.0	4,520.0	13,100.0	10,780.0	7,390.0	18,100.0	14,900.0	8,640.0	23,540.0	19,040.0	10,530.0	29,570.0	23,790.0	13,300.0	37,090.0
	1.8	*1.1*	*1.5*	*1.9*	*1.5*	*1.7*	*2.3*	*1.5*	*1.9*	*2.4*	*1.5*	*2.0*	*2.7*	*1.6*	*2.2*
Canada	2,880.0	1,930.0	4,810.0	3,520.0	2,510.0	6,030.0	3,510.0	3,000.0	6,510.0	4,930.0	3,310.0	8,240.0	6,830.0	4,160.0	10,990.0
	0.6	*0.5*	*0.6*	*0.6*	*0.5*	*0.6*	*0.5*	*0.5*	*0.5*	*0.6*	*0.5*	*0.6*	*0.8*	*0.5*	*0.6*
Russia	1,050.0	2,000.0	3,050.0	1,470.0	3,130.0	4,600.0	1,790.0	4,000.0	5,790.0	2,050.0	3,000.0	5,050.0	2,580.0	3,530.0	6,110.0
	0.2	*0.5*	*0.4*	*0.3*	*0.6*	*0.4*	*0.3*	*0.7*	*0.5*	*0.3*	*0.4*	*0.3*	*0.3*	*0.4*	*0.4*
New Zealand	1,590.0	1,230.0	2,750.0	2,130.0	1,450.0	3,580.0	2,660.0	1,570.0	4,230.0	3,450.0	1,970.0	5,420.0	4,090.0	2,860.0	6,950.0
	0.3	*0.3*	*0.3*	*0.4*	*0.3*	*0.3*	*0.4*	*0.3*	*0.3*	*0.4*	*0.3*	*0.4*	*0.4*	*0.5*	*0.4*
Pakistan	1,780.0	270.0	2,050.0	2,190.0	250.0	2,440.0	2,720.0	300.0	3,020.0	3,180.0	370.0	3,550.0	3,790.0	400.0	4,190.0
	0.4	*0.1*	*0.2*	*0.4*	*0.0*	*0.2*	*0.4*	*0.1*	*0.2*	*0.4*	*0.1*	*0.2*	*0.4*	*0.0*	*0.2*
Sub-Total (Selected Partners)	391,414.0	323,262.7	714,594.6	473,524.5	404,619.9	878,052.7	540,620.5	462,467.4	1003,006.9	641,778.3	538,076.3	1179,775.1	796,015.5	625,077.9	1351,014.0
	82.9	*81.4*	*82.2*	*83.1*	*80.6*	*81.9*	*82.8*	*79.3*	*81.2*	*82.5*	*76.8*	*79.8*	*82.2*	*77.0*	*79.7*
ASEAN World	472,140.0	397,310.0	869,450.0	569,530.0	502,160.0	1071,690.0	652,920.0	582,880.0	1235,800.0	777,920.0	700,520.0	1478,440.0	883,740.0	812,240.0	1695,980.0
Total	*100.0*	*100.0*	*100.0*	*100.0*	*100.0*	*100.0*	*100.0*	*100.0*	*100.0*	*100.0*	*100.0*	*100.0*	*100.0*	*100.0*	*100.0*

Note: Bold italic figures are shares to total ASEAN trade.
Source: IMF (2008), *Direction of Trade Statistics*, December.

Annex 2.3

Joint Media Statement at the Conclusion of Sixth ASEAN–India Consultations

The Sixth Consultations between the ASEAN Economic Ministers (AEM) and India (6th AEM-India Consultations) was held in Singapore on 28 August 2008. The Consultations was co chaired by Mr. Lim Hng Kiang, Minister for Trade and Industry of Singapore and Mr. Kamal Nath, Minister of Commerce and Industry of India. The annual consultations provided the opportunity for Ministers to exchange views on issues and developments affecting global and regional trade, particularly those that are significant to the bilateral trade between ASEAN and India. The Ministers noted that, despite the challenges prevailing in global and regional trade, ASEAN-India bilateral trade continues to grow at impressive rates. From 2005 to 2007, trade in goods between ASEAN and India increased at an average annual rate of 28 percent. ASEAN exports to India during the same period grew at an annual rate of 31 percent on average, the fastest among ASEAN's exports to major trading partners. The share of ASEAN–India trade in relation to total ASEAN trade continued to increase and India remains ASEAN's seventh largest trading partner. On the investment side, in 2007, India's FDI to ASEAN, valued at US$641 million, and was the highest ever recorded since 2000. The other Ministers who attended the meeting were Mr. Pehin Dato Lim Jock Seng, Second Minister of Foreign Affairs and Trade, Brunei Darussalam; Mr. Cham Prasidh, Senior Minister and Minister of Commerce, Cambodia; Mr. Mari Elka Pangestu, Minister of Trade, Indonesia; Mr. Nam Viyaketh, Minister of Industry and Commerce, Lao PDR; Mr. Tan Sri Muhyiddin Yassin, Minister of International Trade and Industry, Malaysia; Mr. U Soe Tha, Minister for National Planning and Economic Development, Myanmar; Mr. Peter B. Favila, Secretary of Trade and Industry, the Philippines; Mr. Pichet Tanchareon, Deputy Minister of Commerce, Thailand; (representing Mr. Chaiya Sasomsub, Minister of Commerce, Thailand); Mr. Nguyen Cam Tu, Vice Minister, Ministry of Industry and Trade, Viet Nam (representing Mr. Vu Huy Hoang, Minister of Industry and Trade, Viet Nam and Mr. Surin Pitsuwan, Secretary-General of ASEAN.

The Ministers announced the conclusion of the ASEAN–India Free Trade Agreement (AIFTA) negotiations for trade-in-goods. The Ministers were pleased that, despite the difficult issues in the negotiations, both sides were able to reach an agreement on the modality for tariff reduction and/or elimination, which is among the key elements that will facilitate the creation of an open market in a region comprising about 1.7 billion people and with a combined gross domestic product of approximately USD2,381 billion as of 2007. The Ministers viewed that the AIFTA could be a major avenue in harnessing the region's vast economic potentials towards sustained progress and improved welfare not only for ASEAN and India but for the greater East Asian region as well. The Ministers agreed that officials finalise the text of the ASEAN-India Trade in Goods Agreement in time for signing during the ASEAN-India Summit in December 2008, together with the ASEAN-India Agreement on Dispute Settlement Mechanism. The Ministers agreed to target implementation of tariff reduction commitments starting 1 January, 2009. The Ministers also instructed officials to commence, as soon as possible, negotiations on trade in services and investment as a single undertaking, and to work towards the conclusion of substantive discussions on these two agreements by 2009 to bring about a complete ASEAN-India Comprehensive Economic Cooperation Agreement. The Ministers also took stock of the latest developments in the Doha Round and emphasised that a stronger multilateral trading system would benefit all Members, especially the developing countries. Since the Doha Round is a Development Round, the developing countries have a special stake in its successful conclusion. The Ministers reaffirmed their commitment to active and constructive engagement in the negotiations to bring about balanced and ambitious outcomes in all areas, especially in agriculture, NAMA and services. The Ministers assured Lao PDR of their continued support in her accession to the WTO.

The Economic Ministers of ASEAN, Australia, the People's Republic of China, the Republic of India, Japan, the Republic of Korea and New Zealand had a productive exchange of views on the areas of cooperation within the EAS framework. The Ministers welcomed the establishment of the Economic Research Institute for ASEAN and East Asia (ERIA) with the Inaugural Governing Board Meeting of ERIA held at the

ASEAN Secretariat on 3 June 2008. The Ministers also welcomed the research activities of ERIA and looked forward to ERIA's practical policy recommendations for deepening economic integration, narrowing development gaps and sustainable development. In particular, the Ministers noted with appreciation the ERIA East Asia Industrial Corridor Project for the region-wide comprehensive development, affirming the importance of linking the infrastructure development and industrial development planning. The Ministers also expressed interests in the ERIA Energy Outlook which demonstrates the importance of enhancing energy efficiency for sustainable development. The Ministers agreed to report the outcome of ERIA's activities to the EAS Leaders.

The Ministers also discussed current regional and international policy issues such as the increase in the energy and foods prices and its impact on the region. In this regard, the Ministers welcomed Japan's proposal to host the symposium on the energy and food security in cooperation with ERIA. The Ministers noted the report of the Track Two Study Group on Comprehensive Economic Partnership in East Asia (CEPEA), which shows greater potential trade and GDP growth if enhanced integration among EAS members is achieved. Consistent with the request of Leaders, the Ministers agreed to convey the report to Leaders at the 4th EAS. The Ministers also agreed to a Phase II Track II Study on CEPEA, detailing the pillars of economic cooperation, facilitation and liberalization as well as institutional developments. The Ministers acknowledged that substantial progress was made during the World Trade Organization (WTO) Mini-Ministerial in July and members came very close to agreement. However, there are still outstanding issues before modalities in Agriculture and NonAgriculture Market Access (NAMA) can be resolved. The Ministers agreed that all economies must work together to preserve what has been achieved to date, and to show constructive and continued engagement to conclude the Round. The Ministers also agreed that a strong and equitable global rules-based trading system is necessary for continued growth. The Ministers also stressed the importance of concluding the round to achieve development objectives and to respond effectively to the global financial and food crisis. The Ministers committed to intensify efforts in the coming weeks to resume negotiations and achieve convergence in the remaining areas before the window of opportunities closes. The Ministers supported WTO DG Pascal Lamy's efforts to bridge gaps among the key economies and his call on these economies to show political commitment and flexibility to work towards a balanced and ambitious outcome. The Ministers agreed that it is important to ensure the integrity of the multi-lateral trading system, and that work on the remaining areas of the single undertaking should resume in Geneva even as modalities in Agriculture and NAMA are being worked out.

CHAPTER 3

The Economics of Regional Integration and Analytical Insights from Negotiations

3.1. Economic Rationale of Regional Integration

The economics of a regional economic integration is often not understood with a positive mindset. The negotiating processes of Regional Trade Agreements (RTAs) also appear to be complicated. Given these, the chapter also presents some important conceptual basis of regional economic integration and offers crucial insights from the negotiating processes (see Das, 2009b, 2009c).

3.1.1. Adjustment cost versus efficiency concerns

In the India-specific context, there was a stage of development when trade liberalization was considered crucial for enhancing efficiency levels through import-competition. However, this posed the risk of a deindustrialization process in the country, as the domestic stakeholders needed some time for adjustment for withstanding import-competition. The RTAs in India provide avenue to balance these seemingly conflicting objectives of addressing efficiency-concerns and phase of transition and adjustment. This is possible due to the very nature of RTAs. The import liberalization is calibrated in terms of the choice of a country (or countries), sectors, and timeframe. It does not open up all the sectors to all the countries at the same time. Moreover, import liberalization is done with reciprocity so that our exports also get market access.

From efficiency to development outcomes: There is a two-way linkage between trade and development. While trade can initiate achieving developmental objectives through scale expansion, productivity gains, employment generation, and consequent poverty reduction, the development process itself enhances trade capabilities and hence can help augment trade flows. This needs to be understood in a regional context by taking into account specificities that are present in a regional trade and economic cooperation agreement, especially through efficiencies as mentioned earlier.

The economics of trade–FDI–poverty reduction is captured in a partial equilibrium framework in a time-neutral setting.[1]

$$RT = \alpha + \beta_1(MA) + \beta_2(TC) + \beta_3(I) + \beta_4(Ts)$$
$$+ \beta_5(K) + \beta_6(ROO) + \mu,$$

where

$$MA = f(T, S) \text{ and } T = f(TB, NTB), \text{ and } I = f(DI, GFDI, RFDI).$$

Furthermore,

$$E = \phi + \gamma_1(RT) + \gamma_2(LP) + \gamma_3(LI) + \gamma_4(S) + \varepsilon.$$

Finally,

$$RT = Net(TC + TD).$$

The complexity of above relationships needs to be elucidated. Any regional free trade agreement (FTA) — this is being used for different forms and levels of regional economic integration — would be able to generate higher regional trade (RT) due to increased market access (MA), decreased transaction costs (TC) through trade facilitation, increased trade in services (due to relationship between trade in goods and services), increased investment, improved knowledge and

---

[1] Das, RU (2007b). Some analytical basis of a regional economic cooperation arrangement, Supported by DIE research program "Anchor Countries as Drivers of Regional Economic Integration" and preliminary version presented at the German Development Institute's conference on "Regional Economic Integration Beyond Europe" in Bonn, December 19–20, 2007.

technology (K), and rules of origin (ROO) effects. The MA would be ensured by reduction in trade barriers (T) in a static scenario and the incumbent scale expansion effect (S) in the dynamic setting. Here, trade barriers include reduction in tariff barriers (TB) and non-tariff barriers (NTB). Conceptually, trade augmenting investment (I) can be a summation of domestic investment (DI), FDI from outside the region, i.e. global FDI (GFDI) and intra-regional FDI (RFDI), all spurred by the possibilities of enhanced intra-regional trade due to reduced trade barriers under the FTA.

The role of technology and knowledge (K) in improving the supply-side efficiency and product-competitiveness needs to be reconciled as per the new growth theories as one of the determinants of RT. The effects of ROO could also be trade (RT) augmenting, especially through its regional cumulation provisions.

The strengthening of trade-investment linkages due to regional economic cooperation may often require efforts more than a mere FTA, but also an agreement to facilitate and promote intra-regional investment.

From trade-investment linkages, their combined employment effect can be derived whereby employment is a function of RT, labor productivity (LP), labor intensity (LI), and scale expansion (S).

The whole formulation becomes complex as finally, RT needs to be viewed in terms of the net effects of trade creation (TC) and trade diversion (TD). Thus, the cross-effects among variables are explained step-by-step below, in cases where they are not obvious. For instance, the obvious effects include market access effects and effects of lower transaction costs.

However, before that the trade–FDI–poverty reduction linkages need to be decomposed. The above may, as the first step, lead to growth convergence and through it, along with employment effects, lead to poverty reduction.

In which case, growth convergence could be captured as:

$$(\log Y_{Tt,I} - \log Y_{0t,I})/n_t = \alpha + \lambda_1 \log(Y_{0t,i}) + \lambda_2(GC) + \lambda_3(OP) + \lambda_4(FDI) + \lambda_5(INF) + \lambda_6(RT) + \varepsilon_{t,I},$$

where, $Y_{Tt,I}$ refers to the real GDP per capita in the last year of period t ($t = 1, 2, 3, 4,\ldots$) the corresponding sub-periods for country i, $Y_{0t,I}$ is the value of real GDP per capita in the initial year of period t, n_t is the number of years, and T the last year in period t. Further, the explanatory variables are Government Consumption (GC) as a percentage of GDP, openness of the economy (OP) measured as imports as percentage of GDP, FDI as percentage of GDP and percentage of annual inflation (INF) as a deflator of GDP. These variables have been chosen on the basis of our own inferences drawn from various economic growth theories and some of them used in other empirical studies on the subject. In this step, it is obvious that the β-convergence would give results on convergence or divergence in a global setting. However, in the context of regional integration, intra-regional trade as a percentage of each regional grouping's total world trade can be taken as an additional variable to see in the presence of high or low intra-regional trade if the convergence or divergence estimates change. FDI in the equation also includes intra-regional FDI.

Now it is possible to go back to some of the explanations of how trade–FDI–poverty reduction can be inter-related in a regional context, as explained further below.

3.1.2. Linkages between trade in goods and trade in services

Trade in goods cannot be stepped up unless institutional mechanisms exist for facilitating concomitant trade in services. For instance, trade in goods is incumbent upon the presence of facilitative services like post-shipment credit, consignment-insurance, bank-guarantees, shipping services, etc., that not only facilitate trade but also contribute to the competitiveness of exports. On the other hand, trade in services in a sector like health is dependent upon trade in goods pertaining to this specific service sector such as medical equipments and medicines that the health service providers are confident of. Thus, any RTA needs to recognize the two-way linkages between trade in goods and services. However, in reality the converse of it could also be observed. Given the increasing trend of disconnect between tangibles and intangibles, for instance in the case of real sector and financial sector, trade in goods and trade in services follow their independent growth dynamics. In any case, the autonomous flows in both trade in goods and services need to be reckoned with.

The added argument stems from the fact that cooperation in upgrading infrastructural services help in reducing the transaction costs by making products cheaper in the regional context.

3.1.3. Trade-Investment linkages

It needs to be further acknowledged that the strengthening of trade-investment linkages is crucial for achieving higher levels of regional trade and for its developmental impact. Such linkages help in improving the export supply capabilities in the countries of a regional grouping. They are also generating employment on a large scale along with the three types of investment that are made to take advantage of trade liberalization, regionally. While an FTA can spur investment flows in terms of efficiency-seeking regional restructuring, it is the trade-creating joint ventures that ultimately have a decisive impact on regional trade flows. The trade-creating joint ventures are in a position to take advantage of the regional FTA.

In this context, if vertical integration and horizontal specialization are also focused upon with the help of cross-country investment flows that strengthen trade-investment linkages, then the gains in terms of higher trade and investment flows leading to greater employment generation become possible. This may essentially mean distribution of different stages of production in a particular industry regionally in an integrated manner viz. the vertical integration and specialization in the same stage of production with the help of product differentiation across the region viz. the horizontal specialization.

3.1.4. Importance of regional economic integration for scale expansion

The data available from the literature on regional trading arrangements analyze the effects of removal of trade barriers in terms of export growth in the context of static and dynamic gains. For instance, reduction in tariffs means greater market access to member countries, which manifests itself in export growth in a static setting. The scenario of a dynamic framework is different in which due to economies of scale — arising on account of enhanced market access — ultimately the manufacturing processes experience gains in terms of cost reductions and improved product competitiveness. Short-run static trade diversion effects, if any, are likely to be outweighed by the long-run positive dynamic effects of regional integration in terms of increased competition, economies of scale, and benefits of intra-industry trade.

To the extent, exports are a part of the national income identity; they contribute to the economic growth process and thus generate employ-ment. However, exports need not always be employment generating if in order to enhance export competitiveness the technique of production becomes less labor intensive. Thus, it is imperative to understand the impact of technological change on employment in the pursuits of achieving export competitiveness even in a regional context of trade integration.

The linkage between trade openness and employment can be exam-ined by looking at the effects on labor productivity; however, the complexity of such a relationship is not always properly understood. It has been argued and confirmed empirically by Das (2007a) that trade to tech-nology linkages may yield higher labor productivity gains. However, it is being translated into increased demand for labor that is dependent upon the possibilities of scale expansion. This is so because in the absence of scale expansion, labor productivity gains could result in a lower demand for labor per unit of output production, precisely since labor has become more productive. Thus, scale expansion becomes a crucial variable for generating positive effects of technology on employment and export expansion in a regional context assumes importance.

An analysis of channels through which trade and investment could influence employment levels and poverty profiles would not be complete unless the issues are posited in the frame of trade creation and diversion.

3.1.5. Trade creation and diversion

One of the arguments against regional groupings since the work of Viner (1950) and subsequently Meade (1955) and Lipsey (1970) has been on the failure bringing about welfare gains, especially in the short run, due to their trade diverting effects. Trade diversion occurs when the participating countries in a regional grouping are not low-cost producers. In this sense, the grouping may be an efficiency-reducing arrangement. Due to regional trade liberalization, the member countries acquire an advantage over the extra-regional countries in terms of lower product prices resulting from reduction in trade barriers. A member country thus switches its imports from the more efficient rest of the world producers to the lesser efficient and higher cost partner member country. This results in resource misallocation and amounts to trade diversion.

3.1.6. Trade diversion not necessarily bad

However, it is often missed out from the analytical debate on the subject that trade diversion in some products could itself lead to trade creation in other products over a period of time. Illustratively, if an intermediate product is cheaper in a member country and it is imported by a partner member country on preferential terms, then it becomes further cheaper in the importing country. This makes the final product highly competitive in the importing country for the production of which the imported input is used. The possibilities of trade creation in the final product increase by generating the forward linkage effect. Similarly, backward linkage effect in the country that produces the intermediate product could also be present. Thus, through their backward and forward linkage effects, trade diversion could lead to trade creation in a dynamic setting[2] (Das, 2006).

3.1.7. Rules of origin: Developmental outcomes

Rules of origin provide yet another channel through which regional trade can have developmental effects, especially on account of employment generation. Whether or not a product has originated in a particular country is decided if the product has undergone substantial transformation. There are three prime ways of determining this. First, the

---

[2] Paper presented at International Conference on "India's Globalisation," organized by MSH and University of Paris X, Paris, September, 2006.

change-in-tariff-heading test implying that the tariff heading of the final product is different from the tariff headings of its inputs. Second, a percentage test is applied according to which a minimum percentage of total value addition should be achieved with the help of domestic inputs. Finally, specified process tests require a product to undergo certain stipulated processes.

One of the prime functions of these rules is to prevent trade deflection in trading arrangements when the three modalities of determining origin of a product aim at substantial transformation in inputs. However, what remains unappreciated is that these rules of origin and their modalities together facilitate value-addition in the country of manufacturing and play a developmental role. Such requirements that check the import content of value addition have the potential for generating backward and forward linkages in a country adhering to the rules. Thus, a member country is prevented from becoming a mere trading country as these requirements act as a deterrent to assembly kind of production activities (Das, 2007, 2004; and Panchamukhi and Das, 2001).

3.1.8. *Some empirical estimates*

Under the β-convergence framework the following equation has been estimated econometrically (Das and Sambamurty, 2006):

$$(\log Y_{Tt,1} - \log Y_{0t,1})/n_t = \alpha + \beta \log(Y_{0t,t}) + \varepsilon_{t,1}, \qquad (3.1)$$

where, $Y_{Tt,1}$ refers to the real GDP per capita in the last year of period t ($t = 1, 2, 3, 4, \ldots$) the corresponding sub-periods) for country i, $Y_{0t,1}$ is the value of real GDP per capita in the initial year of period t, n_t is the number of years and T the last year in period t.

The same set of data was also used to estimate the conditional β-convergence in the fourth step by further augmenting the model with additional variables (data sourced from WB, World Development Indicators). These are Government Consumption (GC) as a percentage of GDP, openness of the economy (OP) as imports in percentage of GDP, the FDI as percentage of GDP (FDI) and percentage of annual inflation

(INF) as a deflator of GDP. These variables have been chosen on the basis of our own inferences drawn from various economic growth theories and some of them used in other empirical studies on the subject. In this step, it is obvious that the β-convergence would give results on convergence or divergence in a global setting. This implies that convergence or divergence would include intra-developing country, intra-developed country, and developing-developed country that is effected in a combined manner.

The following equation was estimated:

$$(\log Y_{Tt,I} - \log Y_{0t,I})/n_t = \alpha + \beta_1 \log(Y_{0t,t}) + \beta_2(GC) + \beta_3(OP) \\ + \beta_4(FDI) + \beta_5(INF) + \varepsilon_{t,I}. \qquad (3.2)$$

The same methodology was used to estimate the equation for the prominent regional groupings viz. EU-15, NAFTA, MERCOSUR, ASEAN, SAFTA, and SADC including both developed world groupings and developing countries groupings across continents. However, in this context, intra-regional trade as a percentage of each regional grouping's of the total world trade was taken as an additional variable to see the presence of high or low intra-regional trade, if the convergence or divergence estimates change.

The estimates of Conditional β-convergence for prominent regional groupings separately are shown in Tables 3.1 and 3.2.

Table 3.1 shows that more integrated regional groupings like EU, NAFTA, MERCOSUR, and ASEAN are converging and lesser integrated groupings like SARRC and SADC are growth diverging when we estimate the same equation. However, the results do not conform to the openness variable in some instance.

Thus, to extend the analysis we included intra-regional exports as a proportion to total world trade of the grouping to a measure the depth of regional integration and such results are presented in Table 3.2.

It is clear that trade integration is a significant factor in reducing the global growth asymmetries. The conditional β-convergence regression for different regions shows a negative and highly significant β-coefficient. It implies that the countries of the sample are converging toward each other

Table 3.1. Panel data regression results for conditional convergence for different regional economic groupings (fixed effects).

Variable	EU-15	NAFTA	ASEAN	MERCOSUR	SAFTA	SADC
Constant	0.033 (1.38)	0.05 (3.51)	0.14 (3.29)	0.09 (3.00)	-0.03 (-0.87)	-0.01 (-0.14)
Initial Per Cap GDP	-0.004 (-0.58)	-0.01@ (-2.63)	-0.04@ (-2.63)	-0.02* (-2.51)	0.03** (2.09)	0.0003 (0.07)
FDI	4.32E-05 (0.26)	0.004*** (2.22)	0.006** (1.98)	-0.0003 (-0.12)	-0.02# (-1.27)	-0.0005 (-1.11)
Govt. Consumption	-0.0005* (-2.49)	0.0003 (0.96)	-0.001 (-0.96)	-0.0003 (-0.51)	-0.002** (-1.81)	-2.42E-05 (-0.06)
Openness	7.00E-05*** (1.56)	-0.0004* (-2.32)	-0.0001 (-0.48)	-0.0005* (-2.37)	0.0008* (2.25)	0.0002@ (2.79)
Inflation	-0.0003*** (-1.73)	-0.0003@ (-4.36)	-0.001** (-2.09)	-5.27E-06 (-0.85)	-0.002* (-1.58)	-0.0002# (-1.48)
R^2	0.31802	0.79505	0.61659	0.48735	0.41764	0.27333
Adjusted R^2	0.249822	0.624266	0.424896	0.231029	0.255869	0.166472
Durbin–Watson Statistic	2.094563	2.640758	2.226182	2.958406	1.914701	1.374469

Note: @99.5% level of significance, *99% level of significance, **97.5% level of significance, ***95% level of significance, #90% level of significance.

Table 3.2. Panel data regression results for conditional convergence for different regional economic groupings (fixed effects).

Variable	EU-15	NAFTA	ASEAN	MERCOSUR	SAFTA	SADC
Initial Per Cap GDP	-2.673147@	-4.990330*	-7.440070@	-7.383730@	-2.649437#	-4.053724
	(-5.803273)	(-2.394842)	(-5.785915)	(-2.612764)	(-1.522123)	(-1.012069)
FDI	0.009232*	0.012439	-0.013774	-0.007713	0.151979	0.001983
	(2.361190)	(0.413688)	(-0.374970)	(-0.151395)	(1.233226)	(0.030715)
Govt. Consumption	-0.096125@	-0.139156@	-0.099492#	-0.058347	0.009181	-0.011574
	(-5.888433)	(-3.675862)	(-1.605896)	(-1.427832)	(0.132478)	-(0.324602)
Openness	0.015940@	0.017721#	0.019460**	0.020979	0.009785	0.009429
	(3.286657)	(1.441796)	(1.973965)	(1.075854)	(0.349963)	(0.526162)
Inflation	-0.033881@	-0.031375@	-0.047225@	-0.000287**	-0.061292***	0.006276
	(-6.026702)	(-3.349175)	(-7.043683)	(-2.155428)	(-3.224152)	(1.487893)
Intra-regional Exports (% of Total Exports to World)	0.004939	0.000558	0.050144	0.020449	-0.025784	-0.017733
	(2.584232)	(1.382015)	(2.298402)	(2.216748)	(-1.843808)	(-0.843272)
R²	0.608129	0.387068	0.701042	0.370187	0.615116	0.108441
Adjusted R²	0.564855	0.238479	0.642551	0.246963	0.482397	-0.042671
Durbin–Watson Statistic	1.167292	2.143394	1.400654	1.737550	2.365883	2.084743
WALD	144.6812	16.89538	59.67342	13.33240	18.70952	2.925624

Note: @99.5% level of significance, *99% level of significance, **97.5% level of significance, ***95% level of significance, #90% level of significance.

with respect to real GDP per capita. From this we can calculate the rate of convergence/divergence.

The rate of convergence for all regions is quite high for the period concerned. It is around 7% for regions like EU, NAFTA, ASEAN, MERCOSUR, and SADC and around 12% for SAFTA. This supports the argument that regional trade integration which has been a new development in the international trade arena will be an effective policy instrument for the countries across the world to follow and remove the asymmetries that are plaguing the rate of growth of many countries. Also, openness defined as Imports as a percentage of GDP also has the expected positive sign. This shows that trade openness along with regional trade integration has played an increasingly important role in reducing the growth asymmetries.

The explanatory power of the independent variables included is also very high for almost all the regressions. The Durbin–Watson statistic also shows that there is no problem of autocorrelation. The Wald test shows that all coefficients of the additional variables in the model are jointly significant in explaining the convergence within the regional trading blocs.

It can be concluded that regional integration leads to growth convergence and openness to both global trade and regional openness captured by intra-regional exports which are important in this regard.

3.1.9. *Tests of stationarity*

The primary motivation behind the application of panel data unit root tests, as opposed to standard univariate unit root tests, is to exploit the extra information provided by pooled cross-section time series data in order to get more powerful procedures. It has been noticed that the unit root test for a single time series, such as the Augmented Dickey–Fuller (ADF) test has low power due to its tendency to overly reject the stationary hypothesis of a time series. During the last decade, several such methods have been developed. The panel data unit root tests have been performed by Levin and Lin,1993; Im, Pesaran, and Shin, 1997; and Hadri, 2000, 2004; in order to make the estimates more powerful in a sequential manner.

3.1.10. *Levin–Lin–Chu test*

The Levin–Lin–Chu (LLC) test assumes that there is a common unit root process such that it is identical across cross-sections. The LLC test considers the following basic ADF specification:

$$\Delta y_{it} = \alpha y_{it-1} \sum_{j=1}^{pi} \beta_{ij} \Delta y_{it-j} + \varepsilon_{it}, \tag{3.3}$$

where i and t stand for cross-section (i.e. country) and time, respectively; y_{it} is the time series variable for all countries that is being tested for stationarity. Δ is a first difference operator; and ε is the error term. Here, we assume a common $\alpha = \rho - 1$, but allow the lag order for the difference terms, p_i, to vary across cross-sections. The null (H_0) and alternative (H_1) hypotheses for the tests are:

$$H_0: \alpha = 0,$$
$$H_1: \alpha < 1.$$

As per the test, under the null and alternative hypotheses there is presence of a unit root and there is absence of a unit root, respectively. The LLC test shows that under the null hypothesis a modified t-statistic for the resulting $\hat{\alpha}$ is asymptotically normally distributed:

$$t^* = \frac{t_\alpha - (NT)S_N \hat{\sigma}^2 \text{se}(\sigma) \hat{\mu}_{MT*}}{\sigma_{MT*}} \rightarrow N(0,1),$$

where t_α is the standard t-statistic for $\hat{\alpha} = 0$, $\hat{\sigma}^2$ is the estimated variance of the error term, $\text{se}(\hat{\sigma})$ is the standard error of $\hat{\alpha}$, and T = no. of time periods $- (\Sigma p_i/N) - 1$.

The remaining terms, which involve complicated moment calculations, are described in greater detail in LLC. The average standard deviation ratio, S_N is defined as the mean of the ratios of the long-run standard deviation to the innovation standard deviation for each individual. Its estimate is derived using kernel-based techniques. The remaining two terms, μ_{MT*} and σ_{MT*} are adjustment terms for the mean and standard deviation.

The major weakness of the LLC test lies in its implicit assumption that all individual AR (1) series have a common autocorrelation coefficient. Consequently, under (H_0, **LLC**) each series has a unit root while under (H_1, **LLC**) each of them is stationary. Thus, the alternative hypothesis becomes too restrictive for practical purposes. The Im–Pesaran–Shin (IPS) Test relaxes this assumption by assuming under the alternative hypothesis that at least one but not necessarily all of the series is stationary.

3.1.11. Im–Pesaran–Shin test

Under the IPS test, a separate ADF regression for each cross-section is specified:

$$\Delta y_{it} = \alpha y_{it-1} \sum_{j=1}^{pi} \beta_{ij} \Delta y_{it-j} + \varepsilon_{it}.$$

The null hypothesis is written as

$$H_0: \; \alpha_i = 0, \quad \text{for all } i$$

while the alternative hypothesis is given by:

$$H_1: \; \alpha_i = 0, \quad \text{for } i = 1, 2, 3 \dots N_1$$
$$\text{or, } \alpha_I < 0, \quad \text{for } i = N + 1, N + 2, \dots, N$$

Let t_i denote the "t-statistic" for α_i. The test statistic as calculated by Im, Pesaran and Shin is given by:

$$Z = \frac{\sqrt{N(t - E(t))}}{\sqrt{\text{Var}(t)}},$$

where $t = (1/N) \sum^N t_i$: $E(t)$ and Var(t) are the mean and variance, respectively.

The LLC and IPS tests described earlier tests the null hypothesis of a unit root against the alternative of at least one stationary series, by using ADF statistic across the cross-sectional units of the panel. By contrast, in a major advancement, Hadri (2000) proposed a Lagrange multiplier (LM) procedure to test the null hypothesis that all of the individual series are stationary against the alternative of at least a single unit root in the panel.

3.1.12. Hadri test

The Hadri panel unit root test is similar to the KPSS unit root test. Like the KPSS test, the Hadri test is based on the residuals from the individual OLS regressions of y_{it} on a constant, or on a constant and a trend. A critical assumption underlying this test is that of cross-section independence among the individual time series in the panel. The IPS test exhibits severe size distortions in the presence of cross-sectional dependence. Hence, in this regard Hadri's test is an improvement over the earlier tests. The panel data model under Hadri's test procedure has been specified by the following model:

$$y_{it} = \alpha_i + \delta_{it} + \varepsilon_{it}$$

where, y_{it} is an observation for cross-section I at time t. $\{\alpha_i, \delta_i\}$ is an intercept and a time trend, respectively, that are specific to cross-section i. Given the residuals $\hat{\varepsilon}$ from the individual regressions, the LM statistic (assuming homoskedasticity across cross-sections) is given by:

$$LM_1 = \frac{1}{N}\left(\frac{\sum_{i=1}^{N}\left(\frac{S_i(t)^2}{T^2}\right)}{f_0}\right),$$

where $S_i(t)$ are the cumulative sums of the residuals, or in other words, $S_i(t) = \Sigma \hat{\varepsilon}_{it}$.

And f_0 is the average of the individual estimators of the residual spectrum at frequency zero:

$$f_0 = \frac{\sum_{i=1}^{N} f_{i0}}{N}.$$

More importantly, an alternative form of the LM statistic allows for heteroskedasticity across i:

$$\mathrm{LM}_1 = \frac{1}{N}\left(\frac{\sum_{i=1}^{N}\left(\frac{S_i(t)^2}{T^2}\right)}{f_{i0}}\right).$$

Hadri shows that under mild assumptions, the panel data test statistic is given by:

$$Z = \sqrt{N(\mathrm{LM}i - \xi)}\,/\,\zeta \to N(0,1), \quad \text{for } i = 1 \text{ and } 2,$$

where $\xi = 1/6$ and $\zeta = 1/45$, if the model only includes constants (δ_i is set to 0 for all i), and $\xi = 1/15$ and $\zeta = 11/6300$, otherwise. Thus, LMi and the LM statistic (as mentioned earlier) are with the homoskedasticity and heteroskedasticity assumption, respectively.

Although the panel variant of the KPSS tests developed by Hadri for the null of stationarity is an improvement over the earlier tests developed, it suffers from size distortions in the presence of cross-section dependence under certain conditions (Giulietti *et al.*, 2005). This aspect is left for future research as it deviates from the main focus of the paper.

As emphasized earlier on the prominent regional groupings across continents that witnessed an increasing tendency toward deeper regional trade integration in 1990s, a continuous time-series and cross-country dynamic panel data set were considered for meaningful estimations of the role of regional trade integration in the context of addressing growth asymmetries in a particular regional grouping. This posed the problem of handling the issue of stationarity in the pooled data framework. Unless the unit root tests are conducted, the interpretation of results would remain deficient. We addressed this problem by applying different tests with increasing power of the robustness of the estimate. The LLC, IPS, and Hadri tests were undertaken and are summarized in Tables 3.3, 3.4, and 3.5, respectively. As evident from the tests there are non-stationarity problems for different variables differently under different tests as well as regional groupings. All that emerges is that the

Table 3.3. Levin–Lin–Chu test results for all the time series variables in all the regional groupings.

Series →	Levin–Lin–Chu Test (LLC)						
	EXP	FDI	GC	INF	LOGD	LOGIN	OP
Regional Groups ↓							
EU-15	NUR	NUR	NUR	NUR	NUR	UR	UR
NAFTA	UR	UR	UR	NUR	NUR	UR	UR
ASEAN	NUR	UR	UR	NUR	NUR	NUR	NUR
Mercosur	UR	UR	UR	UR	UR	UR	NUR
SAFTA	UR	NUR	NUR	NUR	NUR	NUR	NUR
SADC	UR	NUR	NUR	UR	NUR	UR	UR

Note: UR means presence of UNIT ROOT; NUR means NO UNIT ROOT; EXP is intra-regional trade series; FDI is Foreign Direct Investment; GC is Government Consumption; INF if inflation; LOGD is the growth rate of per capita GDP; LOGIN is the initial per cap GDP; OP is openness.

Table 3.4. Im–Pesaran–Shin Test results for all the time series variables in all the regional groupings.

Series →	Im–Pesaran–Shin Test (IPS)						
	EXP	FDI	GC	INF	LOGD	LOGIN	OP
Regional Groups ↓							
EU-15	UR	UR	UR	NUR	NUR	UR	UR
NAFTA	UR	UR	UR	NUR	NUR	UR	UR
ASEAN	UR	UR	UR	NUR	NUR	UR	UR
Mercosur	UR	UR	UR	UR	UR	UR	UR
SAFTA	UR	NUR	UR	UR	NUR	UR	UR
SADC	UR	NUR	NUR	UR	NUR	UR	UR

Note: UR means presence of UNIT ROOT; NUR means NO UNIT ROOT; EXP is intra-regional trade series; FDI is Foreign Direct Investment; GC is Government Consumption; INF if inflation; LOGD is the growth rate of per capita GDP; LOGIN is the initial per cap GDP; OP is openness.

problem is not uniform for all the variables under each test and for each regional grouping.

This helps us in concluding that the broad results of our chapter need to be interpreted with caution due to the presence of non-stationarity,

Table 3.5.   Hadri Test results for all the time series variables in all the regional groupings.

	Hadri Test						
Series →	EXP	FDI	GC	INF	LOGD	LOGIN	OP
Regional Groups ↓							
EU-15	UR	UR	UR	UR	NUR	UR	UR
NAFTA	UR	NUR	UR	NUR	NUR	UR	UR
ASEAN	UR	UR	UR	NUR	NUR	UR	UR
Mercosur	NUR	UR	UR	UR	UR	UR	UR
SAFTA	UR	NUR	UR	UR	NUR	UR	UR
SADC	UR	UR	NUR	UR	UR	UR	UR

Note: UR means presence of UNIT ROOT; NUR means NO UNIT ROOT; EXP is intra-regional trade series; FDI is Foreign Direct Investment; GC is Government Consumption; INF if inflation; LOGD is the growth rate of per capita GDP; LOGIN is the initial per cap GDP; OP is openness.

though the problem is not uniform across variables, tests, and regional groupings.

3.2. Analytical Insights from Negotiations

3.2.1. *"Substantially all trade"*

One of the issues which have had a determining impact on the outcomes of trade negotiations under an FTA relates to defining "substantially all trade." It is a well-known fact that an FTA needs to cover "substantially all trade" in order to be WTO-consistent. However, the definition of "substantially all trade" has remained ambiguous in WTO. While some countries have taken the position of defining it in terms of number of tariff lines covered for tariff reduction/elimination, others have argued for expressing trade coverage in terms of trade volume. Yet others have considered both the criteria simultaneously.

Such vagueness has had two effects on negotiations. First, the negotiations have been long drawn, such as in the case of India–ASEAN FTA. Second, since the negative list (on which no tariff concession is committed) is the residual of all trade minus "substantially all trade," the exact size of it has also remained unclear. This often results in exclusion of a relatively large and relevant portion of trade from the FTA tariff commitments.

3.2.2. Sensitive list

3.2.2.1. *Safeguarding the sensitivities of the agriculture sector: Lessons from RTAs of the ASEAN countries and some developed countries*

In the context of an increasing disagreement over addressing domestic agriculture's sensitivities between India and ASEAN under their FTA negotiations, this section dwells upon the way the different FTAs all over the world adopts to tackle this issue and focuses on the way such sensitivities were addressed within the ambit of the ASEAN Free Trade Agreement (AFTA). It also highlights the way other countries have accommodated these concerns in their negotiations with the ASEAN. Bilateral FTA engagements of some of the prominent ASEAN countries with other countries have also been referred to. It has been found that in some cases inadequate attention to domestic agriculture sensitivities have caused adverse impacts on an ASEAN member. As a consequence, a country like Thailand has opted out of the ASEAN–South. Korea FTA. In the same vein, the modalities and trends in the developed world, including the US and the EU, in addressing their agricultural sector's concerns have also been touched upon. All these have been included to emphasize that India's stance in the India–ASEAN FTA negotiations on matters relating to such sensitivities is neither out of place nor contrary to global practices. Toward the end, some policy suggestions have been given to help resolve the issues in the India–ASEAN FTA negotiations on the basis of the analysis of these facts.

1. *Evolution of AFTA in Addressing Agricultural Sensitivities*

AFTA and its background: AFTA was launched among the ASEAN-6 in January 1992. It planned to reduce tariffs from 0% to 5% in 15 years among the six nations through a Common Effective Preferential Tariff (CEPT). The 5% option was kept to help some member countries to cover the administrative costs of government in handling trade. A mid-phase target of 20% tariffs within 5 to 8 years was also set. The agreement included all manufactured products including capital goods and processed agricultural products. The major exclusion was basic agriculture or unprocessed agricultural products. The agreement also called for the removal of quantitative restrictions (QRs), or to "terrify" all QRs.

ASEAN had expanded and new deadlines were given to the new entrants, Vietnam (in 2006), Lao PDR and Myanmar (in 2008), and Cambodia (in 2010) for implementing the AFTA. The original signatories agreed to accelerate the full implementation of AFTA. Instead of 2008, it was advanced to 2003 in the ASEAN Summit of 1995 and again to 2002 in the ASEAN Summit of 1998.

Common Effective Preferential Tariff (CEPT): The CEPT is the mechanism by which tariffs on goods traded within the ASEAN region were reduced to the range of 0%–5% by the year 2002/2003 (2006 for Vietnam, 2008 for Laos and Myanmar, and 2010 for Cambodia). The tariff reductions are moving ahead on both the "fast" and "normal" tracks. Tariffs on goods in the fast track were largely reduced to the range of 0%–5% by 2000. At present, ASEAN members have the option of excluding products from the CEPT in three cases: (1) Temporary exclusions; (2) Sensitive agricultural products; and (3) General exceptions. Temporary exclusions refer to products for which tariffs will ultimately be lowered to 0%–5%, but which are being protected temporarily by a delay in tariff reductions. This is permissible under the AFTA agreement, and is spelled out under a *Protocol Regarding the Implementation of the CEPT Scheme Temporary Exclusion List*. (Malaysia invoked this protocol in 2000, delaying tariff reductions on completely-built-up automobiles, and automobile knock-down kits, in order to protect its local auto industry.) Furthermore, a small number of sensitive agricultural products were given an extension till the year 2010 for their integration into the CEPT scheme. General Exceptions refer to products, which a country deems necessary for the protection of national security, public morals, the protection of human, animal, or plant life and health, and protection of articles of artistic, historic, or archaeological value. Approximately one percent of ASEAN tariff lines fall into this category. In the longer term, the ASEAN countries have agreed to enact *zero* tariff rates on virtually all imports till 2010 for the original signatories and 2015 for the four newer ASEAN members. (*Source*: http://www.us-asean.org/afta.asp.)

Three points emerge: First, the initial timeframe of AFTA was kept as 15 years, which is longer than the practice of 10-year implementation period. Second, agriculture was excluded initially with some exceptions maintained till now. Third, newer members have been given further phase of transition. The imperatives of safeguarding national economic interests, especially in the farm sector, and addressing developmental concerns over a sufficiently long period of time are best highlighted by the evolution of AFTA itself.

2. ASEAN–China FTA

The number of tariff lines which each Party can place in the Sensitive Track shall be subjected to a maximum ceiling of: (i) ASEAN-6 and China: 400 tariff lines at the HS six-digit level and 10% of the total import value, based on 2001 trade statistics; (ii) Cambodia, Lao PDR and Myanmar: 500 tariff lines at the HS six-digit level; and (iii) Viet Nam: 500 tariff lines at the HS six-digit level, and the ceiling of import value shall be determined not later than December 31, 2004.

Tariff lines placed by each Party in the Sensitive Track shall be further classified into Sensitive List and Highly Sensitive List. However, tariff lines placed by each Party in the Highly Sensitive List shall be subject to the following ceilings: (i) ASEAN-6 and China: not more than 40% of the total number of tariff lines in the Sensitive Track or 100 tariff lines at the HS six-digit level, whichever is lower; (ii) Cambodia, Lao PDR, and Myanmar: not more than 40% of the total number of tariff lines in the Sensitive Track or 150 tariff lines at the HS six-digit level, whichever is lower; and (iii) Viet Nam: shall be determined not later than December 31, 2004 (http://www.aseansec. org/4979.htm).

Reportedly, India and ASEAN have been having maximum problems in the areas of Coffee, Tea (black), Pepper, and Palm oil (Crude and refined). It is interesting to note that under the ASEAN–China FTA, China has been able to meet the above mentioned stipulations even while keeping three out of five HS six-digit items of Coffee and the only two six-digit items of Pepper in the Sensitive List. China has also placed Palm oil both crude and refined in the Highly Sensitive List. Other countries of the ASEAN have also kept several items of the agriculture sector in these sensitive and highly sensitive lists.

However, it must be mentioned that these lists are subject to tariff reduction. In the case of Sensitive list it also entails elimination. In the case of the Highly Sensitive List, tariffs are to be reduced up to 50%. This is different for India's commitment to any tariff reduction on negative list items.

3.   ASEAN–South Korea FTA

The signing of the ASEAN–South Korea FTA recently, without Thailand being a party to it from the ASEAN side, is a glaring example of how countries do not compromise on their agriculture-sector related sensitivities. It is reported that Thailand was left out due to objections to South Korea's barriers on farm products. Thailand decided to step aside rather than hold the rest of ASEAN back over its demand that the FTA with South Korea should cover rice — which is one of Thailand's key exports. This implies that ASEAN minus Thailand has not forced South Korea beyond a point when it came to safeguarding the farm sector by the South Koreans. It may also be highlighted that while the issue of Thai rice exports to South Korea was a major concern, some other agricultural items were also issues of contention.

Reports suggest that South Korea has designated 200 agricultural products that will be exempted from tariff reductions due to their effect on local farmers. South Korea would also hold onto tariffs on 40 *super sensitive* products, while gradually reducing duties on others in the following years. The exceptions to tariff cuts include mostly agricultural products like rice, chili peppers, garlic, beef, pork, chicken, pineapples, apples, and pears. South Korea will maintain the existing level of tariffs on products such as ginseng, powered milk and sweet potatoes until 2015, before cutting tariffs by 20% at beginning of 2016. Similar treatment will apply to corn and orange juice but the rate of cuts will reach only up to 50% of the present levels. This also gives the impression that this FTA too has the provisions of the Sensitive and Highly Sensitive Lists on the lines of the ASEAN–China FTA (*The Nation*, 2006b).

4. *Japan–Philippines Economic Partnership Agreement*

Japan and Philippines decided in 2003 that the two Governments should start negotiations at the beginning of 2004 for a Japan–Philippines Economic Partnership Agreement (JPEPA). Based upon the discussions of the Working Group and the Joint Coordinating Team for the Agreement the two countries confirmed on November 29, 2004, that both sides had reached agreements in principle on major elements of the Agreement.

In terms of one of the outcomes, it was decided that on a major part of agricultural, forestry, and fishery products tariffs will be eliminated within 10 years as far as Market Access Improvement by the **Japanese side** was concerned. However, in terms of the specifics, the following details suggest how Japan could take care of product-specific sensitivities of its agriculture sector.

(a) Sugar:
- Raw cane sugar requires re-negotiation in the fourth year after the entry into force of the JPEPA.
- Cane molasses has a Tariff Rate Quota (TRQ) with in-quota rate as 50% of MFN applied rate.
- Mascovado sugar (a type of un-centrifugal sugar which is produced specifically in the Philippines) for retail sale (not more than 1kg/container) has a TRQ with in-quota rate as 50% of MFN applied rate.

(b) Chicken meat has a TRQ with in-quota rate as 8.5% of MFN applied rate.

(c) Pineapples do not have TRQ with in-quota rate.

(d) Fishery products:
- Fresh, chilled or frozen yellowfin tunas and skipjack will undergo tariff elimination in 5 years after the entry into force of the JPEPA.

- Other specific tuna species will undergo re-negotiation in the 5th year after the entry into force of the JPEPA.

(e) Bananas:

- Small bananas will undergo tariff elimination in 10 years after the entry into force of the JPEPA.
- Other bananas: Winter tariff rate will decrease from 20% to 18% in 10 years and Summer tariff rate will decrease from 10% to 8% in 10 years.

(f) Sensitive Products for Exclusion or Re-negotiation consists of State trading products (such as rice, wheat, barley, and designated dairy products), beef, pork, starches, fishery products under import quota, etc.

- Market Access Improvement by the Philippine side was effected with an immediate tariff elimination on grapes, apples, pears, etc. (http://www.mofa.go.jp/region/asia-paci/philippine/joint0411. html).

5. *Japan–Thailand Economic Partnership Agreement*

On the basis of a series of negotiations since February 2004, Japan and Thailand jointly announced on September 1, 2005, that agreement in principle has reached on all major elements of the Japan–Thailand Economic Partnership Agreement (JTEPA). They expected the JTEPA to be signed in 2006.

It is clear from the details below that just as in the case of the JPEPA, Japan has been able to address its product-specific sensitivities of the agriculture and related sectors vis-à-vis Thailand as well. The Market Access Improvement by **Japan** includes:

(i) Agricultural Products

- Mangoes, Mangosteens, Durians, Papayas, Rambutan, Okra, and Coconut whose tariff on the date of entry into force of the JTEPA will be eliminated.
- Bananas have a duty-free TRQ with in-quota rate.
- Fresh small pineapples have a duty free TRQ with in-quota rate.

- Fresh, frozen vegetables will undergo tariff elimination within 5–10 years
- Prepared, preserved chicken meat will undergo tariff reduction from 6% to 3% in 5 years
- Prepared, preserved pork and ham has TRQ with in-quota rate reduction by 20% of MFN rate
- Rice bran oil will undergo tariff reduction by 55.5% in 5 years
- Pet food will undergo tariff elimination in 10 years
- Cane molasses: Introduction of TRQ on cane molasses in the third year with in-quota rate is reduced by 50% of out-quota rate
- Esterified Starch contains a duty free TRQ with in-quota tariff rate

(ii) Fishery Products

- Fish Fillet and jellyfish, fresh and frozen Mongo Ika will undergo tariff elimination in 5 years
- Prepared, preserved tuna, skipjack, other bonito and crab will undergo tariff elimination in 5 years

(iii) Forestry Products

- Particleboard and fiberboard will undergo Tariff elimination in 10 years

(iv) Exclusion or Re-negotiation includes:

- Rice, wheat, barley, fresh, frozen and chilled beef and pork, raw cane and beet sugar, refined sugar, starches, canned pineapple, plywood, fishery products under import quota, tuna and skipjack, most items of prepared beef and pork, and designated items of dairy products.

(a) Market access improvement by Thailand includes:

* Fishes as Thailand's raw materials in fishery industry
— Yellow fin Tuna, Skipjack Tuna, and Sardines which will undergo tariff elimination in 5 years

(b) Exclusion or Re-negotiation includes: mackerel, tobacco, raw silk, bird's egg, dried egg yolks, and some designated items of fish. (http://www.mofa.go.jp/region/asia-paci/thailand/joint0509/index.html).

6. *Japan–Malaysia Economic Partnership Agreement*

Japan and Malaysia confirmed that agreement in principle has been reached, on major elements of the JMEPA, on May 25, 2005. The Agreement came in force on July 13, 2006. The domestic agricultural sensitivities have been tackled by Japan in similar manner as in the case of their engagements with Philippines and Thailand. This is evident by the following coverage of products and their safeguard modalities.

(i) Market access improvement by Japan

    (a) Agricultural products

- Margarine will undergo a tariff reduction from 29.8% to 25% in 5 years followed by the renegotiation in the 5th year
- Cocoa preparations (not containing added sugar) will undergo tariff elimination
- Bananas contains a duty free TRQ with in-quota rate

    (b) Forestry products

- Plywood: needs renegotiation.
- Cooperation:
    - o national timber quality evaluation system
    - o enhancing trade in wood products from sustainable resources

    (c) Fishery products

- Shrimps, prawns, and jellyfish under tariff elimination

    (d) Sensitive products for exclusion or re-negotiation:

- State trading products (rice, wheat, barley, and designated dairy products), beef, pork, starches, fishery products under import quota, etc.
- Market access improvement by Malaysia

- Immediate tariff elimination on apples, pears and persimmons. (http://www.mofa.go.jp/region/asia-paci/malaysia/joint0505. html).

7. *Thailand–Australia FTA*

As soon as Thailand–Australia FTA (TAFTA) entered into force, Thailand eliminated tariffs on more than 50% of products, accounting for nearly 80% of Australia's exports to Thailand. Tariffs on a further 40% of goods were phased down and eliminated by 2010. Importantly, all remaining Thai tariffs and tariff quotas were subjected to up-front cuts and then were eliminated by 2010 according to agreed phasing time-tables. Imports to Thailand of certain sensitive agricultural products (e.g., dairy, coffee, tea, and potatoes) were governed by TRQs. Under TAFTA, Thailand expanded their access for Australian imports under TRQs over a transition period that varied according to the product, with the eventual elimination of all TRQ restrictions.

Just as in any other similar agreement, this Agreement too included certain safeguard mechanisms against import surge. More importantly, in addition, special safeguards were applied to agricultural products, which both the countries considered as sensitive. The specific products are listed in Annex 5 of TAFTA, which also includes a time limit for application of a special safeguard to each product. If a particular volume level is triggered, the resulting safeguard action allowed additional duties to be imposed to a level up to the "Most-favored Nation" (MFN) tariff rate for the rest of the year. Thailand has access to the special safeguard mechanism for 41 dairy, meat, and horticultural items (Department of Foreign Affairs and Trade, Australian Government.

However, even the above-mentioned measures of safeguard have been proved insufficient. The sensitivities especially towards the agriculture sector have emerged in Thailand since the implementation of its FTAs with China, Australia, and New Zealand. Reports suggested that the agreement covering agricultural goods with China in 2003 has invoked protests from farmers, especially in the Northern provinces that have been flooded by lower priced agricultural products leading to a sharp reduction in local agricultural output. Australian and New Zealand dairy imports have also been the focus of local protests by farmers in recent times. Observations suggest a replacement of Thai products from Thai farms and from the supermarkets by Australian fruits and milk from New Zealand.

8. *US–Thailand FTA*

The first round of US–Thailand FTA negotiations was held in July 2004, with successive rounds held in October 2004 and April 2005. It was expected that this FTA would be mutually beneficial to both the countries. However, the agreement has reached a deadlock due to a lack of consensus on various issues including the treatment accorded to the agriculture sector. The status of present state of negotiations is summarized in the following excerpts from a Report submitted to the US Congress.

The two sides completed their Sixth round of FTA negotiations in Chiang Mai, Thailand on January 10–13, 2006. While US negotiators stated that some progress was made, they also expressed disappointment over the lack of progress in the talks. Major stumbling blocks reportedly include US proposals on IPR and liberalization of the services sector, including distribution, financial services (such as banking, insurance, and securities brokerage), and telecommunications. Thai officials have sought to reduce high US. tariffs on light trucks (25%) and restrictions on sugar imports. In addition, the January 2006, FTA talks reported temporarily were disrupted by an estimated 10,000 Thai protesters. On January 19, 2006, Nitya Pibulsonggram, who was a Thailand's lead negotiator in the US–Thailand FTA talks, resigned. Press reports stated that the resignation was induced in part by political opposition to the FTA by various groups. As a result, it is still unclear whether the US goal of completing the FTA negotiations by spring 2006 was achieved. (Ahearn and Morrison, 2006).

On the other hand, the point of view of the Thais toward the resistance to the US–Thai FTA clearly indicates their quests for safeguarding their national economic interests especially in the general field and agriculture field. The leading academician, Mr. Ath Pisalvanitch, who heads the Center for International Trade Study of Thai Chamber of Commerce University, noted that all sectors in Thailand are not ready for the opening up of the planned Thai–US FTA. "Even Thailand's agricultural sector which is considered mostly ready now for the planned Thai–US FTA, still needs some more time to improve quality, productivity, and standard of Thai farm products; while the banking sector is partly ready and the service sector is not ready at all in terms of developed database, personnel, capital, and advanced technology," he pointed out (MCOT News, 2006a).

Thai negotiators say US demands on drug patents are an unacceptable extension of WTO position. Talks on the agricultural goods sector also remained in flux, as the two sides said that they would exchange a list of goods eligible for tariff cuts in February. In this sector, US had a trade deficit of up to 100 million dollars, with Thailand exporting 670 million dollars and importing 570 million dollars worth of US farm products (*The Nation*, 2006a, 2006b; *MCOT News*).

9. Malaysia–South Korea FTA

A decision to pursue bilateral FTA negotiations between Malaysia and Korea was made in August 2004.

Preparation to commence the bilateral Malaysia–Korea FTA negotiations was discussed among the Ministries, Agencies, and the private sector representatives, simultaneously with preparation for the ASEAN–Korea FTA negotiations.

It was decided that the bilateral negotiations would commence after taking into account developments in the negotiations of the ASEAN–Korea FTA. The FTA in goods between ASEAN and Korea was completed in December 2005, and has entered into force recently, as mentioned earlier.

3.2.2.2. *Treatment of agriculture sector in agreements of the developed countries*

10. US–Australia FTA

The US sugar industry successfully lobbied so that US trade negotiators excluded sugar from the FTA agreement with Australia, the world's fourth largest sugar producing nation.

Likewise, in both the Australia FTA and in other FTAs with agricultural exporting countries, the US has made minimal concessions when it comes to reducing tariffs on agricultural imports (like meat and dairy, in the Australian case).

11. EU FTAs: Treatment to Agriculture

A review of European Union free trade agreements in agriculture — looking at Morocco, Egypt, South Africa, and Chile — and the impact on US interests reveals that they do not cover "substantially all trade," especially while looking at the agricultural sector individually. While the overall trade increased, the percentage of fully liberalized agricultural products was considerably less than those products that continued to incur some restriction to trade.

The apparent impact of these agreements on the competitiveness of US exports was substantial. With the continuation of preferences being given to third countries, the US stands to lose a considerable share in EU and third country markets. Combined with the expansion of the EU, liberalized trade between the EU and third countries will continue to grow and have an adverse effect on US producers (USDA Foreign Agricultural Service, 2005).

12. US–Israel FTA

The US–Israel Free Trade Area (FTA) agreement took effect from September 1, 1985 and is designed to stimulate trade between the US and Israel. The agreement, which has no expiration date, provides for the elimination of duties on merchandize from Israel entering the US. As of January 1, 1995, all eligible reduced rate imports from Israel were accorded duty-free treatment. The FTA does allow the two countries to protect sensitive agricultural sub-sectors with non-tariff barriers including import bans, quotas, and fees. In 2004, both the countries entered into a US–Israel Agricultural Agreement, which is characterized by greater liberalization commitments by Israel than the US. It includes provisions of TRQ for both the countries. However, in terms of tariff liberalization, Israel has also been allowed to maintain high tariff rates on agri-products).

3.2.2.3. *Summary*

The foregoing analysis of facts with respect to various FTAs and Economic Partnership Agreements (EPAs) of ASEAN (either ASEAN as a grouping or individual ASEAN member) with other countries suggests that product-specific sensitivities pertaining to the agriculture sector have been addressed in multifarious ways. This also comes out of the experiences in the developed world as well. The tools and modalities used for this purpose are recapitulated below:

- Exclusions of products from the ambit of tariff liberalization
- Imposition of import bans
- Longer tariff liberalization schedule
- Lower tariff cuts
- Extending the deadlines of liberalization (e.g., in the case of newer ASEAN members)
- Renegotiation provisions
- Tariff rate quotas (TRQs)
- Keeping out-quota rate different from MFN rate in applying TRQs
- Special safeguards on top of safeguards with import quantities specified
- Deferment of liberalization (some kind of back-loading)
- Tariff liberalization taking into account seasonal factors
- State Trading of agricultural products
- Non-tariff Barriers (NTBs) like quality evaluation and products obtained from sustainable sources
- Rules of origin tackling agricultural imports through well-defined criteria of "Wholly-obtained."

Two points are worth-highlighting: First, developed countries with whom an ASEAN member or ASEAN as a grouping has been engaged in FTA negotiations, have been able to tackle their agricultural sensitivities through various policy-tools. Second, ASEAN members have been relatively more liberal in their approach vis-à-vis their agriculture sector in such engagements.

To add to the vagueness of the sensitive/negative/exclusion list are a whole host of factors that make it difficult to negotiate the sensitive list at a fast pace and constrain it in keeping within a reasonable size-limit. Thus, the prime determinants of a sensitive list arise from:

- Exporters' interests
- Importers' interests
- Manufacturers Targeting Domestic Market
- Public Morals, Environment, Archaeological, etc.
- All Trade minus Substantially All Trade
- Stages of Development: S&DT for LDCs

3.2.3. Rules of Origin

Rules of Origin (ROO) have emerged as an area in which consensus is hard to achieve among countries, under any negotiations of India's trading arrangement. Disagreements over rules of origin have often deferred the implementation of several trade agreements, which India has been associated with, in recent times.

Much of such a phenomenon is attributable to a lack of sound understanding of the implications of rules of origin. It is thus imperative to develop a comprehensive view on the subject so as to prevent wastage of negotiating-time, to avoid cumbersome procedures, and to implement the agreements with the intention to reap the economic benefits of such endeavors as fast as possible.

3.2.3.1. The rationale

It is obvious that a country would like to allow goods from a partner country on a preferential duty basis under a trade agreement, provided the goods have originated in the partner country. However, there is always a possibility that third-country goods enter a country's markets through the partner country and that too, on a preferential basis. This phenomenon is well known as "trade deflection," which has the potential to undermine a country's MFN-customs regime. Thus, one of the prime objectives of rules of origin is to check trade deflection. It is also important to bear in mind that rules of origin are not to safeguard against imports *per se* instead they are to check deflected imports from third countries.

Rules of origin influence both our import patterns and export prospects. If they are too stringent, then they may provide import protection and scuttle our export prospects. But if they are too liberal, then the converse may be true. Thus, a combination of different modalities can give the policy space to balance the objectives of export promotion and efficient imports actually originating from the partner countries.

3.2.3.2. Modalities

Global practices have mostly combined the modality of change in tariff classification with local value addition norm, specific process test, regional cumulation, and non-qualifying operations. However, the exact mechanisms differ in NAFTA, agreements between the EC and its partners, MERCOSUR, and FTAs of Japan–Singapore, Australia–Thailand, and Singapore–US among others.

There are different methods of determining the originating status of products. Whether or not a product has originated in a particular country is decided, if the product has undergone substantial transformation. In other words, the final product should be distinct from its constituents. Three kinds of tests are applied to determine this. First, the change in tariff heading test whereby the tariff heading of the final product is different from the tariff headings of its components. Second is the percentage test according to which a minimum percentage of total value addition should be achieved with the help of indigenous inputs. And third, specified process tests that require a product to undergo certain stipulated processes.

However, agreement on implementing these tests is often difficult. For instance, the extent of "substantial transformation" for different products would depend on the level of disaggregation (i.e., HS four or six-digit level) on which tariff-shift is envisaged. Similarly, fixing of percentages of minimum value addition varies between products, depending on the prevailing labor costs and the product-specific import dependence of the country in terms of intermediates.

In terms of the specifics, a combination of change in tariff heading (CTH) at HS four-digit level and local content norm of 40% is neither too stringent to be akin to non-tariff barrier nor too liberal to open the floodgates for trade deflection. This is because on the spectrum of HS nomenclature of tariffs a movement towards a change in tariff classification at two-digit chapter level (CC) would be too stringent and conversely, a change in tariff at six-digit sub-heading level (CTSH) would be too liberal.

Transformation of inputs into output at HS four-digit level (CTH) thus provides the middle level balance in as much as it can check trade deflection and help achieve developmental objectives through enforcing manufacturing without becoming a stringent non-tariff barrier. By the same token, 40% stipulation of local content is neither too stringent to scuttle the prospects of imported inputs used in manufacturing nor too liberal to pave ways for third-country imports coming into any country on a preferential basis without undergoing adequate manufacturing process. A major advantage of combining CTH with 40% local content norm is that when used in conjunction they counter the demerits of each modality applied in isolation. In addition, there is always a scope to build product-specific derogations from such general rules.

A comprehensive approach towards rules of origin issues can therefore help solve several problems of RTA negotiations in which India is presently engaged. Such an approach has yielded straightening of negotiating positions on several occasions in the past including India–Sri Lanka FTA, India–Thailand FTA for the Early Harvest Program and India–Singapore CECA. Similarly, it is expected that a consensus on rules of origin would be arrived at the ongoing negotiations under different FTAs.

As it was mentioned, the twin criteria of rules of origin (change in tariff classification and value-addition percentage requirement) help to offset the well-known demerits of each of the two criteria. In this regard, it may be further highlighted that the change in tariff classification criterion has been found to be the most effective in checking trade deflection while trade creation takes place (Figure 3.1).

3.2.3.3. *Change in tariff heading versus change in tariff subheading*

Since the rules of origin have been decided upon in the context of India–ASEAN FTA negotiations as change in tariff subheading (CTSH)

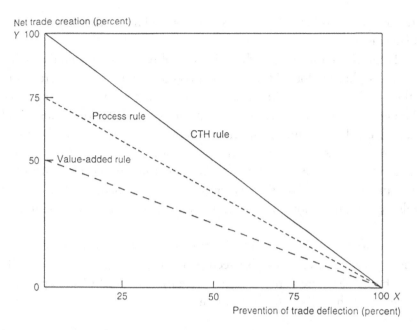

Figure 3.1. Trade off between net trade creation and prevention of trade deflection in an RTA with differing rules of origin.

Source: Stephenson and James (1995).

at HS six-digit level as opposed to change in tariff heading (CTH) at HS four-digit level, along with a 35% value addition norm it is pertinent to highlight some of the merits of CTH in comparison to the CTSH criterion.

The CTH rule enforces bilateral cumulation within a bilateral FTA and enhances bilateral trade. On the other hand, in the case of CTSH application such possibilities are limited. If partner country of India fulfils maximum of its raw material requirements through imports and technically the final product qualifies for a CTSH rule, then stipulating a CTH rule would imply that the partner country necessarily imports its material from India and qualifies for preference under the bilateral cumulation provision.

Second, the CTH rule could also ensure in the partner country the usage of a particular kind of manufacturing-technology in a manner that the raw materials have to be necessarily sourced from other HS four-digit level classifications.

Third, the application of the CTH rule also ensures certain minimum amount of local value addition in that country. Not all manufacturers in other countries produce the final product from basic raw material since different manufacturers are at different stages of production. Thus, CTH can ensure local value addition for granting the originating status to products and extending the tariff preferences. In case of CTSH such value addition possibilities might be compromised. It may be mentioned, that in such cases only the percentage test is applied, but accuracy of value addition is not guaranteed because of likelihood of accounting manipulations.

Accordingly, CTH safeguards national economic interests given the state of technology in different sectors of our country. Thus, the CTSH rule should be applied only in cases where there is a technical impossibility to apply and adhere to a CTH rule.

3.2.3.4. *Rules of Origin as a development policy tool*

It is true that rules of origin would not be redundant when a country, which is a member of different trade agreements, considerably reduces its MFN-tariffs to very low levels. In fact, there is evidence to suggest that stringent rules of origin and liberal tariff regimes are inversely related. The natural question arises as to why be that so?

The answer possibly lies in the fact that rules of origin are not just trade policy instruments aimed at preventing trade deflection. They are used as a developmental tool. First, these rules, executed through different modalities like change in tariff classification, value-addition norms, specific process tests, and non-qualifying operations, enforce domestic manufacturing that is in essence substantial in nature. The three modalities of determining origin of a product aim at substantial transformation in inputs. Thus, rules of origin together, facilitate value-addition in the country of manufacturing. Such requirements that check the import content of value addition, have the potential for generating backward and forward linkages in a country adhering to the rules. Thus, a member country is prevented from becoming a mere trading country as these requirements act as a deterrent to assembly kind of production activities. The rules of origin thus, have important implications for the development of the manufacturing sector as a whole, which in turn, contributes toward enhancing the export supply capabilities of the member country.

Second, it provides an impetus to the necessary commensurate supportive services sector activities. It can be argued that manufacturing activities brought about with the help of rules of origin stipulations in order to export the final product under a preferential trade agreement cannot be possibly executed without the existence of a supportive services sector. For instance, trade in goods is incumbent upon the presence of facilitative services like post-shipment credit, consignment-insurance, bank-guarantees, shipping services, etc. that not only facilitate trade but also contribute to the competitiveness of exports.

Third, rules of origin have been used as instruments to promote investment to boost regional production, especially in NAFTA. It has been highlighted by Rugman (1998) as to how rules of origin have been used in NAFTA to attract foreign investment for talking advantage of the regional market in NAFTA by the non-member countries.

Fourth, through regional/bilateral cumulation provisions of origin-rules regional/bilateral trade flows can be augmented. All these positive effects on manufacturing (and on agriculture, through agriculture-industry linkages), services and investment have important implications for employment and income generation, foreign exchange earnings, and regional integration. In a nutshell, the rules of origin, if used in a comprehensive manner can help achieve developmental objectives. It is in this sense that they can become a developmental tool and have the potential to strengthen trade-development linkages under RTAs/FTAs.

3.2.3.5. *Enhancing the feasibility of welfare-inducing FTA*

Incorporating intermediate inputs into a small-union general-equilibrium model, Duttagupta and Panagariya (2003) developed the welfare economics of preferential trading under the rules of origin demonstrating that a welfare reducing FTA that was rejected in the absence of the ROO becomes feasible in the presence of these rules. Second, a welfare improving FTA that was rejected in the absence of the ROO is endorsed in their presence, but upon endorsement it becomes welfare inferior relative to the *status quo*. This could happen because "the ROO increases the price of the regionally produced intermediate input and hence effectively provides protection to it. The FTA that was unattractive to the input exporter in the absence of a ROO can now become attractive. Therefore, the ROO could make a previously infeasible FTA feasible." One may argue that a combination of different origin-rules contributes to such an effect.

Hence, rules of origin do not lose their significance if tariff levels are reduced. The rules of origin are important also in the context of imposition of anti-dumping duties and countervailing duties. Without them it is difficult to collect even trade statistics. It is not without reason that even for non-preferential trade flows rules of origin are important and there is a WTO Agreement on Rules of Origin.

In the end, it is worth reiterating that rules of origin, if devised and understood adequately, could serve as a development policy tool within the ambit of a regional economic cooperation agreement. It can contribute to trade and investment expansion and through its emphasis on value addition; it has a rich potential for employment and income generation.

3.2.4. Trade in services

3.2.4.1. Uniqueness of services

Services are different in their characteristics as compared to goods. Their unique characteristics also influence the way international transactions in services are conducted. In other words, trade in services has distinct features that need to be analyzed and understood.

3.2.4.2. Major characteristics of services

Services encompass many different economic activities. They can be defined as economic activities that add value either directly to another person or to a good belonging to another person. Services possess three main characteristics that make them very different from goods. First, they are intangible, though often incorporated in tangible products. Second, they are non-storable. Finally, they involve a simultaneous action between the service provider and the service consumer.

Moreover, unlike goods production, ownership of a service is often not transferred during the process of service provision. Hence, services cannot be stored. Instead, the service supplier stores the capacity to provide the service to be rendered at a time when there is a demand for that service. The inability to store means that services mostly are produced and consumed simultaneously.

3.2.4.3. *Theories of trade in services*

There has been little work done in terms of developing a theoretical construct for trade in services. Seth (2006) summarized the theories dealing with trade in goods that fails to capture the dynamics of trade in services: "According to Melvin (1989), when producer services are incorporated into the standard Heckscher–Ohlin framework which is contrary to the conclusion arrived at by Hindley and Smith (1984), it requires modifications; this necessitates the reformulation of the law of comparative advantage because in the context of services, it is difficult to know what is exactly being traded. This problem was also illustrated by him with the help of an example: If there is a productive activity with a production function $Q = f(x_1, x_2)$ where Q stands for output, x_1 and x_2 are inputs one of which is producer service. If production of the product is being organized in Canada and x_1 is supplied by the US, the product here is automobile, x_2 represents Canadian labor and x_1 capital from US, then x_1 represents foreign direct investment by US in Canada, but not trade. If instead, x_1 represents foreign know-how or management service, then x_1 represents trade in services. On the contrary, if Q represents haircut, x_1 represents barbers shops, then Q can be interpreted as US exports of haircut, despite the fact that production of this service is located in Canada. If another example is taken where x_1 stands for Japanese cars then x_2 will stand for Canadian car dealership and Q for number of Japanese cars sold in Canada. Here, Q also stands for imports of car from Japan, though a part of the value has been added by the services rendered by the Canadian car dealer" (p. 174).

"The example given above illustrates the fact that even though the structure of production is the same in the production of Q, it leads to different consequences depending on what is being imported. To avoid the complexity of these situations, if we just pay attention to international payments and accept x_1 as an import, when international payments are made for x_1, ignoring whether it stands for capital, a service, or as an intermediate commodity. Following this logic leads us to believe that x_1 is always an import and Q stands for domestic production. Hence, in the haircut example, the import is barber's services not haircut. This distinction is quite crucial to avoid logical inconsistencies" (pp. 174–175).

"However, according to Hindley (1990), the global integration of markets of services is quite different from global integration of markets of goods. Due to the differences in the nature of integration of markets in goods and services, price equalization, as a consequence of trade, as predicted by Heckscher–Ohlin theory, may not occur in services. This happens because services remain embedded in local economic and regulatory environment, and due to trade in services that involves the use of local as well as imported factors" (p. 175).

Due to the above characteristics, trade in services assumes a special character. The simultaneous nature of service transaction impacts upon the modalities of international transactions in services. Thus, issues relating to trade in services need to be approached differently from trade in goods.

If a service provider in one country possesses a desired service, then the service provider must somehow interact with service consumers in other countries for the trade to take place. Services have in fact often been characterized as non-tradable in the sense that they involve movement in factors of production. For instance, provision of services to global markets often necessitates the movement of capital (economic activities generated through foreign direct investment) or labor (personnel to manage such activities or to provide different types of expertise, including basic labor).

According to Stern and Hoekman (1988) services can be (a) complementary to trade in goods, (b) substitute for trade in goods, or (c) unrelated to goods. Depending on these, implications for services trade would change. The intangibility and non-storability of services imply that in order for them to become tradable, services have to be embodied in objects, information flows or persons. When services are globally traded through crossing borders they are embedded into products such as in the case of computer programs in CD-ROMs, air transport through aircraft, music in digital products, films in videotapes, etc. Some services may be transmitted via the telecommunications networks.

Thus, for services trade to occur, the means of transporting the services often have to be allowed to cross national boundaries. This makes international transaction in services more complex conceptually than international transactions in goods. Most services, however, are supplied directly by their providers in a foreign market, and for this reason cannot be dissociated from international movement of capital or labor, as well as accompanying knowledge, and technology.

It has been acknowledged in the literature that physical proximity in services trade may not be a necessary condition always (see, e.g., Bhagwati, 1984). It is for this reason that international transactions in services have been defined according to four modalities (Mattoo *et al.*, 2008 and Sampson and Snape, 1985) and later set out in Article I of the GATS viz. Cross-border Supply, Consumption Abroad, Commercial Presence, and Supply through Movement of Natural Persons.

- Mode 1 (Cross-border supply), where the service itself crosses the border but consumer does not move (e.g., a company providing Business Process Outsourcing services through electronic means to consumers in another country).
- Mode 2 (Consumption abroad), where the consumer travels to the country where the service is supplied (e.g., a person going abroad to consume tourism or education services).
- Mode 3 (Commercial presence), where the service provider establishes a commercial presence abroad (e.g., an insurance company owned by the citizens of one country establishing a branch by means of FDI in another country).
- Mode 4 (Movement of natural persons), where the provider of the service moves temporarily to the territory of another country to supply a service (e.g., a software professional of one country supplying services through his/her physical presence in another country).

Domestic regulations pertaining to trade in services are akin to tariff or other barriers of trade in goods. Since the tariff route is not available, for the sake of liberalization it is tackled through commitments on Market Access and National Treatment, for each of the services in the various sectors and sub-sectors, for the four different modes. This makes the task quite complex in a plurilateral or multilateral framework. The commitments negotiated through some offers and requests can be horizontal — cutting across all sectors; confined to sectors or sub sectors, or particular modes of supply.

Added to such complexities are sector-specific nuances and intricacies. It is thus imperative to approach the services negotiations based on a sectoral cost-benefit analysis. It is against this background that some of the analytical issues pertaining to regional cooperation in scrvices sector in the SAARC region are highlighted below.

3.2.4.4. *Relevance of services trade integration in SAARC*

With the SAFTA Treaty, the process of SAARC economic cooperation reached a milestone. However, in order to realize full benefits of SAFTA, a developmental and integrated approach towards trade in goods is needed. This stems from the fact that trade in goods and trade in services could be used to reinforce each other. More broadly, trade and investment linkages need to be strengthened. This is perhaps possible, among others, by focusing on one of the several modes of trade in services. All these together, bring the developmental focus to regional trade and investment cooperation, especially in South Asia. It is in this context, that efficiency-seeking regional restructuring becomes important and achieving a South Asian Economic Union becomes realistic, with the help of concentrating on another mode of service delivery.

These only highlight that the SAARC regional economic integration process needs to adopt extensive and intensive approaches simultaneously. The former may entail expanding the scope of SAARC economic cooperation to include trade in services within its ambit. This would help integrate the region in the realms of factors of production including long term capital flows in the form of investment and movement of natural persons, leading to a South Asian Economic Union (see also Dhar, 2010 and Dubey, 2007). The latter would mean expediting these economic integration processes. However, such imperatives do not preclude instituting adequate safeguards to contain any deleterious effects that these might have.

Theoretically, services liberalization may be more easily negotiated among regional partners due to similarity in levels of development, geographical proximity, and cultural ties. This may be attributed to the possibility of a greater degree of reciprocity, thus reducing the free-rider problem, which would be possible through multilateral negotiations (UNCTAD, 2007).

Thus, the economics of neighborhood becomes relevant in this context. For instance, sectors like health services, education, transport, tourism, and others have rich potential to get traded regionally due to simultaneous presence of service consumers and providers. This does not mean that these sectors do not have potential for integration on an extra-regional basis. The short point is that the case for regional integration in such sectors appears to be strong, conceptually. In terms of modes of services trade too, Modes 2, 3 and 4 take a region towards a deeper level of integration, as highlighted earlier.

Similarities among countries in a region also help regulatory cooperation on mutual recognition or harmonization of professional qualifications, licensing certification, technical standards, competition laws, and provisions for labor mobility.

Above all these arguments, in favor of regional services trade liberalization, the arguments in terms of considering regional cooperation as building blocs for multilateral liberalization, contributing to preparedness at a smaller level for global integration, and economies of scale achieved through efficiency-seeking regional restructuring also apply to the services sector just as in the case of goods.

3.2.5. Investment cooperation

It is further acknowledged in India's RTAs that the strengthening of trade-investment linkages is a pre-requisite for achieving economic successes because of the fact that trade deficits between bigger and smaller countries need to be compensated by capital account surpluses wherein outward-FDI from bigger to smaller countries takes place. This kind of linkage helps in improving export supply capabilities of the smaller countries and in the second round there are favorable trade effects.

The real gains from an FTA result from efficiency-seeking industrial restructuring, which also builds productive capacities in relatively lesser-developed economies. Therefore, most of the new age free trade arrangements of India are trying to combine trade in goods and services with investment liberalization (Kumar, 2007b).

The trade-investment linkages also run in both the directions. While a free trade agreement can spur investment flows in terms of efficiency-seeking regional restructuring, it is the trade-creating joint ventures that ultimately have a decisive impact on regional trade flows. The trade-creating joint ventures are in a position to take advantage of the regional free trade agreement. In this context, in a dynamic scenario, vertical integration and horizontal specialization could be focused upon with the help of cross-country investment flows that strengthen trade-investment linkages. This may essentially mean distribution of different stages of production in a particular industry regionally in an integrated manner viz. the vertical integration and specialization in the same stage of production with the help of product differentiation across the region viz. the horizontal specialization (Das, 2004). This is the basis of argument highlighting the imperatives of moving beyond SAFTA to bring in investment cooperation within the ambit of the South Asian economic integration process.

This chapter has provided a synoptic view of some of the conceptual basis for RTAs along with certain related insights into the complex negotiating processes. With this, we move on to assess what some of these RTAs mean in terms of their empirics.

Annex 3.1

Economics of a Free Trade Agreement: A Glossary

Trade Trends

Regionalism includes any formal trading agreements between two or more countries.

Regionalization is a market — bed process of increasing economic interaction by unilateral liberalization, market-oriented reforms, and successful economic growth.

Regionalization came late to Asia as compared to Regionalization which has been building up momentum in Asia for decades. Formal preferential trading arrangements, particularly in the form of FTA's, free trade areas, are being developed to enhance regionalization as part of overall process of economic reform, in most of Asia, to encourage the outward-oriented developed strategies of two region's economies.

Rise of Free Trade Agreements in Asia and the Pacific

The spread of regionalization is one of the most important recent developments in global trade system and trade between FTA partners make up to almost two-thirds of global trade. Though Asia is a latecomer in the move towards FTA's but has seen a dramatic increase from FTA's involving Asian countries in the early 1990's. The factors which have contributed to it include:

(i) a defensive response to the proliferation of trading blocs and FTA's in other major regions,
(ii) uncertainty over progress in global trade talks under WTO,
(iii) the need to improve productivity against competitive pressure from China and India, with respect to economies of scale through market integration,
(iv) the need for deeper integration with trading partners, and
(v) the promotion of "beyond the border" structural reforms as part of a competitiveness strategy.

Among the Asian subregions, East Asia is most active in forming FTA's, almost double the number of FTA's involving central or South Asian countries and the Pacific is the least involved in FTA formation. An important feature of the rise in the number of FTA's in Asia is the growing number of overlapping agreements that has emerged from the proliferation of bilateral and plurilateral FTA's in the region.

According to ADB (Asian Development Bank) estimates, Asian countries are involved in 156 bilateral and 48 plurilateral FTA's in various stages of implementation. Many of these agreements are with countries outside the region, which itself shows the importance of external markets for the export of final products.

Why Enter into a Free Trade Agreement? — Political and Economic Goals

While economics may be an important motivation in setting up an FTA, political circumstances also dominate.

Gains from Trade

This concept was developed by economist "David Richards" and has been used to promote the need for trade liberalization. As a country specializes in the products that it produces most efficiently, and then trades the goods in surplus, it is able to improve its standard of living. The country uses its resources in the most productive way; so on the supply side, efficient structural adjustment takes place. On the demand side, consumers are able to purchase imports at the lowest price and firms are able to source the most cost — effective inputs. When all countries specialize in their "comparative advantage" products, the entire world is better off and global prosperity is maximized.

Economic integration changes from inter-industry trade to intra-industry trade. Recent trends in East Asia show this process. At first, trade was inter-industry, but after the Asian crisis, East Asian countries have engaged more in intra-industry trade, that is responsible for rising intra-regional trade share and greater economic symmetry, which leads to distinction between "horizontal" and "vertical" specialization.

Horizontal specialization relates to production according to comparative advantage.

Vertical specialization focuses on the many parts processes that make up the production of a final good i.e., the "value chain."

Static Effects of FTA's refers to the effect on price changes induced by preferential tariff liberalization. Free trade areas remove discrimination between partner countries and domestic firms, hence home and country prices of tradable goods that tends to be equalized as barriers to trade are reduced. However, FTA's create a new form of discrimination between the exports of partner and non-partner countries. Thus, the net (static) effects of an FTA depend on the degree of trade creation compared with trade diversion. Here trade liberalization is the "first best" option and regionalism is the "second best" option.

Dynamic Effects refers to the medium and long term implication of regional integration and tends to be more significant. They are also more pervasive, affecting almost all the areas that relate to an economy's competitiveness. The most important dynamic effects in content to FTA's are — *economies of scale, technology transfer and foreign direct investment (FDI), and structural policy change and reform.*

Economies of scale its importance in context of FTA's is by creating a larger market for firms operating in partner countries, an FTA will allow producers to take advantage of a larger customer base and hence, produce at a lower average cost on all sales. Firms will even be able to lower prices for existing customers — the "cost-reduction effect." As a result, they become more competitive not only at home but also in foreign market.

Economics of Consolidation/Harmonization

Does regionalism support unilateral or multilateral reform goals?

Several possible negative policy consequences emerge also from an FTA, while other tendencies are consistent with multilateral goals and market-friendly domestic liberalization.

Stumbling Blocs

- Maximizing terms-of-trade gains. Regional integration increases the size of an economic zone and hence increases market power. The larger the grouping, the larger the potential improvement in terms of trade.

- Special interests manipulating the contents and scope of the agreement — this is a problem in context of accords between developed and developing countries, in which former have an upper hand, as special interests tend to be far better organized and funded.

- Waste of scarce negotiating resources. Particularly in case of developing economies, the scarcity of well-trained and well-experienced experts in trade negotiations implies an opportunity cost of less resources being devoted to multilateral negotiations if all talent is engaged in regional deals.

Building Blocs

- Locked-in policy change.
  Regional integration can be seen as a blue print for market friendly reform and increased competitiveness in the international market place.

- Improved negotiating power for smaller units.
  The possibility of small countries joining together and working as one cohesive unit in trade negotiation has always been considered as an advantage of regionalism. This applies both to smaller countries as well as larger units.

- Competitive liberalization to attract international capital as well as a positive "threat."
  By reducing transaction costs across countries, an FTA can enhance to attractiveness to MNC's. As an FTA deepens and policy externalizes because that is increasingly important, the incentive to internalize them through monitoring, information, sharing, closer cooperation, etc., increases.
  Both the stumbling block and building bloc arguments have theoretical merit. But in practice, the inclination of regional accord tends to be extremely important. If outward-oriented economies were to form a regional grouping, regionalism is likely to promote the goals of domestic policy reform and multilateral liberalization.

Annex 3.2: Asian RTAs in Brief

RTA	Description	Type	Status	Year	Tariffs (Goods)	Rules of Origin (Goods)	Standards (Goods)	Specific Sectors Covered (Services)	Investment (Others)
ACFTA	Agreement on Trade in Goods of the Framework Agreement on Comprehensive Economic Cooperation between the Association of Southeast Asian Nations and the People's Republic of China	Free Trade Agreement	In force since	2005	Tariff reduction or elimination program under this Agreement shall include all tariff lines not covered by the Early Harvest Program under Article 6 of the Framework Agreement (see ASEAN-China FA) Normal track (details in Annex 1) and Sensitive track (details in Annex 2) Tariff reduction and elimination undertaken by each party (subject to Annex 1 and Annex 2) shall be applied to all other parties.	Article 5 or the FTA and Annex 3. Rules of origin applicable to the products covered under the FTA and the Early Harvest Program of the Framework Agreement. The Agreement uses the ASEAN rules of origin.			No

(Continued)

Annex 3.2 *(Continued)*

RTA	Description	Type	Status	Year	Tariffs (Goods)	Rules of Origin (Goods)	Standards (Goods)	Specific Sectors Covered (Services)	Investment (Others)
ACFTA-Services	Agreement on Trade in Services of the Framework Agreement on Comprehensive Economic Cooperation between ASEAN and the People's Republic of China	Free Trade Agreement	In force since	2007	n.a.	n.a.		This agreement is just a platform agreement setting the stage for negotiations of specific commitments. Parties endeavor to achieve commitments beyond GATS (Article 21).	No
AJCEP	Agreement on Comprehensive Economics Partnership among Japan and the Member States of the ASEAN	Free Trade Agreement	In force since	2008	Based on positive lists — schedules for each member available at http://www.mofa.go.jp/policy/economy/fta/asean/annex1.html	http://www.mofa.go.jp/policy/economy/fta/asean/annex2.pdf Chapter 3 of the agreement	SPS measures in chapter 4 of the agreement; Standards and technical regulations in chapter 5 of the agreement		Yes. Article 51 referring to future negotiation on investment
AKFTA	Agreement on Trade in Goods under the Framework Agreement on	Free Trade Agreement	In force since	2007	Negative List; Normal and sensitive list tracks of the tariff reduction or elimination	Minimum content 40% FOB of product value or tariff heading change at			Yes

(Continued)

Annex 3.2 *(Continued)*

RTA	Description	Type	Status	Year	Tariffs (Goods)	Rules of Origin (Goods)	Standards (Goods)	Specific Sectors Covered (Services)	Investment (Others)
	Comprehensive Economic Cooperation Among the Governments of the Member Countries of the Association of Southeast Asian Nations and the Republic of Korea.				program; tariff elimination under normal track by 2010 (2016 for Vietnam, 2018 for Cambodia, Lao, PDR and Myanmar) — details in Annex 1 No provisions for coverage of agricultural goods.	4-digit level Specific manufacturing process specified for Textile and Garment			
ANZCERTA	Australia–New Zealand Closer Economic Relations Trade Agreement	Free Trade Agreement	In force since	1983	Negative list; tariff elimination by 1990 Tariff reduction through negotiation Agriculture is covered by Article 10 (Agricultural stabilization and support) and by Annex E.	New Rules of Origin entered into effect on January 1, 2007. The new rules are largely based on satisfying a "change in tariff classification"™, or CTC, rather than the previous 50% "regional value	Calls for harmonization	Negative list approach. See sectors excluded.	No

(Continued)

Annex 3.2 (*Continued*)

RTA	Description	Type	Status	Year	Tariffs (Goods)	Rules of Origin (Goods)	Standards (Goods)	Specific Sectors Covered (Services)	Investment (Others)
						content* ™ threshold. Under the agreement exporters will have the option of using the old rules based on value content until 2012.			
APTA	Asia-Pacific Trade Agreement (previously known as Bangkok Agreement)	Preferential Trade Agreement	In force since	1976	Positive list (with each country's National List of Concessions - Annex Concessions effective upon signature of the agreement Possibility of further tariff reduction through negotiation (yearly reviews)	No tariff heading change necessary Minimum content: 45% (35% for LDC's) No specific manufacturing process required	n.a.	—	No
ASEAN–CER	ASEAN–ANZCERTA Free Trade Agreement	Free Trade Agreement	Under negotiation since	2004	n.a.	n.a.	n.a.	—	No

(*Continued*)

Annex 3.2 (*Continued*)

RTA	Description	Type	Status	Year	Tariffs (Goods)	Rules of Origin (Goods)	Standards (Goods)	Specific Sectors Covered (Services)	Investment (Others)
ASEAN–CHINA FA	Framework Agreement on Comprehensive Economic Cooperation between the Association of South–East Asian Nations and the People's Republic of China	Framework Agreement	In force since	2003	Positive list. Normal track — tariff elimination by 2010 for ASEAN-6 and China, 2015 for new ASEAN members Protocol to Amend the Agreement on Trade in Goods of the Framework Agreement signed December 8, 2006; see http://www.aseansec.org/19219.htm	Change in tariff classification is not an option Minimum content: 40% No specific manufacturing process required	n.a.	ASEAN-China Agreement on Trade in Services signed in 2007 covers (a) business services, (b) construction and engineering services, (c) tourism and travel services, (d) transport and educational services, (e) tele-communication services, (f) health-related and social services, (g) recreational, cultural, and	Yes. Article 5 talks about measures to promote investment: negotiations to progressively liberalize the investment regime; strenghten cooperation in investment, facilitate investment and improve transparency of investment rules and regulations, provide for the protection of investment

(*Continued*)

Annex 3.2   (*Continued*)

RTA	Description	Type	Status	Year	Tariffs (Goods)	Rules of Origin (Goods)	Standards (Goods)	Specific Sectors Covered (Services)	Investment (Others)
ASEAN-EU	ASEAN–European Union Free Trade Agreement	Free Trade Agreement	Under negotiation since	2007	n.a.	n.a.		sporting services, (h) environmental servies, and (i) energy services	No
ASEAN-INDIA FTA	ASEAN–India Free Trade Agreement	Free Trade Agreement	In force since	2010	Except a small sensitive list most of the goods covered for tariff reduction/ elimination.	CTSH+ 35% and PSRs	n.a.	Negotiations ongoing	Negotiations ongoing
ASEAN-KOREA FA	Framework Agreement on Comprehensive Economic Cooperation Among the Governments of the Members Countries of the Association of the Southeast Asian Nations and the Republic of Korea	Framework Agreement	In force since	2006	Liberalization of trade in goods is regulated with an additional Agreement on Trade in Goods (TIG) signed in August, 2006. (http://www. aseansec.org/ akfta.htm)	n.a.	n.a.	n.a.	Yes

(*Continued*)

Annex 3.2 (*Continued*)

RTA	Description	Type	Status	Year	Tariffs (Goods)	Rules of Origin (Goods)	Standards (Goods)	Specific Sectors Covered (Services)	Investment (Others)
ASEAN Goods-AFTA	ASEAN Free Trade Area	Free Trade Agreement	In force since	1993	Progressive reduction of tariffs based on mixture of positive list (CEPT Inclusion List) and negative list (Temporary Exclusion List, Sensitive List and Highly Sensitive List) Tariff reduction (to 0%–5% level) implemented in ASEAN-6, under way in new ASEAN members; working towards the elimination of non-tariff barriers. Goal to completely eliminate tariffs on all except products covered by the Protocol on Sensitive and Highly Sensitive Products by 2010 for ASEAN 6 and 2015 for CLMV	No tariff heading change necessary Minimum content 40% FOB No specific manufacturing process specified; product specific rules under negotiation	Creates the ASEAN Consultative committee for Standards and Quality		Yes. ASEAN Investment Area http:// www. aseansec. org/6462. htm

(*Continued*)

Annex 3.2 (*Continued*)

RTA	Description	Type	Status	Year	Tariffs (Goods)	Rules of Origin (Goods)	Standards (Goods)	Specific Sectors Covered (Services)	Investment (Others)
ASEAN Services-AFAS	ASEAN Framework Agreement on Services	Framework Agreement	In force since	1996	n.a.	n.a.	n.a.	Air transport; business services; construction; financial services; maritime transport; tele-communication; tourism MRAs are being negotiated in engineering, architecture, accountancy, surveying, and tourism	No
AUSFTA	United States–Australia Free Trade Agreement	Free Trade Agreement	In force since	2005	Negative list Tariffs scaled back, according to category, in up to 10 years. See Annex 2A Agriculture is covered in export subsidies (Art 3.3), safeguard measures (Art 3.4), TRQ (Art 3.5), and review of dairy market access in 20 years (Annex 2-B).	Change in tariff classification (2-to 6-digit level). Value added 35% to 50% on FOB value. No specific manufacturing process necessary	Calls for cooperation and recognition of the other party's regulations as long as they claim "same goals"	Negative list approach. Tele-communications, Financial Services	Yes

(*Continued*)

Annex 3.2   (Continued)

RTA	Description	Type	Status	Year	Tariffs (Goods)	Rules of Origin (Goods)	Standards (Goods)	Specific Sectors Covered (Services)	Investment (Others)
AUSTRALIA–CHINA	Australia–China Free Trade Agreement	Free Trade Agreement	Under negotiation since	2005	n.a.	n.a.	n.a.	n.a.	No
AUSTRALIA–JAPAN	Australia–Japan Trade and Economic Framework	Framework Agreement	Under negotiation since	2003	Under consultation and study	n.a.	n.a.		No
AUSTRALIA–MALAYSIA	Australia–Malaysia Free Trade Agreement	Free Trade Agreement	Under negotiation since	2005	n.a.	n.a.	n.a.	n.a.	No
AUSTRALIA–THAILAND	Thailand–Australia Free Trade Agreement	Free Trade Agreement	In force since	2005	Positive list and schedule Tariff elimination by 2010; Calls for consultations in order to accelerate the schedule Agricultural export subsidies (Art 208),	Change in Tariff heading (4- or 6-digit level). Value Added Content: 40%–55% FOB value No Specific Manufacturing Process Required	Chapter 6, including SPS		Yes, Chapter 9

(Continued)

Annex 3.2 (*Continued*)

RTA	Description	Type	Status	Year	Tariffs (Goods)	Rules of Origin (Goods)	Standards (Goods)	Specific Sectors Covered (Services)	Investment (Others)
BHUTAN–INDIA	Bhutan–India Free Trade Agreement	Free Trade Agreement	In force since	2006	No list available Tariff elimination since signing of the agreement	n.a.	n.a.	—	No
BIMSTEC	Bay of Bengal Initiative for Multi-Sectorial Technical and Economic Cooperation	Framework Agreement	In force since	1997	Negative list Tariff elimination by 2012 (2017 for LDCs)	ROO's in the agenda for further negotiation	under negotiation	The parties agree to enter into negotiations to progressively liberalize trade in services with substantial sectoral coverage through a positive list approach.	Yes
CHINA–HONG KONG, SAR	Mainland and Hong Kong Closer Economic Partnership Agreement	Free Trade Agreement	In force since	2004	Positive list Tariff elimination by 2005 Every year new products can be included in the non-tariff list (every October 1st)	Change in tariff heading (four-digit level) Minimum value content 30% FOB Some manufacturing processes accepted	n.a.	Positive list approach for China. See Annex IV for sectors covered	No

(*Continued*)

Annex 3.2 (*Continued*)

RTA	Description	Type	Status	Year	Tariffs (Goods)	Rules of Origin (Goods)	Standards (Goods)	Specific Sectors Covered (Services)	Investment (Others)
CHINA–KOREA	China–Korea Free Trade Agreement	Free Trade Agreement	Under negotiation since	2005	n.a.	n.a.	n.a.	n.a.	No
CHINA–MACAO, SAR	Mainland and Macao Closer Economic Partnership Agreement	Free Trade Agreement	In force since	2004	Positive list, can be reviewed annually tariff elimination by 2006	Change in tariff classification Value added 30% Specific manufacturing process required	n.a.	Positive list approach for China. For sectors covered see Annex IV	No
CHINA–PAKISTAN	Free Trade Agreement between the Government of the People's Republic of China and the Government of the Islamic Republic of Pakistan	Free Trade Agreement	In force since	2007	Progressive elimination according to Annex 1. Tariff reduction modality and the lists reviewed and modified every five years based on consultations. http://www.commerce.gov.pk/PCEHP.asp	n.a.	Chapter VI covers SPS; Chapter VII TBT	n.a.	Yes. Chapter IX on promotion and protection of investment and separate Articles 53 and 54 on settlement of disputes between parties

(*Continued*)

Annex 3.2 (*Continued*)

RTA	Description	Type	Status	Year	Tariffs (Goods)	Rules of Origin (Goods)	Standards (Goods)	Specific Sectors Covered (Services)	Investment (Others)
EFTA–KOREA	Free trade agreement between the EFTA States and the Republic of Korea	Free Trade Agreement	In force since	2006	Positive list-products in categories 25–97 of the HS, excluding those in Annex III and including those processed agricultural products as provided in Annex IV and fish and marine products as provided in Annex V There are separate individual agreements for agricultural products between Rep. of Korea and Each and EFTA State	Sufficient working and processing — Appendix 2 product group specific	Article 2.7 (SPS) and Article 2.8 (Technical regulations)	Financial services; tele-communication services. Positive list approach	Yes. Agreements on investment separately concluded between Rep. of Korea, on one hand, and Iceland, Liechten-stein and Switzerland, on the other. See http:// secretariat. efta.int/ Web/ External Relations/ Partner Countries/ Korea/KR/ KR%20Inv% 20Agr/ KR_Inv_Ag. pdf

(*Continued*)

Annex 3.2 (*Continued*)

RTA	Description	Type	Status	Year	Tariffs (Goods)	Rules of Origin (Goods)	Standards (Goods)	Specific Sectors Covered (Services)	Investment (Others)
EFTA–SINGAPORE	Free Trade Agreement between the EFTA States and Singapore	Free Trade Agreement	In force since	2003	Positive list of products covered, but with exceptions Tariff elimination by signing of the agreement 2-year revision of the	Change in tariff classification not considered Value added, 50% for some products Some products have to go through a specific process to be considered originating	Subject to WTO Agreement on SPS	Positive list approach.	Yes. Asset based-open list: includes FDI, portfolio investment and various forms of tangible and intangible property.
GSTP	Global System of Trade Preferences among Developing Countries	Preferential Trade Agreement	In force since	1989	Positive list for tariff concessions Three rounds of negotiations to exchange concessions, third round in 2004 Article 17 stipulates Special treatment for LDCs.	Minimum value of content not less than 50% FOB value of the products produced or obtained, for LDC not less than 40%. Accumulation			No

(*Continued*)

Annex 3.2 (*Continued*)

RTA	Description	Type	Status	Year	Tariffs (Goods)	Rules of Origin (Goods)	Standards (Goods)	Specific Sectors Covered (Services)	Investment (Others)
						where aggregate contents originating in the members is not less than 60% FOB value of the products produced or obtained Single certificate of origin			
INDIA–CHILE	Preferential Trade Agreement between the Republic of India and the Republic of Chile	Preferential Trade Agreement	Pending country ratifi-cation		Elimination of tariffs based on positive list provided in Annexes A and B Acceleration of elimination or reduction of tariffs or inclusion of new products to annexes upon consultation.	Set out in Annex C	Article XII on Technical Barriers to Trade. Article XIII on SPS measures		No

(Continued)

Annex 3.2 *(Continued)*

RTA	Description	Type	Status	Year	Tariffs (Goods)	Rules of Origin (Goods)	Standards (Goods)	Specific Sectors Covered (Services)	Investment (Others)
INDIA–GCC	Framework Agreement on Economic Cooperation between the Republic of India and the Member States of the Cooperation Council for the Arab States of the Gulf	Framework Agreement	In force since	2006	Free trade agreement under negotiation	n.a.	n.a.	—	No
INDIA– MERCOSUR	India–Mercosur Preferential Trade Agreement	Framework Agreement	Pending country ratification	2005	Positive list does not consider full tariff elimination	60% minimum	Calls for cooperation	—	Yes
INDIA–NEPAL	Indo–Nepal Treaty of Trade	Preferential Trade Agreement	In force since	1991	Positive list Preferential treatment for Nepal's products.	Change in tariff classification Value added minimum 35% No specific process required	n.a.	—	No

(Continued)

Annex 3.2 *(Continued)*

RTA	Description	Type	Status	Year	Tariffs (Goods)	Rules of Origin (Goods)	Standards (Goods)	Specific Sectors Covered (Services)	Investment (Others)
INDIA–SINGAPORE	Comprehensive Economic Cooperation Agreement Between the Republic of India and the Republic of Singapore	Free Trade Agreement	In force since	2005	Positive list into India, all goods free into Singapore. Full tariff elimination or reduction by 2010 Further liberalization through negotiation	Change in tariff heading at the four-digit level Minimum content 40% No specific process required	Cooperation towards mutual recognition	Positive list Approach: Air services, e-commerce, media, Education	Yes. Asset based-open list: includes FDI, portfolio investment and various forms of tangible and intangible property.
INDIA–SRI LANKA	Free Trade Agreement between the Republic of India and the Democratic Socialist Republic of Sri Lanka	Free Trade Agreement	In force since	2001	Positive/negative List. Full 100% margin advantage in 3 to 8 years	Change in tariff classification Value Added Minimum 35%. No specific manufacturing process necessary	—	—	No

(Continued)

Annex 3.2 (*Continued*)

RTA	Description	Type	Status	Year	Tariffs (Goods)	Rules of Origin (Goods)	Standards (Goods)	Specific Sectors Covered (Services)	Investment (Others)
INDIA–THAILAND	India–Thailand Framework Agreement for establishing a FTA	Framework Agreement	In force since	2004	There is an early harvest scheme with 82 products to be liberalized in 2004. Free trade agreement under negotiation	Change in tariff classification Value added minimum 40% No specific manufacturing process required.	n.a.	—	Yes
JAPAN–BRUNEI	Japan–Brunei Darussalam Economic Partnership Agreement	Free Trade Agreement	In force since	2008	http://www.mofa.go.jp/region/asia-paci/brunei/epa0706/annex1.pdf	Chapter 3 of the agreement Product-specific rules at http://www.mofa.go.jp/region/asia-paci/brunei/epa0706/annex2.pdf		Financial services — http://www.mofa.go.jp/region/asia-paci/brunei/epa0706/annex6.pdf	Yes. Chapter 5 of the agreement
JAPAN–INDIA	Japan–India Economic Partnership Agreement	Framework Agreement	Under negotiation since	2007	n.a.	n.a.			No

(*Continued*)

Annex 3.2   *(Continued)*

RTA	Description	Type	Status	Year	Tariffs (Goods)	Rules of Origin (Goods)	Standards (Goods)	Specific Sectors Covered (Services)	Investment (Others)
JAPAN–INDONESIA	Japan–Indonesia Economic Partnership Agreement	Free Trade Agreement	In force since	2008	Positive list http://www.mofa.go.jp/region/asia-paci/indonesia/epa0708/annex1.pdf. Goods under X are excluded from any commitments. Immediate tariff elimination for goods under category "A". For "B" goods categories, tariff elimination spread over 4 to 16 annual installments For other goods categories (P, Q, R) tariff elimination postponed.	Laid out in Chapter 3 of the Agreement text. Product specific rules http://www.mofa.go.jp/region/asia-paci/indonesia/epa0708/annex2.pdf. Minimum data requirements http://www.mofa.go.jp/region/asia-paci/indonesia/epa0708/annex3.pdf		Financial services provisions http://www.mofa.go.jp/region/asia-paci/indonesia/epa0708/annex7.pdf	Yes. Chapter 5 of the Agreement text. Reservations are set out in Annex 4 http://www.mofa.go.jp/region/asia-paci/indonesia/epa0708/annex 4.pdf. Additional provisions on energy and mineral resources related investment: http://www.mofa.go.jp/region/asia-paci/indonesia/

(Continued)

Annex 3.2 (*Continued*)

RTA	Description	Type	Status	Year	Tariffs (Goods)	Rules of Origin (Goods)	Standards (Goods)	Specific Sectors Covered (Services)	Investment (Others)
									epa0708/annex12. pdf. Also additional provision on settlement on investment disputes http://www.mofa.go.jp/region/asia-paci/indonesia/epa0708/annex6.pdf No
JAPAN–KOREA	Japan–Korea Free Trade Agreement	Free Trade Agreement	Under negotiation since	2004	n.a.	n.a.	n.a.		
JAPAN–MALAYSIA	Japan–Malaysia Economic Partnership Agreement	Free Trade Agreement	In force since	2006	Positive list Tariff elimination schedule varies for every product group, maximum 10 years. There is an Early Harvest Schedule	n.a.	n.a.	Positive list approach.	Yes. Asset-based-open list: includes FDI, portfolio investment and various

(*Continued*)

Annex 3.2 (*Continued*)

RTA	Description	Type	Status	Year	Tariffs (Goods)	Rules of Origin (Goods)	Standards (Goods)	Specific Sectors Covered (Services)	Investment (Others)
									forms of tangible and intangible property. Yes. Chapter 8
JAPAN–PHILIPPINES	Agreement between Japan and the Republic of the Philippines for an economic partnership	Free Trade Agreement	In force since	2008	Positive list http://www.mofa.go.jp/region/asia-paci/philippine/epa0609/annex1.pdf Elimination sequenced over 5–11 years from the date if force of the agreement, with some duties (items classified as B4) to be full eliminated by January 1, 2010	Value-added method (article 4, Chapter 3); product specific	http://www.mofa.go.jp/region/asia-paci/philippine/epa0609/annex4.pdf	http://www.mofa.go.jp/region/asia-paci/philippine/epa0609/annex6.pdf Annex on Financial services http://www.mofa.go.jp/region/asia-paci/philippine/epa0609/annex5.pdf	Yes. Chapter 8

(Continued)

Annex 3.2 (*Continued*)

RTA	Description	Type	Status	Year	Tariffs (Goods)	Rules of Origin (Goods)	Standards (Goods)	Specific Sectors Covered (Services)	Investment (Others)
JAPAN–SINGAPORE	Agreement between Japan and the Republic of Singapore for a New-Age Economic Partnership	Free Trade Agreement	In force since	2002	Positive list Full tariff elimination Foresees inclusion of more goods in the list	Change in tariff classification necessary Value Added: Minimum 60% No specific process necessary	Calls for mutual recognition, and sets out the standards to register new conformity assessment bodies in the Sectorial Annexes	Specific chapters for cooperation on: Financial Services, Information and Communication Technology, and Tourism. Japan uses negative list for national treatment for mode 3.	Yes. Asset based-open list; includes FDI, portfolio investment and various forms of tangible and intangible property.
JAPAN–THAILAND	Agreement between Japan and the Kingdom of Thailand for an Economic Partnership	Free Trade Agreement	In force since	2007	Schedule at http://www.mofa.go.jp/region/asia-paci/thailand/epa0704/annex1.pdf Electric products http://www.mofa.go.jp/region/asia-paci/thailand/epa0704/annex4.pdf	Product-specific ROO http://www.mofa.go.jp/region/asia-paci/thailand/epa0704/annex2.pdf		All the sectors and sub-sectors in WTO document W/120 will appear in the schedule of commitments. See more details in http://www.mofa.go.jp/region/asia-paci/thailand/epa0704/annex5.pdf	Yes. http://www.mofa.go.jp/region/asia-paci/thailand/epa0704/annex6.pdf

(Continued)

Annex 3.2   (*Continued*)

RTA	Description	Type	Status	Year	Tariffs (Goods)	Rules of Origin (Goods)	Standards (Goods)	Specific Sectors Covered (Services)	Investment (Others)
JAPAN–VIET NAM	Agreement between Japan and Viet Nam on Economic Partnership	Framework Agreement	Under negotiation since	2006	n.a.	n.a.			No
KOREA–EU	Framework Agreement for Trade and Cooperation between the European Community and its Member States and the Republic of Korea	Framework Agreement	In force since	2001	n.a.	n.a.			No
KOREA–INDIA	Korea–India Comprehensive Economic Partnership Agreement	Framework Agreement	Under negotiation since	2006	n.a.	n.a.	n.a.		No

(Continued)

Annex 3.2 (*Continued*)

RTA	Description	Type	Status	Year	Tariffs (Goods)	Rules of Origin (Goods)	Standards (Goods)	Specific Sectors Covered (Services)	Investment (Others)
KOREA– SINGAPORE	Free Trade Agreement Between the Government of the Republic of Korea and the Government of the Republic of Singapore	Free Trade Agreement	In force since	2006	Positive list. Tariff elimination in 10 years time; Tariff concessions from Korea cover 91.6 trade in goods, immediately 59.7%) and from Singapore 100% of all the goods traded Ensure that excise taxes and other charges are not levied in an unjust manner that will result in discrimination against imported products.	Waive the requirement for a certificate of origin for low-value originating goods An advance ruling on the eligibility of originating goods for preferential tariffs and tariff classification.	n.a.	Negative list approach except for financial services for which a positive list adopted.	Yes. Asset based-open list: includes FDI, portfolio investment and various forms of tangible and intangible property.

(*Continued*)

Annex 3.2　(*Continued*)

RTA	Description	Type	Status	Year	Tariffs (Goods)	Rules of Origin (Goods)	Standards (Goods)	Specific Sectors Covered (Services)	Investment (Others)
KOREA–UNITED STATES	Korea–US Free Trade Agreement	Free Trade Agreement	Pending country ratification		Tariff concession from Korea will cover 99.7% of goods trade (with immediate effect for 80.4%) and from the US 100% (immediate effect for 82.1%). ROK agrees to address specific auto non-tariff barriers. Reciprocal duty-free access form most textile and clothing goods.	The FTA adopts the "yarn forward" rule.	Strong binding to WTO commitments and establishes a bilateral committee to strengthen FTA and WTO commitments on TBT. Chapters 8 and 9 cover SPS and TBT	Financial services, tele-communication, broadcast, health care, education, legal, postal and other services.	Yes. Establishes a stable legal framework for US investors to operate in ROK.
LAO, PDR–THAILAND	Lao PDR–Thailand Preferential Trading Arrangement	Preferential Trade Agreement	In force since	1991	n.a.	n.a.	n.a.	—	No
MALAYSIA–KOREA	Malaysia–Korea Free Trade Agreement	Free Trade Agreement	Under negotiation since	2005	n.a.	n.a.	n.a.	n.a.	No

(*Continued*)

Annex 3.2 (*Continued*)

RTA	Description	Type	Status	Year	Tariffs (Goods)	Rules of Origin (Goods)	Standards (Goods)	Specific Sectors Covered (Services)	Investment (Others)
MALAYSIA– NEW ZEALAND	Malaysia– New Zealand Free Trade Agreement	Free Trade Agreement	Under negoti- ation since	2005	n.a.	n.a.	n.a.	—	No
MALAYSIA– PAKISTAN	Agreement on the Early Harvest Program for the Free Trade Agreement between the Government of Malaysia and the Government of the Islamic Republic of Pakistan	Free Trade Agreement	In force since	2008	Tariffs <5% eliminated; those between 5% and 10% receive 50% preferences Malaysia offers 114 products, Pakistan 125	Interim rules apply during implementation of the early harvest program Product-specific rules on textile and clothing and jewellery 40% of the local content	n.a.		No
MALAYSIA– UNITED STATES	Trade and Investment Framework Agreement between the Government of the United States of America and the Government of Malaysia	Framework Agreement	In force since	2004	n.a.	n.a.	n.a.	—	No

(*Continued*)

Annex 3.2 (*Continued*)

RTA	Description	Type	Status	Year	Tariffs (Goods)	Rules of Origin (Goods)	Standards (Goods)	Specific Sectors Covered (Services)	Investment (Others)
NEW ZEALAND–CHINA	New Zealand–China Free Trade Agreement	Free Trade Agreement	In force since	2008	Positive list Annex 1 provides tariff schedules http://chinafta.govt.nz/1-The-agreement/2-Text-of-the-agreement/20-Annexes/01-Annex-1.php See the tariff finder at http://www.china fta.govt.nz/2-For-businesses/2-Tools-and-resources/3-Tariff-finder/index.php n.a.	Product specific ROO at http://chinafta.govt.nz/1-The-agreement/2-Text-of-the-agreement/20-Annexes/05-Annex-5.php	Chapter 7 on SPS and Chapter 8 on TBT of the Agreement	Positive list approach	Yes. Chapter 11 of the Agreement
NEW ZEALAND–GCC	New Zealand–Gulf Cooperation Council Free Trade Agreement	Free Trade Agreement	Under negotiation since	2007	n.a.	n.a.			No

(*Continued*)

Annex 3.2 (*Continued*)

RTA	Description	Type	Status	Year	Tariffs (Goods)	Rules of Origin (Goods)	Standards (Goods)	Specific Sectors Covered (Services)	Investment (Others)
NEW ZEALAND–HONG KONG SAR	Hong Kong–New Zealand Closer Economic Partnership	Framework Agreement	Under negotiation since	2001	n.a.	n.a.			No
NEW ZEALAND–SINGAPORE	Agreement between New Zealand and Singapore on a Closer Economic Partnership	Free Trade Agreement	In force since	2001	Tariff elimination by the signing of the agreement	No change in tariff heading necessary Value added percentage: minimum 40% No specific manufacturing process necessary	Mutual and unilateral recognition and harmonization of standards	No specific sector covered in the text. Positive list but no carve-out sectors.	Yes. Asset based-open list: includes FDI, portfolio investment and various forms of tangible and intangible property. Yes
NEW ZEALAND–THAILAND	New Zealand–Thailand Closer Economic Partnership Agreement	Free Trade Agreement	In force since	2005	Positive List Tariff elimination by 2014 (see annexes for details) Tariff elimination acceleration is encouraged.	Change in tariff classification Value added minimum variable depending on the product Specific process required	Calls for harmonization	—	Yes

(*Continued*)

Annex 3.2 (*Continued*)

RTA	Description	Type	Status	Year	Tariffs (Goods)	Rules of Origin (Goods)	Standards (Goods)	Specific Sectors Covered (Services)	Investment (Others)
PAKISTAN– SRI LANKA	Free Trade Agreement Between the Islamic Republic of Pakistan and the Democratic Socialist Republic of Sri Lanka	Free Trade Agreement	In force since	2005	Negative list phased elimination of tariffs based on exclusion of products in three categories in Annex A and B. See notes below. Tariff elimination/ reduction in 3 years Pakistan, 5 years Sri Lanka Elimination of all non-tariff barriers and equivalent measures on the movement of goods and services from the date in force	Change of tariff heading at the six-digit level 35% minimum content No specific process required	Article IV list general exceptions (GATT Arts. XX and XXI) and the SPS Agreement		No

(*Continued*)

Annex 3.2 (*Continued*)

RTA	Description	Type	Status	Year	Tariffs (Goods)	Rules of Origin (Goods)	Standards (Goods)	Specific Sectors Covered (Services)	Investment (Others)
SAFTA	South Asian Free Trade Area	Free Trade Agreement	In force since	2006	Negative list (Sensitive List) Tariff reduction to 0–5% in 7 years (8 years SLK, 10 years LDCs) Calls for accelerated reductions; Trade Liberalization Program in effect since January 1, 2006 except for Nepal (from August 1, 2006) and Sri Lanka (September 16, 2006).	Minimum content 40% (30% for LDCs) Diagonal cumulation	Calls for harmonization	—	Yes
SINGAPORE–AUSTRALIA	Singapore–Australia Free Trade Agreement	Free Trade Agreement	In force since	2003	Negative list Tariff elimination by entry in effect of the agreement.	Change in tariff classification is not an option Value added content, minimum 50% (some products as low as 30%) No specific manufacturing process necessary	Based on the previous Mutual Recognition Agreement on Conformity Assessment. Calls for Harmonization within APEC, WTO guidelines.	Financial Services, Tele-communications.	Yes

(*Continued*)

Annex 3.2 (*Continued*)

RTA	Description	Type	Status	Year	Tariffs (Goods)	Rules of Origin (Goods)	Standards (Goods)	Specific Sectors Covered (Services)	Investment (Others)
THAILAND–UNITED STATES	Thailand–United States Free Trade Agreement	Free Trade Agreement	Under negotiation since	2004	n.a.	n.a.	n.a.	—	Yes. Asset based-open list: includes FDI, portfolio investment and various forms of tangible and intangible property (United States proposal)
TRANS-PACIFIC SEP	Trans-Pacific Strategic Economic Partnership Agreement (Brunei, Singapore, New Zealand and Chile)	Free Trade Agreement	In force since	2006	Negative list approach. Different schedules for each member. Article 3.11 provides for elimination of export subsidy for agricultural goods	Tariff sub-heading change minimum value content 45% No specific process necessary	Calls for cooperation	negative list approach	No. Investment chapter under negotiation
UNITED STATES–INDONESIA	USA–Indonesia Free Trade Agreement	Free Trade Agreement	Under negotiation since	2006	n.a.	n.a.	n.a.		No

(*Continued*)

Annex 3.2 (*Continued*)

RTA	Description	Type	Status	Year	Tariffs (Goods)	Rules of Origin (Goods)	Standards (Goods)	Specific Sectors Covered (Services)	Investment (Others)
UNITED STATES–LAO PDR	Agreement between the United States of America and the Lao Peoples Democratic Republic on Trade Relations	Preferential Trade Agreement	In force since	2005	Negative list for elimination of tariffs and non-tariff measures (Annex A lists exclusions to this provision) Customs calculation based on transaction values transparency for barter trade	No provisions		Positive list approach	No
UNITED STATES–PAKISTAN	US–Pakistan Trade and Investment Framework Agreement	Framework Agreement	Under negotiation since	2004	n.a.	n.a.	n.a.		No
UNITED STATES–PHILIPPINES	US–Philippines Free Trade Agreement	Free Trade Agreement	Under negotiation since	2006	n.a.	n.a.	n.a.		No

(*Continued*)

Annex 3.2   (*Continued*)

RTA	Description	Type	Status	Year	Tariffs (Goods)	Rules of Origin (Goods)	Standards (Goods)	Specific Sectors Covered (Services)	Investment (Others)
UNITED STATES– SINGAPORE	US–Singapore Free Trade Agreement	Free Trade Agreement	In force since	2004	Positive list and schedule Tariff elimination in 10 years at the most (depending on the staging category) New products/services can be included through negotiation	Change in tariff classification Minimum content between 30%– 60% depending on the product No specific process necessary	Enhance cooperation in standards, certification, and conformity assessments	Tele communications, Financial Services (different regulation from other services). Negative list approach.	Yes. Asset based- open list: Includes FDI, portfolio investment and various- forms of tangible and intangible property.

(*Continued*)

Annex 3.2 *(Continued)*

RTA	Description	Type	Status	Year	Tariffs (Goods)	Rules of Origin (Goods)	Standards (Goods)	Specific Sectors Covered (Services)	Investment (Others)
UNITED STATES–VIET NAM	Agreement between the United States of America and the Socialist Republic of Viet Nam on Trade Relations	Preferential Trade Agreement	In force since	2001	Tariff cuts on a positive list approach detailed in Annexes to Chapter I. Typical cuts on Vietnamese side by 1/3 to 1/2 in first three year period. QR on industrial and agricultural products listed eliminated over a period of 3–7 years Viet Nam eliminates discretionary import licensing	No provisions customs valuation based on the transaction value of the imported merchandize on which duty is assessed, or of like merchandize	In accordance with WTO standard, technical regulation and SPS measures applied on national treatment basis	Positive list approach.	Yes. Chapter III on Development of Investment Relations, Annex I on TRIMs illustrative list. Joint ventures with 100% US ownership in 7 years from time agreement in force.
UNITED STATES–AFGHANISTAN	Agreement between the Governments of the United States and Afghanistan concerning the Development of Trade and Investment Relations	Framework Agreement	In force since	2004	n.a.	n.a.			No

(Continued)

Annex 3.2 (*Continued*)

RTA	Description	Type	Status	Year	Tariffs (Goods)	Rules of Origin (Goods)	Standards (Goods)	Specific Sectors Covered (Services)	Investment (Others)
UNITED STATES–ASEAN	Trade and Investment Framework Arrangement between the United States of America and the Association of Southeast Asian Nations	Framework Agreement	In force since	2006	n.a.	n.a.			No
UNITED STATES–CA TIFA	Framework Agreement between the Government of the United States of America, and the Governments of Kazakhstan, Kyrgyz/Republic, Tajikistan, Turkmenistan, and Uzbekistan concerning the Development of Trade and Investment Relations	Framework Agreement	In force since	2004	n.a.	n.a.			No

Source: Excerpted from UNESCAP (2009).

CHAPTER 4

Empirical Estimation of Economic and Welfare Gains

This chapter provides an overview of the empirical estimates in terms of the plausible effects of Regional Trade Agreements (RTAs) of India on an illustrative basis. This includes the methodologies relating to computable general modeling exercises, intra-industry trade, trade complementarities, costs of non-cooperation, and trade projections. So, this suggests that these are the only methodologies for making similar assessments.

4.1. Computable General Equilibrium Modeling Estimates (GTAP Simulations)

The combined economic gains from India engaging in different FTAs at different levels and depth of integration have been estimated using a multi-sector Computable General Equilibrium (CGE) model.[1] This is the standard Global Trade Analysis Project (GTAP) model, coordinated by the Center for Global Trade Analysis, Purdue University. The basic model is documented in Hertel (1997).

The data is obtained from the GTAP database (version 7) which contains 113 countries/regions and 57 sectors. For computation of the data, the aggregation of different country/region with 19 sectors including agriculture, manufactures, and the services sectors was done. The estimations were made for four scenarios such as Scenario 1 that covers reduction of import tariffs by 50% among the members, Scenario 2 that represents reduction of import tariffs by 50% and also institution of trade facilitation measures, Scenario 3 that covers reduction of import tariffs by 100% among the FTA members, and last but not the least, Scenario 4 that

---

[1] Based on Das (2010) which may be referred to for technical details.

represents reduction of import tariffs by 100% along with the application of the trade facilitation measures.

Trade facilitation, which is incorporated by the import that augments technical progress in our model, is assumed to occur among the FTA member countries. Specifically, the annual average rate of such import is assumed to be 0.1% from 1997 to 2009 (see Urata and Kiyota, 2003).

The rationale for these scenarios needs to be understood. The negotiating experience of different trading arrangements suggests that even if a trade agreement is aimed at creating an eventual free trade regime amongst its members, the trade liberalization process is often a calibrated one. Thus, it is imperative that the economic gains are estimated first in a scenario of 50% reduction in import tariffs and thereafter for a totally free trade regime. It also makes clear that mere tariff reduction does not create a sufficient condition for trade-augmentation. One of the important steps for translating tariff liberalization into increased trade flows is by trade facilitation measures. It is with this understanding that estimates of economic gains have been simulated for the above-mentioned four scenarios.

4.2. Effects of Tariff Reduction and Trade Facilitation

4.2.1. Simulation results

The broad contours of the results of the simulation exercised under the four scenarios of the FTAs under implementation are encouraging. The economic gains have been estimated both at the macro and sectoral levels. At the macro level, GDP and welfare gains have been observed along with expansion in exports and imports. Implications for macro variables like saving and investment as well as net capital inflows into the partners are also favorable. There are also interesting trends at the sectoral level, both in the context of intra-grouping trade and exports to the world from the grouping. These results are summarized below.

4.2.1.1. GDP and welfare gains

It is discernible from Table 4.1 that under Scenario 1 with 50% imports tariff liberalization, the change in value of GDP comes out as 0.83%

Table 4.1. Economic gains from India's all FTAs under implementation.

	Scenario 1	Scenario 2	Scenario 3	Scenario 4
	50% import tariff reduction	50% import tariff reduction and trade facilitation	100% import tariff reduction	100% import tariff reduction and trade facilitation
Change in Value of GDP (%)	0.83	0.85	1.65	1.68
Total Welfare (US$ million)	9,541.69	9,908.92	19,083.38	19,450.61
Current Net Rate of Return on Capital Stock (%)	0.78	0.8	1.56	1.58
Expected Net Rate of Return on Capital Stock (%)	0.04	0.04	0.09	0.09

per annum. It increases to 0.85% with the adoption of trade facilitation measures (Scenario 2). Even the figures increase to 1.65% and 1.68% in Scenarios 3 and 4, respectively. Going by the standard CGE simulation results, the extent of these gains can be considered as significant.

The overall welfare gains turn out to be quite significant, ranging from US$9 billion (Scenario 1) to US$20 billion (Scenario 4), considering the fact that these simulations pertain to a comparative static framework. In a dynamic setting, the welfare gains would be much larger.

4.2.1.2. Trade gains

The percentage changes in both exports and imports in the pre-FTA and post-FTA regimes suggest that while the exports would increase from 2.18 to 4.39%, the imports would increase between 2.67% and 5.37% for Scenarios 1 and 4, respectively. It is noticeable from Table 4.2 that trade deficit would also increase. This has implications for FDI inflows, which are analyzed in the following.

Table 4.2. Trade gains (US$ million).

	Export	Import	Total
Scenario 1			
FTA (Pre)	916,144	−940,480	−24,336
FTA (Post)	936,119	−965,546	−29,427
Change (%)	**2.18**	**2.67**	**20.92**
Scenario 2			
FTA (Pre)	916,144	−940,480	−24,336
FTA (Post)	936,406	−965,936	−29,530
Change (%)	**2.21**	**2.71**	**21.34**
Scenario 3			
FTA (Pre)	916,144	−940,480	−24,336
FTA (Post)	956,093	−990,612	−34,519
Change (%)	**4.36**	**5.33**	**41.84**
Scenario 4			
FTA (Pre)	916,144	−940,480	−24,336
FTA (Post)	956,380	−991,002	−34,622
Change (%)	**4.39**	**5.37**	**42.27**

4.2.1.3. *Saving, investment, and net foreign capital inflows*

Trade deficit has a bearing on the capital account and net inflows of foreign capital like FDI. In the GTAP model, the expected rate of return is inversely related to the level of gross investment. Thus, the hypothesis is that a reduction in the expected rate of return in FTA countries must be matched by an increase in the amount of investment, which is being excess of the saving that resulted in an increase in the net capital inflows.

This is exactly what the results show. As per Table 4.3, saving and investment would increase. Special focus can be placed on the investment trends, as this would have a bearing on the FDI inflows to the participating countries. While investment is expected to increase from 1.91% to 3.86% between Scenarios 1 and 4 in pre-FTA and post-FTA regimes, the resource gap (S-I) is expected to widen up from 20.92% to 42.27% across the scenarios. As mentioned earlier, this should be matched by a fall in the expected rate of return which is evident from Table 4.1 (falling from 0.78% to 0.04% in Scenario 1 and from 1.58% to 0.09% in Scenario 4 vis-à-vis current rate of return).

Table 4.3. Savings, investment, and net foreign capital inflows (US$ million).

	Saving	Investment	Total
Scenario 1			
FTA (Pre)	469,345	−493,680	−24,336
FTA (Post)	473,674	−503,101	−29,427
Change (%)	**0.92**	**1.91**	**20.92**
Scenario 2			
FTA (Pre)	469,345	−493,680	−24,336
FTA (Post)	473,797	−503,328	−29,530
Change (%)	**0.95**	**1.95**	**21.34**
Scenario 3			
FTA (Pre)	469,345	−493,680	−34,336
FTA (Post)	478,003	−512,521	−34,519
Change (%)	**1.84**	**3.82**	**41.84**
Scenario 4			
FTA (Pre)	469,345	−493,680	−24,336
FTA (Post)	478,126	−512,748	−34,622
Change (%)	**1.87**	**3.86**	**42.27**

Coming back to the issue of increasing the resource gap, it may be stated that the gap would be bridged by net inflow of foreign capital. This has important positive implications for FDI inflows from the rest of the world to FTA countries, as FDI may come in to take advantage of the duty-free regime amongst the FTA members.

4.2.1.4. *Intra-FTA imports and prospects for exports to the world*

Some of the sectors that are emerging as prominent ones in the context of intra-FTA include, in a descending order, cereals, automobiles and parts, processed food, vegetables and fruits, leather products, garments, paddy, wood products oilseeds, etc. (as shown in Table 4.4). There are also rich prospects for increasing exports from the FTA members to the rest of the world. This is observed in Table 4.5 whereby the potential sectors can be identified such as cereals, automobiles and parts, oilseeds,

Table 4.4.   Change in intra-FTA imports in percentage.

	Scenario 1	Scenario 2	Scenario 3	Scenario 4
Paddy rice	5.64	5.73	11.29	11.38
Wheat	2.11	2.14	4.22	4.25
Cereals	9.32	9.37	18.65	18.69
Veg-fruits	7.44	7.5	14.87	14.94
Oilseeds	4.11	4.15	8.23	8.26
Other primary products	2.25	2.29	4.5	4.54
Processed foods	8.51	8.58	17.01	17.09
Textiles	4.26	4.29	8.52	8.55
Garments	6.07	6.18	12.15	12.26
Leather products	6.6	6.71	13.2	13.31
Wood products	4.64	4.72	9.28	9.36
Paper products	2.37	2.41	4.74	4.78
Chemrubpla	2.02	2.04	4.03	4.05
MinMet products	3.13	3.18	6.26	6.31
Auto	8.85	8.92	17.69	17.76
Transport equipment	2.86	2.92	5.72	5.78
Electronic equipment	1.02	1.04	2.03	2.06
Machinery equipment	1.95	1.99	3.89	3.93

wheat, processed food, chemical, rubber and plastic products, and textiles. It is interesting to note that in some products like garments, leather products, and wood products, there is a possibility of decline in exports. This is perhaps due to the fact that more of the trade in these products is of trade diverting nature toward the FTA members, as they were prominent imports in the context of intra-FTA imports (see Table 4.4). However, this issue requires further analysis.

4.3. Bilateral FTA

4.3.1. India–Thailand FTA[2]

4.3.1.1. *The model and assumptions*

The GTAP model needs some further explanation. GTAP is a comparative static, multi-commodity, and multi-region CGE model of the world

---

[2] See Das *et al.* (2002) for details.

Table 4.5. Total exports to the world percentage change between pre-FTA and post-FTA.

	Scenario 1	Scenario 2	Scenario 3	Scenario 4
1 Paddy rice	2.97	2.97	5.73	5.73
2 Wheat	6.10	6.22	12.15	12.33
3 Cereals	24.28	24.34	48.57	48.63
4 Veg-fruits	2.82	2.82	5.64	5.64
5 Oilseeds	6.78	6.78	13.52	13.52
6 Other primary products	0.52	0.53	1.03	1.05
7 Processed foods	4.86	4.88	9.72	9.74
8 Textiles	3.30	3.31	6.60	6.61
9 Garments	−1.92	−2.00	−3.85	−3.92
10 Leather products	−0.06	−0.09	−0.13	−0.15
11 Wood products	−0.78	−0.80	−1.55	−1.57
12 Paper products	2.65	2.69	5.32	5.35
13 Chemrubpla	3.57	3.61	7.13	7.18
14 MinMet products	3.13	3.18	6.25	6.30
15 Auto	23.11	23.19	46.21	46.29
16 Transport equipment	2.36	2.36	4.72	4.73
17 Electronic equipment	0.99	1.07	1.98	2.06
18 Machinery equipment	2.55	2.59	5.10	5.15
19 Othr manufacturings	2.72	2.77	5.44	5.49

economy. A region may be either a single country or a composite region consisting of many countries. Each region produces a commodity that has its own distinctive variety. This is imperfectly substitutable with the varieties produced by other regions of the same commodity. Within each region, the commodity is produced by a single-product industry with the help of inputs sourced from domestic and global markets. The primary factors are considered as skilled and unskilled labor, capital, land, and natural resources. Each input to a particular industry has an ad valorem tax associated with it. Further, industry inputs of each composite commodity and primary factor have technical efficiency terms associated with them. Thus, in the model one can vary intermediate input taxes, primary factor input taxes, and the efficiency with which inputs are used.

Industries source each primary factor from a fixed regional endowment of that factor. The supplies of skilled and unskilled labor and capital are perfectly transformable between industries. On the other hand, land is supplied with a transformation elasticity of one and natural resources with transformation elasticity being so small that its supply to each industry is essentially fixed. Hence, wages for both the categories of labor and the user price of capital are uniform across industries. However, the rental prices of land and natural resources can vary from industry to industry. This is definitely a restrictive design.

Products of each region are either used as intermediate inputs in production that are consumed as inputs to final demand, or exported. It comes from the standard theory that there are three categories of final demand: investment, government consumption, and private consumption. Each of these consumes composite commodities that are Constant Elasticity of Substitution (CES) combinations of the domestic and the imported variety, similar to composite commodity inputs to industries. This is again a restrictive condition. Furthermore, another restrictive feature of the model is in terms of the fact that composite commodity inputs to investment are taken as fixed proportion to aggregate real investment. Composite commodity inputs to government consumption are determined by the maximization of a Cobb–Douglas utility function of these inputs, while a Constant Difference Elasticities (CDE) utility function is used for private consumption. All these add to the list of unrealistic assumptions.

Aggregate government and private consumption are determined by the allocation of net (of depreciation) national income between government consumption, private consumption, and net (of depreciation) saving to maximize a Cobb–Douglas utility function. Therefore, nominal government consumption, private consumption, and net (of depreciation) savings are each a fixed share of nominal national income. Foreign income flows in GTAP are zero, so that national income is equal to primary factor returns plus tax revenue minus subsidies.

On the other hand, aggregate investment can be determined by one of the two mechanisms that can be configured. In the first mechanism, the global net saving can be allocated between regions in fixed shares. In the second, elasticities of future expected rates of return with respect to future capital stocks can be postulated, and in each region determined so as to equalize the future expected rates of return. It is worth noting that investment does not add to the capital stock available for productive use, but does add to the future capital stock, which may be relevant in determining the level of investment.

Exports fall into two categories: commodities that are sold to other regions, and sales to an international pool of freight and insurance services that is used to convey internationally traded commodities. This international pool is a Cobb–Douglas aggregate of the contributions from all industries in all regions. So the contributions of most industries will be zero. Only services sectors, such as trade, transport, and insurance, produce outputs that could contribute to such a pool. The quantity of freight and insurance services used to convey a particular commodity from a source to destination region is proportional to the quantity of commodity transported which is subjected to a change in the efficiency of conveyance for that commodity and trade route.

The total regional imports of each commodity are a CES composite of imports of the commodity from each exporting region. The price that determines the allocation of total imports among exporters is the domestic market price in the exporting region, which includes export taxes (subsidies), the price of international freight and insurance costs per unit of the commodity, and import tariffs. Thus, the choice among sources of imports occurs at the economy-wide level, while the choice between the domestic and the imported (aggregated across sources) varieties of each commodity occurs at the level of agents within the economy, that is, industries and final demands.

A detailed discussion of GTAP Model and further improvements in it in terms of treating the FDI flows can be found in Hanslow *et al.* (2000), among other subsequent works.

4.3.1.2. *Impact not captured by the model*

Apart from the macro level and sectoral impacts of the FTA that are highlighted earlier, it would be pertinent to mention some of the other possible dimensions of analysis which are usually not captured by a CGE model. Since an analysis of these dimensions is also important to probe into the question as to whether the FTA is a feasible proposition or not, a snapshot view of them is provided in the following.

The FTA might influence the trade and production sectors further if the potentials of trade expansion are taken into consideration while implementing the FTA. Such impacts remain uncaptured by the model but are briefly explained now. First, the potential of trade expansion could be immense in terms of possibilities of tapping the potential intra-industry trade i.e. trade between the two countries in the same sector. Second, potentials of trade expansion in terms of exploiting trade complementarities in products where a country has a price advantage over its competitors and by not exploiting these countries incur substantial costs of non-cooperation. Third, the model also does not capture the impact of FTA under different tariff liberalization scenarios at a disaggregated level of product/tariff lines. Finally, the model also does not capture the possible tariff revenue loss at the disaggregated level.

Macroeconomic impact under FTA: CGE modeling results

This section evaluates the economic impact of the India–Thailand FTA. An attempt has been made to quantitatively analyze the impacts of import tariff elimination between India and Thailand on macroeconomic variables and trade flows. A free trade area will theoretically improve the welfare of the countries through the benefits of better market access and cost reduction derived from tariff cuts. However, there might be instances of output compression in some sectors due to increased import competition.

Model and data

The Global Trade Project (GTAP), a static CGE model, has been used to approximate this potential gain from FTA. This model has been widely used to analyze a number of international trade policies under different research programs. This model has been constructed by economists at the Purdue University, USA in collaboration with economists at Monash University, Australia.

The macroeconomic impact of FTA on India

The results from GTAP simulation show that India–Thailand FTA will lead to a decline in price level due to the reduction of India's import tariff rates. In addition, the FTA will result in higher demands for the Indian exports due to the reduction of Thailand's tariff rates and greater competitiveness of Indian products in the world market. Higher export demand leads to greater demand for primary inputs such as labor and land. As a result, the average wage rate will increase by 0.07% while land rent will increase by 0.15%. In addition, the import tariff cut will result in a decline of rental price for capital and average intermediate input prices. The GDP deflator which acts as the average price level will decline by 0.02% in India.

Tariff elimination between Thailand and India will boost the India's total exports by 102%. The trade creation effect will lead to a rise in India's exports to Thailand by 42.78%. In addition, the exports to other countries will slightly expand due to cost reduction from import tariff cuts and the resultant strengthening of competitiveness of India's products in the world market.

The India–Thailand FTA may also cause trade diversion that will help India to increase its import value from Thailand by 113.8% while decrease its import value from Japan by 0.94%, Indonesia by 1.99%, and China by 2.11%.

The FTA has impacts not only on external demand but also on internal demand. Higher export income and lower commodity prices will increase private consumption in India by 0.03%. Aggregate savings will rise by 0.04%. Private investment is expected to increase by 0.16%, which is mainly due to the greater export opportunities. Overall, the welfare of India will improve by US$74.89 million.

The macroeconomic impact of FTA on Thailand

The India–Thailand FTA will benefit Thailand mainly by increasing its market access in India's huge market. A rise in Thailand's exports will increase the demand for the primary factors of production. Wage and rental price of land will also rise by 0.39% and 0.52%, respectively, while the rental price of capital will increase by 0.03%. This leads to a 0.09% increase in the GDP deflator. This shows that the higher demand for Thailand's export will raise the export price index by 0.12%.

The India–Thailand FTA could result in significant trade creation. It is expected that there will be a 113.87% surge in Thailand's exports to India, while Thailand's imports from India will rise by 42.78%. There will also be an increase in the total exports of Thailand by 0.52%. Due to the cheaper products from India and expansion of overall economy, Thailand's total imports will increase by 0.66%.

On the other hand, the FTA will cause some trade diversion effects. The exports of Thailand to ASEAN members will decline from 0.29% to 0.43%. The exports to China and Japan are expected to drop by 0.53% and 0.41%, respectively.

The FTA would expand not only the external sector but also the internal sector of Thailand. Gross domestic investment in Thailand will rise by 0.47%, while the private consumption and savings will increase by 0.41% and 0.39%, respectively. As a result, the real GDP will increase by 0.34%. This would lead to a US$545.2 million increase in the welfare of the country.

It may be summed up that the international trade between India and Thailand has been limited, regardless of positive factors such as size of economies and location. The high import tariff is one of the important trade barriers between these two countries. The results of the GTAP simulation show that the India–Thailand FTA will increase both countries' welfare. The main benefits of FTA are through substantial trade creation between the two economies. Even though the impact of India–Thailand FTA is positive, the size of impact is relatively small for both countries. One factor behind limited benefit is the current small trading activities between India and Thailand. Our study, which is a market analysis of substantial tariff cut, could underestimate the true impacts of FTA. Therefore, this analysis has been supplemented with other techniques of impact assessment which brings out the high potential for economic gains and trade expansion between India and Thailand, if the FTA is set into place. Moreover, it should be noted that current high tariffs mean high adjustment of the cost of economies. This analysis does not take this high adjustment cost into account.

4.3.1.3. *Potential areas of trade expansion*

An attempt has been made here not only to identify the potential areas of cooperation in the realm of merchandize trade but also to make an assessment of the extent of potential trade expansion. Our empirical analysis is focused toward highlighting that even without tariff liberalization, tremendous potential exists for trade expansion between India and Thailand.

On top of it, if tariff liberalization under the proposed FTA is undertaken, then advantages would be much more like the CGE results mentioned earlier.

The potentials of trade expansion are brought out with the help of computing a Trade Complementarity Index and a Production Similarity Index. This analysis has been further extended by computing the intra-industry Trade Index and Costs of non-cooperation between the countries under consideration.

Trade complementarity and production similarity

One of the ways of ascertaining potentials of trade cooperation between a pair of countries is by comparing their exports and imports vectors at a point of time and brings out the matching between the two. A matching such as this between the export supply of one country and import demand of the partner country can be captured by constructing a Trade Complementarity Index. One way of undertaking this is by calculating what is known in the literature is the *Cosine Measure* (Linnemann, 1992) as given below:

$$\mathrm{Cos}_{(IxTm)} = \frac{\Sigma_I \, E_{Ii} \cdot M_{Ti}}{\sqrt{\Sigma_I \, E_{Ii}^2 \cdot \Sigma_I \, M_{Ti}^2}},$$

where trade complementarity between India's exports with Thailand's imports is given by $\mathrm{Cos}_{(IxTm)}$, E = Exports to world, M = Imports from world, I = India, T = Thailand, i = product at HS six-digit level. Similarly, trade Complementarity Index between Thailand's exports and India's imports can also be calculated. The value of the index varies between zero and one, with the former implying no complementarity and the latter implying perfect complementarity. The index is denoted by $\cos(\theta)$, when the two axes x (exports) and y (imports) match perfectly, the angle between the two is zero degrees but the value of $\cos(0)$ is one. This situation implies perfect

Table 4.6.　Trade complementarity and production similarity (2006).

Trade Complementarity between India's Exports and Thailand's Imports ($Cos_{(IxTm)}$)	Trade Complementarity between Thailand's Exports and India's Imports ($Cos_{(TxIm)}$)	Production Similarity between India and Thailand ($Cos_{(TpIp)}$)
0.16	0.34	0.89

complementarity. When the vectors do not match completely, it could be the other extreme situation of 90 degrees between the export (x) and import (y) and the value of index would be zero as cos(90) is zero.

The computed trade complementarity indices of the two types are given in Table 4.6. These were calculated by matching the export and import vectors of the two countries that were arrived at by taking the average over the period 1995–2006. It is evident that the trade potential exists between the countries; however, the trade complementarity is not very high. This phenomenon needs a little explanation. Low trade complementarity could be explained in terms of moderate diversification of export supply and import demand in the countries under consideration.

In the event of high trade diversification or high trade concentration in similar products, the complementarity may turn out to be high. Assuming, that the export and import structures of both India and Thailand are moderately diversified at the present juncture, not very high trade complementarity index is a plausible proposition. This assumption is also not unrealistic as it is corroborated by our observation on export concentration Hirschmann index of the two countries presented in the Table 4.7.

Thus, the trade complementarities exist between India and Thailand, however, it is not very high. We have provided an explanation for this phenomenon. We probe into the issue further by examining whether the production structures of the two countries are similar. It may be argued that even if the production structures are similar, the potentials for trade expansion would be very high. In fact, the higher the production similarity the higher would be the potential for intra-industry trade. One may hasten to add that a majority of global trade are presently of the intra-industry variety and not of the inter-industry type as envisaged in the traditional

Table 4.7. Export Concentration Indices.

Countries	Export Concentration Indices		
	1980	1990	1999
Japan	0.118	0.139	0.137
US	0.064	0.078	0.089
UK	0.083	0.061	0.085
India	0.112	0.142	0.161
Thailand	0.201	0.098	0.108

Source: UNCTAD (2001).

Hecksher–Ohlin framework of trade theories. Hence, it is worthwhile to explore the issue of production similarity between the two countries so as to pin down the argument that potentials for trade expansion of the intra-industry variety exist. The index of production similarity is calculated by applying the cosine measure to the production data of the two countries. Table 4.7 reveals that our calculations do suggest the immense possibility of intra-industry trade expansion between the two countries. This is further corroborated by our calculations as analyzed below.

Potential Intra-industry trade

The phenomenon of the two countries that are trading with each other in a particular industry or sector is known as intra-industry trade (IIT) as opposed to inter-industry trade. The index of IIT (Grubel–Llyod Index) is commonly calculated as the following:

$$\text{IIT Index} = 1 - [\,|\,X_{iA} - M_{iB}\,|\,]/[X_{iA} + M_{iB}],$$

where X is exports, i is a product, and A is exporting country, B is importing country, and M is imports. The index varies from zero to one with the former implying no IIT and the latter as maximum IIT. The index is sensitive to the definition of industry. The higher is the level of aggregation, the higher would be IIT and vice versa. Therefore, as the literature suggests, the four-digit level of SITC classification is close to optimum level on which the industry bias of the index is minimum.

Thus, we have calculated the IIT at SITC four-digit level but with a novel application. Usually, the IIT is calculated for the existing trade flows between partners. We have calculated the index for India and Thailand for products that are being exported by one country to the rest of the world but not being imported by another country, instead it is being imported from the rest of the world. The index in such a situation captures the potentials for intra-industry trade between the two countries. Thus, low trade complementarities as captured by the cosine measure and production similarity do not act as a constraint on future trade flows. Our calculations suggest that there is ample scope for intensifying intra-industry trade linkages between India and Thailand and this aspect needs to be taken into account while evaluating the feasibility of an FTA between the two. The tables reveal that there are several product categories that are displaying high or medium levels of IIT index implying the rich potential for such trade flows.

There is an added advantage of focusing on potential IIT products as they can facilitate tremendous amount of foreign exchange savings for the two countries. Having observed the rich potential for trade expansion, we extend the analysis further by calculating the *Costs of non-cooperation* by comparing the prices of exports of one country to the prices of imports of another country which is also an aspect which has not been captured so far in our analysis. Such an exercise would also throw light on the extent of trade complementarity between India and Thailand through a different analytical and methodological route.

Costs of non-cooperation

A comparison is made of the items that India presently exports to the world but not to Thailand along with the items that are presently being imported by the Thailand from world but not from India at SITC four-digit level. The results are further reported by identifying the items that fall in these SITC categories at HS six-digit level in the case of India and HS 10-digit level in the case of Thailand along with their respective tariff levels. This has been accomplished so as to facilitate the policy-making process in terms of identifying items for the annexure of tariff liberalization schedules of the proposed FTA. The results suggest immense potential to augment India's export of these items to Thailand because these items are being exported by India to the rest of the world at unit values lower than that of the unit values of Thailand's imports when sourced from the rest of the world. If Thailand sources these items from India, then it could amount to a saving of US$7.9 billion for Thailand. It may be mentioned that this is without taking into account the proposed tariff liberalization under the FTA. If tariff liberalization is also taken under consideration, the competitiveness of India's export products would increase further in the Thai market.

On the other hand, India would gain in terms of foreign exchange earnings through increased exports. Thailand would gain in terms of foreign exchange saving as mentioned earlier, which would in turn improve Thailand's competitiveness in its manufacturing process as several such products under consideration fall in the category of raw materials and semi-finished goods.

Similarly, it has been worked out as to what kind of gains would be possible by comparing India's imports and Thailand's exports that are taking place vis-à-vis rest of the world but not bilaterally. It is estimated that India could save US$4.6 billion of foreign exchange if it sources those items from Thailand that are presently not being imported from Thailand but are being exported by Thailand to the rest of the World. In this case, there would be potential increase in Thailand's exports to India as well. If these products are subjected to tariff liberalization then there would be improvements in the competitiveness of Indian products.

4.3.2. India–Malaysia FTA[3]

4.3.2.1. Bilateral exports projection

Three alternative methods have been used for export projection over the next five years under a possible India–Malaysia FTA. Detailed simulation-exercises using the CGE have been conducted and presented at a later stage in this chapter.

The estimated projections of India's exports to Malaysia suggest that the exports from India to Malaysia could be in the range of US$556 million to

---

[3] Based on Das (2007).

Table 4.8.   Projected exports from India to Malaysia (US$ million).

Year	Methodology I: Linear Growth Projection		Methodology II: Compound Growth Projection		Methodology III: Auto regression Method Projection	
	Lower Bound	Upper Bound	Lower Bound	Upper Bound	Lower Bound	Upper Bound
2012	646.6	1,029.9	1,328.2	4,625.3	556.3	2,132.5
2011	620.9	996.8	1,175.7	4,042.4	405.6	1,888.1
2010	595.2	966.7	1,044.6	3,534.0	260.1	1,604.4
2009	569.5	936.6	889.8	2,876.8	339.2	1,464.6
2008	543.6	906.6	791.7	2,525.8	402.7	1,335.7
2007	517.7	876.7	704.3	2,218.4	451.4	1,217.3

US$1.3 billion by 2012 (see Table 4.8). In terms of percentages, the projections are in a broad range which could be partly due to the volatile trade between India and Malaysia in the past.

The upper bound estimates of India's exports to Malaysia are in the range of US$1.0 billion to US$4.6 billion by 2012. It may be also mentioned that these estimates are on the basis of past trends in the bilateral trade and the aspect of tariff liberalization has not been taken into account.

The lower bound estimates of the three methodologies suggest that the exports from Malaysia to India would be in the range of US$1.4 billion to US$1.8 billion by 2012 (see Table 4.9). The upper bound estimates of Malaysia's exports to India are in the range of US$3 billion to US$11 billion by 2012.

4.3.2.2. *Computable General Equilibrium Simulations*

The economic gains of the proposed CECA have been estimated using a multi-sector CGE model. This is the standard Global Trade Analysis Project (GTAP) model, coordinated by the Center for Global Trade Analysis, Purdue University. The data is obtained from the GTAP database (version 6). This exercise was done to complement other empirical exercises aiming to assess the potential gains from the CECA. The estimations were made for four scenarios (see Table 4.10).

Table 4.9. Projected exports from Malaysia to India (US$ million).

Year	Methodology I: Linear Growth Projection		Methodology II: Compound Growth Projection		Methodology III: Auto Regression	
	Lower Bound	Upper Bound	Lower Bound	Upper Bound	Lower Bound	Upper Bound
2012	1,494.2	3,351.6	1,467.0	11,848.5	1,880.0	4,711.9
2011	1,477.2	3,343.2	1,399.7	10,155.8	1,787.4	4,690.2
2010	1,414.0	3,267.3	1,328.3	10,022.2	1,714.1	4,655.9
2009	1,421.1	3,256.6	1,223.7	9,016.6	1,657.0	4,481.2
2008	1,347.5	3,162.1	1,126.8	8,116.1	1,606.0	4,309.2
2007	1,273.3	3,068.1	1,037.0	7,309.6	1,565.3	4,138.8

Table 4.10. Economic gains.

	Scenario 1	Scenario 2	Scenario 3	Scenario 4
	50% Import Tariff Reduction	50% Import Tariff Reduction and Trade Facilitation	100% Import Tariff Reduction	100% Import Tariff Reduction and Trade Facilitation
Change in Value of GDP (%)	0.55	1.25	1.16	2.6
Total Welfare (US$ million)	661.69	1,101.32	1,200.30	2,240.00

Under Scenario 1 with 50% import tariff liberalization; the change in value of GDP comes out as 0.55% per annum. It increases to 1.25% with the adoption of trade facilitation measures (Scenario 2). The figures increase to 1.16% and 2.6% in Scenarios 3 and 4, respectively. These gains can be considered significant. The overall welfare gains range from US$662 million (Scenario 1) to US$2.24 billion (Scenario 4).

The percentage changes in the bilateral exports in the pre-CECA and post-CECA period, as illustrated in Table 4.11, suggest that the exports from India to Malaysia would increase from 26% to 57%, and the exports

Table 4.11. Trade gains percentages in trade for India and Malaysia under CECA.

	Exports (%)
Scenario 1	
India	25.58
Malaysia	29.17
Scenario 2	
India	28.00
Malaysia	32.11
Scenario 3	
India	51.18
Malaysia	58.45
Scenario 4	
India	56.66
Malaysia	65.89

from Malaysia to India would increase between 29% and 66% between Scenarios 1 and 4, respectively.

4.3.2.3. *Gains from the EAS Process*

The studies conducted by RIS have found considerable evidence of complementarities between EAS countries in their production and trade structures (Kumar *et al.*, 2008; Sinha-Roy *et al.*, 2004). Formation of an RTA may help in the exploitation of these complementarities for mutual advantage. Furthermore, trade policy liberalization needs to be accompanied by additional measures such as free capital mobility, harmonization of customs procedures and product standards, and mechanisms to ensure an equitable distribution of gains.

By now, a number of studies conducted independently of each other have reported the substantial potential of regional cooperation in increasing the welfare gains for the region (as summarized in Table 4.12). The RIS studies conducted using a CGE model have shown that trade liberalization within the framework of an RTA in JACIK could produce gains of worth US$147 billion. However, when an RTA is combined with investment liberalization and mobility of skilled manpower, the gains

Table 4.12. Welfare gains from economic integration in East Asia.

Study	Scope of Economic Integration	Estimated Welfare Gains for the Scenario of Deepest Integration	Remarks
RIS (Mohanty et al., 2003)	JACIK	US$210 billion	Every country benefits; potential for rest of the world also gaining
ADB (Brooks et al., 2005)	Developing Asia	Much larger gains than multilateral trade liberalization	Smaller countries can share the dynamism of China and India
ADBI (Kawai and Wignaraja, 2007)	ASEAN+6 (EAS members)	US$284 billion	Every country benefits
RIS (Mohanty and Pohit, 2007)	ASEAN+6 (EAS members)	US$178 billion	Welfare gains vary between 1.5% of GDP (Singapore) to 4.7% (Indonesia); much higher gains for poorer countries as a % of GDP
Ando (2008)	ASEAN+6 (EAS members)	US$188 billion	Full liberalization with technical assistance
Das (2009)	ASEAN+6 (EAS members)	US$243 billion	Welfare gains for all and the rest of the world. Smaller countries benefit more due to trade facilitation effects

Source: Das (2010) and Kumar (2007).

from integration add up to US$210 billion, representing more than 3% of the combined GDP of JACIK economies. Moreover, all the JACIK countries benefit from integration. Interestingly, the welfare of the rest of the world also improves by US$109 billion in Scenario 3 suggesting that Asian economic integration will be Pareto optimal, i.e. benefiting all.

A more recent exercise at RIS with a more up to date database and with the scope of the integration extended to EAS has also corroborated these findings.

Furthermore, the exercise finds that the welfare gains are proportionately higher for relatively poorer countries than for the richer countries, thus presenting a potential for economic convergence. These findings have been corroborated by Asian Development Bank (ADB) and ADB Institute studies as summarized in Table 4.12.

Using the Global Trade Analysis Project database (GTAP 6) with the World Bank's LINKAGE model, the ADB study (see Brooks *et al.*, 2005) generated projections of income and trade to 2025 under different scenarios in order to examine the relative impact of regional integration vis-à-vis global trade liberalization. The findings suggest that regional trade and integration could offer great potential for rapid and sustained growth to Asia. The ADB study also finds that much of Asia's gains from global trade liberalization could be realized by a regional initiative alone. Significantly, it finds that the combined gains from removing tariff and structural barriers to Asian trade far outweigh those from global tariff abolition. Hence, regionalism should have a very high priority for Asia. Furthermore, the ADB study suggests that regional integration would promote Asian economic convergence, raising average growth rates and benefiting poorer countries. In particular, greater regional integration would propagate commercial linkages and transfer the stimulus of Asia's rapid-growth economies, particularly China and India, to their lower income neighbors. A more recent ADBI study has also reported substantial potential welfare gains of nearly US$284 billion from regional economic integration in EAS or ASEAN+6 framework.

Furthermore, creation of regional institutional infrastructure to mobilize even a small proportion of the region's considerable savings of about US$3 trillion for investment in regional public goods, such as transport infrastructure, gas and oil pipelines, satellites, and broadband cables has the potential to generate additional output and welfare gains. These gains could amount to hundreds of billions of dollars in view of the substantial underutilized capacity in Japan, Republic of Korea, and other Asian countries in the engineering and construction industries.

In the most recent study Das (2010) finds that the EAS process can generate much bigger welfare gains both for the region and the rest of the world, if trade facilitation effects are modeled more accurately. Due to this, the gains are also expected to accrue to smaller countries more and thus the process augurs well for the lesser developed economies. This is due to three prime reasons. First, the smaller countries would have greater market access in the bigger countries of the region due to trade liberalization. Second, the improved trade facilitation infrastructure would help facilitate intra-regional trade linkages of the smaller countries and thirdly, it would further provide the boost to their trade linkages with the rest of the world.

In a nutshell, different methodologies and different combinations of RTAs, covering the whole spectrum of a bilateral FTA to a pan-Asian FTA, make it clear that the trade and economic gains from such engagements are substantial and are worth pursuing.

Annex 4.1

India–Malaysia Bilateral Export Forecasting

Analytical Rationale and Methodology

In the literature, there are various methods on forecasting that are used including univariate forecasting, single-equation models, multi-equation macro-models, CGE, etc. Recent times have witnessed an increasing emphasis on univariate forecasting due to the emergence of more sophisticated techniques in the time-series analysis. In addition, single-equation models are being increasingly used to forecast variables due to procedural simplicity without compromising on the dimension of accuracy.

In univariate forecasting, there are problems of trend, seasonal, cyclical, and irregular components. Thus, there are different methods that attempt at smoothing data through arithmetic and exponential moving averages, Holt–Winters and Hodrick–Prescott Filter, etc. Seasonal adjustments are also made using fixed and variable weights, etc. Furthermore, the techniques of ARIMA/Box–Jenkins are also used.

However, it may be argued that a single-equation model of forecasting has its own merits as it brings an opportunity to apply economic logic as opposed to univariate projections in which technical refinements take precedence. The single-equation models are being preferred also for their simplicity and time-saving characteristics without necessarily compromising on accuracy in contrast to multi-equation macro-modeling that are time-consuming and very demanding in terms of data requirements.

Considering the above, an attempt has been made to forecast bilateral exports of India and Malaysia to each other for the next five years, i.e., 2007–2012. In doing so, three methodologies have been used viz. Linear Univariate Forecast, Compound Growth Univariate Forecast, and Single-equation Forecast with Autocorrelation Adjustment.

In the single-equation forecasting, the recent advances in the literature were taken into account while selecting the equation and variable-specification. It can be argued that the supply-side factors like unit labor costs in labor-abundant economies, unit value of exports need to be combined with demand-side factors like the partner country's GDP per capita and import barriers captured as tariff revenue as a proportion of imports in partner country. Additionally, GDP per capita in the exporting country can be included as an activity variable. Some of these variables are used in the gravity modeling framework. It has been found that exchange rate emerges as a significant variable in determining exports in the long run but not in the short run. Since, our forecasts were to be targeted at a five-year short run horizon this variable was not included.

Methodology I: Linear Univariate Forecast
Exports are modeled as a linear function of time.

$$\text{Exports} = \alpha + \beta(t) + \mu$$

Methodology II: Compound Growth Univariate Forecast

$$\ln(\text{Exports}) = \ln(\alpha) + \ln(\beta) \cdot (t) + \mu$$

Methodology III: Single-equation Forecast with Autocorrelation Adjustment

$$\text{Exports} = \alpha + \beta_1(X_1) + \beta_2(X_2) + \beta_3(X_3) + \beta_4(X_4) + \beta_5(X_5) + \mu$$

where $X_1 = $ GDP per capita of the exporting country, $X_2 = $ GDP per capita of the partner country, $X_3 = $ unit labor cost of the exporting country, $X_4 = $ import barrier (import tariff revenue as percentage of imports) in partner country and $X_5 = $ unit value of exports of the exporting country.

It is a well-known fact that time series data has the possibility of presence of autocorrelation and overstatement of t-ratios occurs when autocorrelation is present. We have made autocorrelation adjustment to correct for first-order autoregressive errors with the help of the Cochrane–Orcutt method which is the most widely used estimation procedure for this purpose.

CHAPTER 5

Policy Implementation Issues in Regional Trading Arrangements

As emphasized in the previous chapters, signing of a trade and economic cooperation agreement is a necessary condition for setting in place policy implementation mechanisms. This chapter focuses on the crucial implementation issues that are related to trade circumvention, rules of origin, and customs regulations.

5.1. Circumvention

5.1.1. *Objective to check unfair trade practices*

5.1.1.1. *Anti-dumping Duty (AD): Price-discrimination*

Rationale

The act of a company exporting a product at a price less than its value in the domestic market is known as "dumping" the product. The objective of the Anti-dumping Agreement of the WTO is to discipline governments that allow anti-dumping. Dumping is often considered to an "unfair trade practice" as it artificially lowers the price of an exportable product in a particular market, akin to price discrimination vis-à-vis other markets. This has been a major area of concern even in the context of RTAs.

At the level of application, the two main problems encountered in antidumping cases include establishing a causal link between imports and domestic injury with the latter entailing certain degree of ambiguities and calculation of the dumping margin. The different ways of calculating dumping margins incumbent upon the intensity/degree of dumping that adds further uncertainty to the whole exercise.

Table 5.1.   Number of cases.

Year	1980–1985	1986–1990	1991–1995	1996–2000	2001–June 2004
Developing Countries					
Low	0	0	21	169	212
			(4)	(34)	(61)
			[1.7]	[12.3]	[21.0]
Middle	0	0	66	278	293
			(13)	(56)	(84)
			[5.3]	[20.2]	[29.1]
Upper	0	63	369	351	115
		(13)	(74)	(70)	(33)
		[9.4]	[29.8]	[25.6]	[11.4]
Developed Countries					
OECD	930	605	774	553	379
	(186)	(121)	(155)	(111)	(108)
	[100]	[90.6]	[62.4]	[40.3]	[37.6]
Non-OECD	0	0	10	21	9
			(2)	(4)	(3)
			[0.8]	[1.5]	[0.9]
Total	930	668	1,240	1,372	1,008
	(186)	(133)	(248)	(274)	(288)
	[100]	[100]	[100]	[100]	[100]

Source: Aggarwal (2008).

As evident from Table 5.1, around 11 countries accounted for over 80% of the use during 1996–2000. Out of which, five were developing countries viz India, South Africa, Brazil, Argentina, and Mexico (Aggarwal, 2008).

Cost of AD Application

There is huge cost involved in investigating AD cases. The total expenditure for fighting the dumping case, which is likely to be filed against the imports of shrimp from India and other developing countries by the US, is expected to be $1.5 million (Rs. 7.5 crore) for Indian firms alone (Aggarwal, 2008). Exports suffer due to high cost of searching new markets which then internally affects employment and growth.

Furthermore, anti-dumping measures are misused under the domestic pressures of protectionist tendencies. Apart from the rent-seeking micro behavior, the problem is compounded to certain macro level considerations of economic downturns, unemployment, and sluggish growth. Sometimes, antidumping measures pose implementation challenges while trying to check unfair trading practices. The only way to tackle this issue is by stating the "rules" clearly and implementing them in true spirit.

5.1.1.2. *Countervailing duty: Foreign export subsidy*

Countervailing duty is yet another measure to check "unfair practice" of lowering the export price and taking recourse to foreign export subsidies. In this case too, the issues of application remain the same as providing a causal link between imports and injury, and subsequently arriving at a margin that can be bridged by imposing a countervailing duty.

5.1.2. *Circumvention of rules: Case studies*

5.1.2.1. *Tariff-rate quota*

Tea and Garments: India–Sri Lanka Free Trade Agreement

Tea

Pursuant to the signing of a Free Trade Agreement, a meeting between the two sides was held on February 2, 2000, to operationalize the Agreement. In that meeting it was decided, *inter alia* that the import of tea into India from Sri Lanka under the Tariff Rate Quota Arrangement would be through Calcutta and Cochin Ports. Sri Lanka requested for the inclusion of Mumbai as an additional port of entry. They further proposed the discussion of the details during the forthcoming JMC meeting.

The following four related issues were discussed during the meeting:

(1) Quota Allocation;
(2) Monitoring of the Quota by Indian side, particularly by Tea Board of India;
(3) Certificate of Origin; and
(4) Quality Assurance.

Quota Allocation

For the year 2000, the Sri Lanka Tea Board fixed the quota for export of Tea (to India) at 11.25 m.kgs. The Board allocated the quota under tariff concessions and upon allocating the individual quotas to the Sri Lankan exporters, informed the Tea Board of India, the following:

   (i) Name and address of the exporter
  (ii) Name and address of the Indian tea importer
 (iii) Port of entry in India
 (iv) Allocated quantity

After that the Sri Lanka Tea Board issued a certificate as per Annexure-A indicating the allocation of quota to each exporter along with the certificate of origin issued by the Director General of Commerce, Government of Sri Lanka with every consignment. A copy of both the certificates was sent to the Tea Board of India.

Sri Lanka also informed regarding the publication of the details containing quota allocation on their website which would be accessed by Indian authorities' viz. Tea Board of India, Department of Customs and High Commission of India, Colombo, Sri Lanka.

Monitoring of Quota: Tea Board of India, after receiving the receipt of the above information from Sri Lanka Tea Board, monitored the utilization of the quota in liaison with the Customs Authorities of Calcutta and Cochin. With respect to the quota allocation for any year, the date of Bill of Lading/Airway Bill was taken into account. The ports of entry were allowed under the Agreement for Calcutta sea, Calcutta air, Cochin sea, and Cochin air.

The Sri Lanka Tea Board also monitored the allocations and actual exports on a regular basis.

Garments

Pursuant to the FTA, a meeting between the two sides (India and Sri Lanka) was held on the February 2, 2000, to operationalize the Agreement, wherein, it was decided that Sri Lanka could export eight million pieces (pcs.) of apparel articles to India that falls under chapters 61 and 62 of the

Harmonized System of Nomenclature (HSN), on the payment of preferential import duty. Apart from sourcing fabrics from India, the manufacture of six million pieces to Sri Lanka out of these eight million pieces of apparel articles was also accepted in the meeting. It was further agreed that not more than 1.5 million pieces will be under one product category.

The above preferential tariff quota for the calendar year 2000 was capped at a total of 6.67 million pieces, of which a minimum of five million pieces were manufactured to Sri Lanka out of the fabrics of Indian origin. The other condition stated that the export of such apparel articles by Sri Lanka to India should not exceed 1.5 million pieces with respect to a single product category stands.

With regard to the six million pieces of apparel articles, where the said conditionality of sourcing of fabrics from India (for the manufacture of such apparel articles in Sri Lanka) has been stipulated, the import of such fabrics from India to Sri Lanka and the resultant export of apparel articles from Sri Lanka to India will be confined to manufacturer-exporters in Sri Lanka. However, while ordinarily this will relate to direct manufacturer-exporters, in exceptional cases one change of hand (transfer) must be provided subject to the transferee who is also a manufacturer-exporter. The designated authority in Sri Lanka will ensure that there is a one-to-one co-relation between the apparel articles exported from Sri Lanka by a manufacturer-exporter and the fabrics imported from India for the manufacture of such apparel articles. For this purpose, the conversion factors (adopted from the European Union/United States of America models) in respect of the ratio, in unit terms, of the fabrics exported from India to the garments manufactured thereof in Sri Lanka and exported consequently to India, as also indicated in Annexure-B, will be taken into account by the designated authority of Sri Lanka while certifying that the apparel articles exported from Sri Lanka into India correspond thus with the quantity of fabrics imported from India. For instance, a manufacturer-exporter of apparel articles in Sri Lanka will have to import from India and use 100 kg of fabrics for the manufacture and resultantly export 648 pieces of category 1 apparel articles (see Annexure-B) back to India.

In terms of the FTA, the import of apparel articles from Sri Lanka to India was allowed through the designated ports of Chennai and Mumbai. The latter also includes the Jawaharlal Nehru Port (JNP) in Nhava

Sheva. For this purpose, such imports were through sea and air modes in Chennai and Mumbai.

In 2007, India and Sri Lanka signed a MoU to finalize the procedural arrangements for operationalization of tariff rate quota for import of three million pieces of apparel articles covered under the India–Sri Lanka FTA. In pursuance of the FTA that came into force on March 1, 2000, it was decided that Sri Lanka could export three million pieces of apparel articles on duty-free basis to India in one calendar year, without any restriction on entry points and sourcing of fabrics.

India–Nepal Trade Treaty: The validity of the India–Nepal Trade Treaty was extended by another five years from March 6, 2002 until March 5, 2007. However, detailed rules of origin were adopted for "trade deflection" (third country goods into the Indian market) that occurred due to an absence of rules of origin. A safeguard clause was also inserted to permit appropriate remedial measures in tune with international norms to deal with surge in imports that may constitute injury or threat of serious injury to domestic industry. Tariff Rate Quotas (TRQs) in the case of four sensitive commodities (vanaspati, acrylic yarn, copper products, and zinc oxide) were also introduced which would permit duty free imports of these commodities, however, only up to a certain ceiling.

India–Sri Lanka FTA: Copper exports from Sri Lanka to India have also been controversial, since businesspersons have imported copper scrap to Sri Lanka without paying any import duty, and then melted and reshaped this into ingots for sale to the users in India. Sri Lanka has no copper mines of its own, and there have been allegations that these smelters violated the Rules of Origin (ROO) in the FTA by not adhering to the stipulated value addition norms of around 35%. A total of 20 secondary copper smelters were set up in Sri Lanka by Indian businesspersons after the FTA. After India slashed import duties on copper scrap in 2006, most of these smelters became unviable and had to shut down. Imports of copper items by India from Sri Lanka subsequently jumped from less than US$2 million in 2000–2001 to nearly US$19 million in 2002–2003 and US$82 million in 2003–2004.

5.1.3. *Are rules necessarily bad?*

A general view on the FTA-implementation has been presented earlier. The issue which needs to be examined in this context is whether the rules pertaining to different dimensions are necessarily bad. This needs to be approached with a balanced perspective. Such an approach would also bring to the fore the content and direction of modification of rules.

For instance, it needs to be distinguished whether the rules are bad or their implementation. As emphasized above, the properly formulated and implemented rules can only be trade facilitating and possibly in the developmental interests of RTA members. At times, it is quite possible that the objective sought to be achieved is correct and it is a lack of proper implementation of a well-designed rule which becomes a barrier to trade. Hence, rules *per se* need to be approached with a developmental perspective.

5.2. Improving Implementation

Improving implementation could mean adopting a three-step approach. The first and foremost is having well-formulated rules by themselves. Most important of this would be to have unambiguous rules with clearly defined terms used in any provision. The second step could involve simplified implementation mechanisms. This could be achieved by appropriate use of information technology with online-embedded software that is customized to secured data-sharing and obtain necessary clearances, unless physical verifications are an absolute necessity. The third step could entail surveillance and penalties in cases of circumvention of rules and infringements.

5.2.1. *Harmonization of codes, valuation, and procedures*

To improve implementation, one of the most important dimensions is to harmonize customs codes, valuation, and procedures among the RTA partners.

The Multilateral Approach at WTO: For importers, the process of estimating the value of a product at customs presents problems that can be just as serious as the actual duty rate charged. The WTO agreement on customs valuation aims for a fair, uniform, and neutral system for the valuation of goods for customs purposes — a system that conforms to commercial realities, and which outlaws the use of arbitrary or fictitious customs values. The agreement provides a set of valuation rules that expands and gives greater precision to the provisions on customs valuation in the original GATT. This has important implications for the RTA partners as well.

A related Uruguay Round ministerial decision gives customs administrations the right to request further information in cases where they have reason to doubt the accuracy of the declared value of imported goods. If the administration maintains a reasonable doubt, despite any additional information, it may be deemed that the customs value of the imported goods cannot be determined on the basis of the declared value. The Committee on Customs Valuation of the Council for Trade in Goods (CGT) carries out work in the WTO on customs valuation (WTO website accessed, 2009).

Customs valuation is a customs procedure that is applied to determine the customs value of imported goods. If the rate of duty is *ad valorem*, the customs value is essential to determine the duty to be paid on an imported good. The Article VII of the General Agreement on Tariffs and Trade laid down the general principles for an international system of valuation. It stipulated that the value for customs purposes of imported merchandize should be based on the actual value of the imported merchandize on which duty is assessed, or of like merchandize, and should not be based on arbitrary or fictitious values. Although Article VII also contains a definition of "actual value," it still permitted the use of widely differing methods of valuing goods. In addition, "grandfather clauses" permitted continuation of old standards which did not even meet the very general new standard.

Starting in the 1950s, customs duties were assessed by many countries according to the Brussels Definition of Value (BVD). Under this method, a normal market price, defined as "the price that a good would fetch in an open market between a buyer and seller independent of each other," was determined for each product, according to which the duty was assessed. Factual deviations from this price were taken into account where the declared value was higher than the listed value. But the downward variations were taken into account up to 10%. This method caused widespread dissatisfaction among traders, as price changes and competitive advantages of firms were not reflected until the notional price was adjusted by the customs office after certain periods of time. New and rare products were not captured often in the lists, which made determination of the "normal price" difficult. The USA never became part of the BVD. It was clear that a more flexible and uniform valuation method was needed which would harmonize the systems of all countries.

The Tokyo Round Valuation Code, or the Agreement on Implementation of Article VII of the GATT that was concluded in the year 1979, established a positive system of Customs Valuation based on the price actually paid or payable for the imported goods. Based on the "transaction value," it was intended to provide a fair, uniform, and neutral system for the valuation of goods for customs purposes, conforming to commercial realities. This differs from the "notional" value used in the BVD. As a stand-alone agreement, the Tokyo Round Valuation Code was signed by more than 40 contracting parties.

The Tokyo Round Code was replaced by the WTO Agreement on Implementation of Article VII of the GATT 1994 following the conclusion of the Uruguay Round. This Agreement is essentially the same as the Tokyo Round Valuation Code and applies only to the valuation of imported goods for the purpose of levying *ad valorem* duties on such goods. It does not contain obligations concerning valuation for purposes of determining export duties or quota administration based on the value of goods, nor does it lay down conditions for the valuation of goods for internal taxation or foreign exchange control.

The Agreement stipulates that customs valuation except in specified circumstances shall be based on the actual price of the goods to be valued, which is generally shown on the invoice. This price along with the adjustments for certain elements listed in Article 8, equals the transaction value, which constitutes the first and most important method of valuation referred to in the Agreement.

For cases that lacks transaction value, or where the transaction value is not acceptable as the customs value because the price has been distorted as a result of certain conditions, the Agreement lays down five other methods of customs valuation, to be applied in the prescribed hierarchical order.

The Indian Practice

The Indian Budget of 2007 had laid down significant changes in the provisions relating to Customs valuation. It addresses several changes as the draft Customs Valuation Rules 2007 (CVR) which have also been issued concurrently by the government for public comment.

Existing subsection (1) of Section 14 of the Customs Act, 1962, in relation to valuation, was based on the concept of the "deemed value" of goods, whereas subsection (1A) of Section 14 mandated that the price of the imported goods would be determined in terms of the rules formulated there under. The existing CVR were based on the concept of "Transaction Value" (TV), as enshrined in the WTO Valuation Agreement. The question of whether to give primacy to the wordings of the Section 14(1), which referred to "deemed value," or to the CVR which prescribed TV gave rise to practical difficulties for importers as the department rejected the transaction value in instances where the invoices indicated values which were lower than those of contemporaneous imports or were below the ruling market prices of such goods. While some decisions of the Courts regarded Section 14(1) as primary and hence held that the TV must meet all the conditions of deemed value, other decisions have upheld the TVs as declared by the importers. The issue was finally settled by the Apex Court in the case of Eicher Tractors Ltd. versus. Commissioner of Customs, Mumbai (2000 (122) ELT 321), wherein it held that subject to the three conditions laid down in Section 14(1); namely those of time, place, and absence of special circumstances, the price of imported goods was to be determined under Section 14(1A) in accordance with the CVR framed for the purpose. The Supreme Court clarified that while the CVR that is framed under Section 14(1A) were subject to the condition of Section 14(1), the Customs authorities were bound to assess the duty on the basis of the declared TV unless the transaction fell within the exceptions specified in the CVR.

The Budget of 2007 replaced the Section 14 entirely. The replaced Section states that the value of both imported and exported goods shall be the TV of such goods as determined, in accordance with the separate rules made for the purpose.

Draft rules have been issued laying down independent principles for valuation of imported and exported goods. More importantly however, revised Section 14 now states that the TV of imported goods shall include, besides the price paid or payable for goods when sold for export to India, costs and services which the buyer is liable to pay, in addition to the above price. Thus, the TV is now to be determined in relation to the price of the imported goods when sold for export to India, as opposed to the erstwhile provision which required the TV to be determined based on the price of such goods for delivery at the time and place of importation. This shift on the basis of determination of the TV is further reinforced by the corresponding provisions of Rule 4 of the draft rules for imported goods.

However, Rule 11 seems to contradict this position and suggests that the *status quo* in relation to determination of the TV on the basis of the price for delivery at the time and place of importation remains in effect. This is a significant amendment and ensures that the Indian Customs valuation provisions are fundamentally in line with the WTO Agreement. However, the section also suggests that the additional costs and charges payable by the buyer are to be included in the value and these illustratively extend to commissions, assists, engineering and design work, and royalty and license fees. The problem is that these costs and charges are supposedly to be included automatically without any condition, as long as the buyer incurs them. If this is so, then it would very importantly change the manner of valuation that is laid down under the WTO Agreement. However, if the provisions of Rule 11 of the draft rules, in relation to various costs paid by the buyer that were to be analyzed, then it would be seen that the erstwhile conditions underlying the inclusion of such costs in the TV continue to remain.

Thus, there appears to be a direct contradiction between revised Section 14 and the draft rules. This point is valid in relation to commission, engineering and design work, and royalty and license fees.

The most significant concern is in relation to royalty and license fees, which are only to be included in the TV, if they are required to be paid as a condition for the sale of the imported goods. Given the extensive litigation currently prevalent, it is imperative that the government clarifies the inclusion of royalty and fees in the TV continues to be governed by this fundamental condition.

This will also give an insight into the harmonized way of interpretation. The explanation on royalties that is inserted in Rule 11 suggests that such fees are a condition of sale of the imported goods; they would nevertheless be added to the TV, even if they were to relate to a process which would be carried out in relation to the imported goods, subsequent to importation. This amendment is perhaps of equal significance but is unexceptionable.

Another important amendment relates to Rule 13, which corresponds to erstwhile Rule 10A, pertaining to rejection of a declared TV. An explanation to his revised rule now clearly states that it cannot be used to determine the TV but only provides a mechanism and procedure for rejection of the declared TV in certain situations. Thereafter, in any event, the TV has to be determined by proceeding sequentially through Rules 5 to 10 of the draft rules. This is a salutary amendment as erstwhile Rule 10A was substantially misused by the departmental authorities.

The TV of export goods will now be the price for the goods when sold for export from India for delivery at the place of exportation provided the sale is under fully competitive conditions and where price is the sole consideration. In case the value cannot be determined as above, the draft rules state that the TV must then be determined by a process of sequentially proceeding through Rules 4 to 6. Special mention must be made here of the range of adjustments that the authorities are required to make, especially those in relation to the present market value of the goods, the maximum retail price printed on such goods, if any, and the domestic price of the goods, as per the exporter's price list/catalogue.

To conclude, significant amendments to the Customs valuation provisions in relation to both imported and exported goods are proposed. While ostensibly these amendments are being made to bring the Indian Customs valuation principles in line with the WTO Agreement, there are several significant deviations which are required to be urgently addressed before these provisions become law (Madhavan, 2007, http://www.business-standard.com/india/news/key-changes-in-customs-valuation/283650/).

5.2.2. E-implementation

The literature data available on this subject has a very different tradition and, instead of looking at quantifiable benefits, trade policy, and instruments, it looks at the use of Information and Communication Technologies (ICT). It largely focuses on building case studies, highlighting the benefits of ICT in trade, and the merits of sharing common standards. It draws strongly on UN Recommendation No. 1 (UN/CEFACT 1981), encouraging the alignment of trade paper documents to a common standard as well as to the more recent electronic standards for EDI and XML promoted through national trade facilitation committees and international organizations such as UNECE or WCO.

This work also includes Robert Schware and Paul Kimberley's (1995) which is a collection of 20 brief country studies, where information technology is used to help trade facilitation efforts. Similarly, Robert Mulligan's (1998) case study looks at three UK companies and their use of EDI in trade transactions, consolidating the illustrative findings into one paper. Applying case study methodology, other research looks at Singapore's TradeNet system, which is frequently propagated as a leading example of the Single Window concept (e.g., UN/CEFACT 2004). This research includes the three Harvard Business School case studies (King, 1990; Neo *et al.*, 1993, 1995; and Teo *et al.*, 1997). They report on the strategic decisions by the Singapore government to enhance its island as a trading hub. While the Harvard Business School's work is presented as a narrative account for class discussion, the latter is based on observations and interviews. Finally, Mei and Dinwoodie's (2005) study looks at exploring the potential for electronic shipping documents in China by drawing on survey data. ICT is the driver in many policy initiatives. Considering the trade facilitation by the organizations have been encouraging ICT programmes since the mid 1960s (Raven, 2005) and that it lies at the heart of many policy initiatives — such as the revised Kyoto Customs Convention (WCO, 1999) and the EU customs' modernization programme (COM (2003) 452 final and

Grainger, 2004) — it is surprising that so little literature on the subject has been produced.

In summing up, it is possible to underscore one single point that while the merits of RTAs have been well understood and their potentials estimated empirically, the policy implementation issues leave much to be desired for. It is possible to state that if concerted efforts are made on implementation issues, RTAs may well address the genuine concerns of spaghetti bowl effects.

CHAPTER 6

Issues for Further Negotiations

Usually, countries worldwide have gained relatively greater degree of negotiating experience when handling modalities of tariff cuts, trade coverage of tariff liberalization, the differential pace of tariff liberalization under different categories of goods, and so on. However, there are several areas in which standards of negotiations are still evolving to bring about a greater extent of clarity in concepts, improved objectivity in terms of their impacts and better-understood implementation of the implications.

Against this backdrop, the chapter probes into such issues on which negotiations are much more difficult due to the inherent complexity that prevails in different countries' trade and economic regimes. These include non-tariff barriers, restrictive practices, custom administrative practices, technical barriers to trade, rules of origin for services, and investment cooperation.

6.1. Non-Tariff Barriers[1]

Despite a long history of non-tariff barriers (NTBs) in international trade, the special attention they have got only in the early 70th (Quinn and Slayton, 1980) century when the discussion of the NTB was explicitly scheduled in the framework of Tokyo Round of the GATT negotiations. Various rounds of GATT and later WTO have led to drastic reductions in tariff rates for various lines of products available in member countries. This has increased the importance of NTBs as a trade restricting instrument. These barriers are less transparent, more flexible, and extremely

---

[1] Based on Das and Kathuria (mimeo).

variable; these characteristics make NTB as an important substitute for country's tariff regime.[2]

Many a time, an NTB is defined as any barrier to international trade which is not tariff. Such a definition is quite vague and it increases the complexities involved in dealing with NTBs. Researchers such as Baldwin (1970), Walter (1972), Mayer and Gevel (1973), and Deardorff and Stern (1997) have provided their definitions of this phenomenon. Moreover, several international organizations like UNCTAD and GATT/WTO (2001) have also contributed to the formulation of the term "non-tariff barriers." Careful review of these definitions as well as study of NTB *per se* allowed Movchan and Eremenko (2003) to propose the following definition:

> NTBs are measures, other than tariffs that are tightly connected with state (administrative) activity and influence prices, quantity, structure, and/or direction of international flows of goods and services as well as resources used to produce these goods and services.

This definition highlights various characteristics of NTBs. Here, the emphasis is made on the role of the state in imposing NTBs, although some researchers propose to consider actions of private persons (entrepreneurs) as NTB source (Baldwin, 1970; Walter, 1972). As per this definition, NTBs are expected to affect prices, quantity demanded and sold, allocation of resources, and structure & direction of trade. This definition does not cover another important feature of the NTB, namely their influence on the general level of world welfare or on potential real world income (Baldwin, 1970; Mayer and Gevel, 1973). The absence of judgment criterion is dictated by twofold nature of the NTB. Although traditionally the NTBs are considered as sources of dead weight loss that reduces the level of social welfare, it could be the case that total effect of the NTB is positive. This situation arises when social and private marginal utility functions do not

---

[2] Deardorff (1987) has argued that government generally prefer NTBs over tariffs. If the object is to assist firms and workers who purportedly are being injured by imports, then only an explicit quantitative (non-tariff) restriction can be relied on to do the job in an uncertain world.

coincide due to information asymmetry. For instance, it could be shown that mandatory state certification is necessary for selected types of goods (Movchan, 1999). Types of NTBs are so many that various organizations have divided them into different categories. The different types and categories of NTBs have been discussed later in this chapter.

NTB are quite difficult to get identified and their presence in the economy affects many macro and micro level decisions, therefore it is important to know the complexities involved in the working of NTB. The available literature on NTBs provides important insights into the working of nontariff barriers that are discussed in the next section.

The issue of NTBs has various dimensions. Each dimension has some economic implication. Extensive literature is available on this particular issue that highlights these dimensions.

Michalopoulos (1999) has used Frequency-type Measures for calculating the existing NTB. There exist two common types of frequency measures: frequency ratio and import coverage ratio (Laird and Yeats, 1990). Both of them are based on calculation of the ratio of commodity lines subject to at least one NTB in total number of lines for the respective group of trade nomenclature. The frequency ratio, F, is calculated by formula:

Frequency Ratio

$$= \frac{\text{Number of product categories subject to NTBs in group } i \times 100}{\text{Total number of product categories in each HS group}}.$$

For import coverage ratio, the value of imports of commodities that is subject to at least one NTB is used as a weight instead of number of categories. That allows introduce time factor in the measurement of NTB, as well as better evaluate importance of particular NTB for the trade as a whole. The Import Coverage Ratio (IC) is calculated by formula:

Import Coverage Ratio

$$= \frac{\sum \text{Value of imports of a commodity } j \text{ in a group } i \text{ subject to NTBs} \times 100}{\text{Total imports in HS commodity group } i}.$$

The frequency measures are useful in directing attention to the frequency of occurrence of various types of NTBs. However, these measures have a number of drawbacks. First, according to OECD (1997), the reporting of NTBs is somewhat uneven, and there may be problems arising from the way NTBs are defined and the level and type of aggregation used in calculating commodity and sectoral ratios. Second, the F and IC ratios do not provide any information on the possible deterrent effects that NTBs may have upon the pricing or quantity decisions of foreign exporters. Third, the F and IC/PF ratios refer primarily to border measures and thus ignore the entire range of internal governmental measures and the restrictive actions of imperfectly competitive firms that we discussed earlier. Finally, and most importantly, the frequency-type measures provide no information on the economic impact that NTBs may have on prices, production, consumption, and international trade.[3] But as non-availability of data does not pose a problem in their calculation and they are quite easy to calculate, many studies have applied them.

OECD (2002, 2003, 2003a, and 2004), KITA (various years), KIEP (2000), KIIET (2002), and Kim (2003) have applied inventory based approach to calculate NTBs. This approach can be used both in a quantitative perspective and in a qualitative perspective to assess the importance of domestic regulations as trade barriers (Beghin and Bureau, 2001). Various types of NTBs such as export duties, export restrictions, non-automatic import licensing, prohibitions, and quotas are catalogued under this approach. Three sources of information can be used for this: (i) data on regulations, such as the number of regulations, which can be used to construct various statistical indicators, or proxy variables, such as the number of pages of national regulations, (ii) data on frequency of detentions; and (iii) data on complaints from the industry against discriminatory regulatory practices and notifications to international bodies about such practices. Even this approach is useful for directing attention to the frequency of occurrence and the trade or production

---

[3] See Leamer (1990a, b) for efforts to use the NTB coverage data to assess the impact of NTBs on trade flows in 1983 for the major industrialized and developing countries.

coverage of various types of NTBs. But data availability is a major problem here. Moreover, this approach does not provide a quantification of the effect of regulations on trade *per se*.

Veronika Movchan and Igor Eremenko (2003) have measured Compound NTB Index. They have given some arbitrary values to the NTB imposed on a particular product line (depending upon the type of NTB, for e.g., Technical Barriers have been given a value of 25 whereas Prohibitions have been given a value of 100) and then have used that value as a weight. The Index is calculated as

$$\text{INTB}_j = \frac{\sum \text{NTB}_{ij} \times \text{IM}_j}{\sum \text{IM}_j},$$

where INTB_j is an index of NTB for commodity j, NTB_{ij} is a weight of NTB i to commodity j, IM_j is the value of import of commodity j; $i = 1, \ldots, I, j = 1, \ldots, J$, where I is a number of NTB, and J is the total number of commodities (groups of commodities).

Several authors including Sazanami *et al.* (1995); Kawai and Tanaka (1996); JETRO (2000); Kataoka and Kuno (2003); Harrigan (2003); Ando and Fujii (2002) have used Price Differential Approach (also known as Price-Wedge Method). This approach calculates the differential between the import price and the domestic price and the domestic price of each commodity at a disaggregated level and subtracts the tariff rate on the commodity from this differential. The result is treated as a NTB. The price-wedge method has several limitations (Beghin and Bureau, 2001). First, the method makes it possible to quantify the effect of a set of NTBs present in the market but seldom makes it possible to identify what those NTBs are precisely. Second, formulas that measure the NTBs as a percentage price-wedge between imports and domestic prices are valid only under the assumption that imported goods are perfect substitutes. The main limitation of the method lies in its practical difficulties. For large-scale studies, the available data always reflect differences in the quality of the imported goods. The authors Deardorff and Stern (1998) and Messerlin (2001) have calculated tariff equivalents of NTBs by calculating the price-wedge between the imported goods and the comparable product in the domestic market.

Many others have conducted surveys among exporters to know the various types of NTBs faced during export of commodities. But it is a costly approach and it requires special skill to design and administer surveys.

6.2. Major Categories of Non-tariff Measures and Related Policies[4]

6.2.1. *Quantitative restrictions and similar specific limitations*

1. *Import quotas*: Restrictions on quantity and/or value of imports of specific commodities for some given time period; administered globally, selectively, or bilaterally.
2. *Export limitations*: Same as above but with reference to exports.
3. *Licensing*: Some system of licensing is required to administer the foregoing restrictions. Licensing may be discretionary and also used for statistical purposes.
4. *Voluntary export restraints*: Restrictions imposed by the importing country but administered by the exporting country that are administered multilaterally and bilaterally; requires system of licensing; essentially similar to an orderly marketing arrangement.
5. *Exchange and other financial controls*: Restrictions on receipts and/or payments of foreign exchange which is designed to control international trade and/or capital movements; will generally require some system of licensing that may involve multiple exchange rates for different kinds of transactions.
6. *Prohibitions*: May be selective with respect to commodities and countries of origin/destination that includes embargoes which may carry legal sanctions.
7. *Domestic content and mixing requirements*: Requires that an industry use a certain proportion of domestically produced components and/or materials and labor in producing final products.

---

[4] Excerpted from Deardorff and Stern (1997).

8. *Discriminatory bilateral agreements*: Preferential trading arrangements that may be selective for a commodity and a country including preferential sourcing arrangements.

9. *Counter-trade*: Arrangements involving barter, counter purchases of goods, and payments in kind.

6.2.2. Non-tariff charges and related policies affecting imports

1. *Variable levies*: Based on a target domestic price of imports, a levy is imposed so that the price of imports reaches the target price irrespective of the cost of imports.

2. *Advance deposit requirement*: Some proportion of the value of imports must be deposited in advance of the payment, with no allowance for any interest accrued on the deposit.

3. *Anti-dumping duties*: Imposition of a special import duty when the price of imports is alleged to lie below some measure of the costs of production of foreign firms then minimization of the foreign prices may be established to "trigger" antidumping investigations and actions.

4. *Countervailing duties*: Imposition of a special import duty to counteract an alleged foreign government subsidy to exports; normally require that the domestic injury be shown.

5. *Border tax adjustments*: When indirect (e.g., sales or value added) taxes are levied on the destination principle then the imports are only subjected to such taxes and not the exports. As a result, the effects on trade will be neutral except in cases involving adjustments for more than the compensation for the taxes imposed or exempted, or when the size of the tax differs across commodities.

6.2.3. Government participation in trade, restrictive practices, and more general government policies

1. *Subsidies and other aids*: Direct and indirect subsidies to export and import competing industries, including tax benefits, credit concessions, and bilateral tied aid programs.

2. *Government procurement policies*: Preferences given to domestic over foreign firms in bidding on public-procurement contracts, including explicit cost differentials and informal procedures favoring procurement from domestic firms.

3. *State trading, government monopolies, and exclusive franchises*: Government actions which may result in trade distortions, including government-sanctioned discriminatory international transport agreements.

4. *Government industrial policy and regional development measures*: Government actions designed to aid particular firms, industrial sectors, and regions to adjust to changes in market conditions.

5. *Government financed research and development and other technology policies*: Government actions designed to correct market distortions and aid private firms; includes policies relating to intellectual property (patents, copyrights, and trademarks) and technological spillovers from government programs, such as defense and public health.

6. *National systems of taxation and social insurance*: Personal and corporate income taxation, unemployment insurance, social security, and related policies which may have an impact on trade.

7. *Macroeconomic policies*: Monetary/fiscal, balance-of-payments, and exchange rate actions which have an impact on national output, foreign trade, and capital movements.

8. *Competition policies*: Antitrust and related policies (e.g., intellectual property regulations) designed to foster or restrict competition and which may have an impact on foreign trade and investment.

9. *Foreign investment policies*: Screening and monitoring of inward and/or outward foreign direct investment (FDI), including performance requirements affecting production and trade.

10. *Foreign corruption policies*: Policies designed to prohibit or restrict bribes and related practices in connection with foreign trade and investment.

11. *Immigration policies*: General or selective policies designed to limit or encourage international movement of labor that may have an impact on foreign trade and investment.

6.2.4. *Custom procedures and administrative practices*

1. *Customs valuation procedures*: Use of specially constructed measures of price rather than the invoice or transaction price for the purpose of levying tariffs.
2. *Customs classification procedures*: Use of national methods of customs classification rather than an internationally harmonized method for the purpose of levying tariffs.
3. *Customs clearance procedures*: Documentation, inspection, and related practices which may impede trade.

6.2.5. *Technical barriers to trade*

1. *Health and sanitary regulations and quality standards*: Technical regulations designed for domestic objectives but which may discriminate against imports.
2. *Safety and industrial standards and regulations*: See above
3. *Packaging and labeling regulations, including trademarks*: See above
4. *Advertising and media regulations*: See above

The upshot of above is that NTBs are a very complex set of policy instruments and these are one of the relatively more important components of future negotiations as they do not provide a clear picture of what actually they mean in terms of their effects in an RTA. In addition, the categories presented above of the possible NTBs fail to distinguish between the non-tariff measures that are possibly in the interest of trade partners and those that hinder trade. This dimension makes the NTBs even more complicated and a subtle negotiating approach needs to be evolved.

6.3. Trade in Services

Trade in services is yet another area in which negotiating strategies in RTAs are still not well-developed despite the fact that services have emerged as crucial economic activities for the developed as well as developing country economies. The rapidly expanding services sector is contributing more and more towards economic growth and job creation worldwide. This sector accounts for around 60% and 50% of the gross domestic product (GDP) for the developed and developing worlds, respectively. Thus, a set of multilateral trading rules under the WTO was envisaged and the General Agreement on Trade in Services (GATS) came into being.

6.3.1. GATS framework

The GATS regime is much more complex than the GATT and the WTO disciplines as in many ways, it represented an unexplored territory. The principle of the Most-Favored Nation Treatment (MFN) is embedded in both. However, under GATT, limitations on market access and national treatment could be effected through the mechanism of import restrictions, tariffs, subsidies, and regulatory regimes relating to payments in foreign exchange, export, and local content obligations etc; though most of these policy instruments are being gradually phased out or limited in their application in pursuance of the progressive trade liberalization objectives under WTO. Under GATS, tariffs are not the relevant instruments for progressive liberalization of trade in services. Therefore, it is the regulatory framework, which is the center of discussions under the GATS.

The negotiations under GATS throw light on the rules and framework for liberalization of trade in services. Countries individually choose the sectors in which binding commitments are to be made, as well as those in which commitments are not to be made. This is known as a positive list approach. The negotiations are conducted on the basis of requests and offers whereby countries request each other to consider liberalization in particular sectors in order to respond with offers. The negotiations that began in 2000 are still continuing. Further, work on the implementation of the decisions made during Doha Round is going on, in spite of the fact that the various deadlines for finalizing request-offer lists have been missed.

The GATS covers several services sectors such as telecommunications, business services, transport, health services, audio-visual services, tourism and travel, distribution, financial, and education.

6.3.2. Approaches to trade in services liberalization[5]

Conceptually, as argued earlier in a regional context, on account of the economics of neighborhood, it may be easier to negotiate services sector trade liberalization in a regional economic grouping than multilaterally. Yet, achieving this would require a conscious effort as services trade is complex by its very nature, covering those sectors that are diverse and uniquely placed in terms of governance through domestic regulations serving a wide range of policy objectives. The modes of services delivery also vary among sectors, public and private entities, and different market structures. The electronic mode of delivery poses its own special problems along with its associated benefits. Thus, any negotiations among a set of countries bilaterally, regionally or multilaterally also becomes intricate and nuanced due to country-specific contexts.

There are several dimensions on which consensus-based negotiating approaches have to be designed in the context of services trade liberalization. Some of the dimensions are briefly highlighted below.

6.3.2.1. Economic Needs Tests

Economics Needs Tests (ENTs) are most commonly found in commitments related to mode 3 (establishment) and mode 4 (movement of natural persons). In the absence of a clear definition of ENTs under the GATS, ways to improve the transparency of ENTs are required.

6.3.2.2. Negotiating modalities

The use of formulas should be aimed at the efficient conduct of services negotiations. Thus, formulas need to be flexible, supportive and complementary to the request-offer approaches. Both quantitative and qualitative formulas could be considered, though the latter is considered more appropriate for services negotiations. Standardized approaches in the GATS, such as model schedules and references papers, could also be

---

[5] Refers to OECD (2001).

considered and a possible "measures-based" formula that aims at reducing the incidence of certain types of measures across the four modes of supply may be contemplated upon. Such a measures-based formula could apply across all sectors or to individual sectors, and a combination of cross-sectoral and sector-specific formula approaches may be required.

6.3.2.3. *Approaches to interrelated services sectors*

Consideration has to be given also to the way groupings or "clusters" of related services might be defined. This may include terms of commercial linkages on the one hand and relevant regulatory frameworks, on the other. They will also be examined as to how they would relate to the existing services sectoral classification which is used for negotiating specific commitments. Clusters could be used to make specific commitments as well as form the basis for a model schedule. The benefits and problems of these approaches would have to be explored.

6.3.2.4. *Transparency in domestic regulation*

The issue of transparency in trade-related domestic regulation to facilitate trade in services assumes great importance. The dimensions on which a consensus would be needed include standardized notification procedures including the purpose of regulation, the provisions related to services, contact details for relevant authorities, and information on the regulatory process.

In short, trade in services negotiations are still in the process of evolution and with increased prominence of services; they would form a significant portion of research and negotiate time in future.

6.3.3. *Rules of origin for services*[6]

As trade in services has increased in recent times, various trade policy measures are being devised to facilitate it. Since trade in services is not always similar to trade in goods the need for evolving trade policies

---

[6] See also Das and Ratna (2011).

specific to the services sector is increasingly realized. The academic research as well as the policy making process on Rules of Origin has primarily focused mainly on Rules of Origin for goods.

However, with increasing cross-border trade in services, determination of the origin of service providers has become important. As integration of service markets often necessitates physical presence of service-suppliers in the country that is seeking services, any preferential treatment to them within a regional trading arrangement, would require setting in place the origin norms for services. It is in this light that some of the relevant issues in this regard are highlighted below that could serve as the basis for evolving origin norms for the services sector as a part of the overall Rules of Origin system.

(i) *Goods versus Services*: So far rules of origin have been applied to flow of goods or in other words trade in tangible products. However, with the intensification of integration of services markets among countries determination of the origin of producers viz. natural and legal persons has emerged as an important policy issue. Trade in several services is not analogous to trade in goods because service providers or producers often have to physically be present in the country that is importing services. Any preferential treatment extended to different services would have to identify the sources of services and determine the origin of producers. One point that has been almost missed is regarding services contributing to the value of goods. Similarly, it goes without saying that usage of different goods contribute to value addition in service activities. These linkages are often not taken into account while devising Rules of Origin either for goods or services.

(ii) *Originating Norms*: In the case of goods, Rules of Origin focuses on processing activities in terms of substantial transformation. This is determined by applying three tests viz. change in tariff heading, percentage test, and specified process test. Several tradable services involve processing activities and contribute to value addition. Obviously, enough substantial transformation based on change in tariff heading cannot be applied for the determination of origin of services. Non-storability of services often renders all the services which are sold as substantial transformation simply because that particular service might not have been existed before. In the same manner physical content requirements also become irrelevant as services tend to be both intangible and indivisible.

Thus, origin norms for services would have to be based upon nationality or value added criteria. There are several parameters that are looked into in different international treaties and trading agreements while determining origin of producers (corporations) that include place of incorporation; nationality of control; nationality of ownership; principal place of business and location of headquarters, or center of management/decision making.

Different agreements use one or many parameters and their combination for determining the origin of producers (Box 1). Since determination of nationality is often difficult there is need for applying the value added criterion for the products that an enterprise produces in determining the origin of the enterprise. The practical difficulty of this type has been experienced in the context of anti-dumping and safeguard actions, the problem is that since enterprises source their inputs from all over the world it would be very difficult to consider an enterprise as a domestic enterprise if the origin norms take into account the value added in production by local firms. That is why quite often along with the value added test, specific process test is also used in determination of the origin of products and in turn origin of enterprises.

What comes out of the forgoing discussion is that in order to evolve origin norms for the services sector, Rules of Origin would have to be applied to both the products as well as services providers. While for determination of origin of products change in tariff heading, percentage test, and specific process tests are applied for the purposes of origin determination of services providers of the three criteria pertaining to products as well as the nationality criteria applied on enterprise would have to be used together.

However, one may hasten to add that the value added criterion used for service providers may induct some kind of ambiguity and subjectivity into the system as indivisibility of services creates difficulties in making an objective assessment of the extent of value addition in a particular enterprise in a particular country.

Origin determination in the realm of services trade is yet another dimension on which the existing knowledge base is limited and needs adequate policy attention.

Box 1: Approaches to Services Trade Liberalization Under Different RTAs

I. Dimensions: RTAs have adopted distinct approaches in respect of (i) scope; (ii) modalities for liberalization; (iii) depth of commitments; and (iv) regulatory cooperation.

Sectoral and modal coverage: Existing RTAs tend to provide universal sectoral coverage, with the exclusion of sensitive sectors such as air and maritime transport and audiovisual services. Liberalization may be based on a progressive approach with an implementation period, especially for DCs (10 years in MERCOSUR). Some agreements provide for separate treatment of investment (NAFTA-type RTAs, MERCOSUR, EU) and movement of persons (NAFTA). Some sector-specific provisions can also contain a liberalization element, including financial services, air, maritime and land transport, telecommunications, professional services, and mode-4-type movement.

Modalities of liberalization: RTAs generally follow either a negative or a positive list approach. In the negative list approach, countries list those sectors and modes of supply that they wish to be excluded from the general obligation of not restricting services imports, and remaining restrictions may be subject to negotiated elimination (in some cases with the "ratchet mechanism," which automatically binds unilateral liberalization of new services under the agreement). The positive list approach consists in listing those sectors and modes of supply to whose liberalization countries commit. This approach can, in theory, provide the same level of liberalization as the negative list approach but provides greater flexibility in designing the scope and pace of liberalization commitments. The negative list approach was adopted in NAFTA-type RTAs (CAN, CARICOM), Europe Agreements and EU-Mexico, while the positive list approach was adopted in EU-Chile, ASEAN, MERCOSUR, CACM, Japan–Singapore and United States–Jordan. The definition of rules of origin for services providers is important in determining the level and depth of regional services liberalization vis-à-vis third country services/suppliers.

Depth of commitments: Countries' regional commitment as well as general and sectoral disciplines provided under an RTA would affect the extent to which RTAs can generate effective service towards liberalization. Liberalization commitment may result either in standstill or rollback of

(Continued)

Box 1: (*Continued*)

restrictive measures. This is important, since RTAs can go beyond GATS commitment to provide "preferential" market access conditions for regional partners. A series of measures are included to promote effective market access, including improved transparency obligations.

Regulatory cooperation: Domestic regulation measures such as qualification requirements also determines the level of liberalization, since such requirements often constitute important market entry barriers to services trade, for example trade in professional services. Harmonization and mutual recognition are pursued under some RTAs (MERCOSUR, NAFTA (accountancy, architecture, engineering), CARICOM), but often on a best-endeavor basis. RTAs can contain market access commitments in government procurement in services and disciplines regarding ESM, monopoly, and competition policy.

II. *Experience in Asia*: Most Asian RTAs adopt a GATS approach, which contains provisions on national treatment, market access, modes of delivery, and domestic regulation. However, there are notable differences from a GATS approach. For instance, while the schedules of country-specific commitments in most Asian RTAs, such as ASEAN, follow a positive list approach, some Asian FTAs follow a negative list approach (FTAs between the Republic of Korea and Singapore, and the Republic of Korea and Chile). Most bilateral agreements contain well-defined services provisions, including separate chapters for key services sectors. The India–Singapore agreement has separate investment and services chapters with extensive coverage of the movement of professionals, air services, and e-commerce. In view of the Philippines' and India's skilled English-speaking workforces, both the India–Singapore FTA and the Japan–Philippines EPA have extensive provisions for the movement of natural persons.

Source: Based on UNCTAD (2007).

6.4. Investment Cooperation

Empirical evidence on causality between trade and FDI is mixed. A part of the literature points to trade promoting FDI. Assuming this was the case, trade liberalization in an RTA which includes investment rules would increase trade and FDI jointly. Hence, there would be complementarity between these flows. Another part of the empirical literature argues that if trade barriers are eliminated, firms will no longer invest in foreign locations, preferring to serve a foreign market through export. Here, trade and FDI flows are assumed to be related through substitution. There has been a very rich development of empirical evidence documenting the relationship between international trade and FDI.

Having recognized the developmental role of investment, developing countries in general have been forging more and more investment cooperation links in recent times (see Box 2). Agreements on investments between developing countries have increased substantially in both number and geographical coverage over the past decade, according to UNCTAD (2004). This wave of South–South International Investment Agreements (IIAs) includes 653 Bilateral Investment Agreements (BITs), 312 Double Taxation Treaties (DTTs) and 49 Preferential Trade and Investment Agreements (PTIAs) between developing countries.

Bilateral investment treaties (BITs) aim at protecting and promoting foreign investment flows. DTTs aim to avoid having the same income taxed by two or more States. PTIAs — both bilateral and regional in nature — aim at creating preferential market access and other forms of economic integration among the signatory States.

On the other hand, different regions such as the South Asian region has not been able to keep pace with such global trends despite the fact that in the age of globalized production networks and supply chains such initiatives are considered crucial. These policy mechanisms are also important in the context of investment cooperation on a regional basis.

What is more, the imperatives of instituting such measures are much more pronounced than before. As highlighted earlier, the need for forging stronger trade-investment links in the South Asian region is crucial for bringing about the desired results of the South Asian regional integration process and SAFTA.

It is in this sense that cooperative initiatives and negotiating skills require greater amount of clarity with adequate understanding of the trade-investment linkages.

Box 2:   The Rising Tide of South–South Investment Agreements

In total, 113 developing countries have entered into BITs with another developing nation. China, Egypt, and Malaysia have each signed more than 40 such agreements, and have also signed more agreements with other developing countries than with developed countries. Asia — followed by Latin America — accounts for 68% of South–South BITs, constituting the largest part of the South–South BITs network.

This phenomenon is occurring as developing countries are increasingly becoming home countries of FDI flows and as their companies start to figure more prominently among the world's major transnational corporations. Since the late 1990s, FDI flows from developing countries appear to be growing faster than those from developed to developing countries (see UNCTAD/PRESS/PR/2004/017/Corr.1 of October 20, 2004). The share of total outward FDI stock in developing economies that is protected by a BIT was estimated to be 27% in 2000, according to UNCTAD data. Looking specifically at South–South FDI stock, roughly 20% was covered by South–South BITs in force as of 2003, based on data for nine developing economies that report outward FDI stock by destination (Hong Kong; China; India; Kazakhstan; Malaysia; Pakistan; Singapore; South Africa; Thailand; and Tunisia). These nine economies represent about 58% of the total outward FDI flows of developing countries. The 20% figure would double if one counted all BITs, including signed BITs that are not yet in force.

A similar, though less pronounced, trend emerges for South–South DTTs. Since the first-ever such South–South treaty was signed in 1956 between India and Sierra Leone, the number has grown slowly, reaching 96 by 1990. During the 1990s, 172 new DTTs were signed between 73 developing countries. The growth rate continued until this year, by which time 312 DTTs had been undertaken between 94 developing countries. Today, 14% of all double taxation treaties are between developing countries. South–South DTTs are concluded by countries in all geographical regions, but mainly in South–East Asia and to a lesser extent in Latin America and Africa. India, China, and Malaysia accounted for the largest number of such treaties that followed closely by other Asian countries, while Tunisia stands out among the African and Arab countries.

Another important indicator for the rise in South–South cooperation on investment is the increase in PTIAs. The first South–South PTIA was signed in 1970 (by seven Arab countries), and the number grew rather slowly in the decade that followed. By 2004, however, the total number of PTIAs

(Continued)

Box 2: (*Continued*)

among developing countries rose to 49, and 31% of all current PTIAs concluded between or among developing countries. There are marked
regional variations within the group of PTIAs. Latin America and Asia are
the most active regions, with 25 and 14 such agreements, respectively.
African PTIAs are modest compared to the initiatives in Latin America and
Asia. This regional distribution corresponds largely to the pattern of
South–South outward FDI flows.

- As a rule, South–South BITs deal mainly, and exclusively, with investment
  protection and promotion (i.e., they do not grant free access and establishment, unlike the western hemisphere BITs); they refrain from explicitly
  prohibiting performance requirements; and they limit transparency
  requirements to the stage after the adoption of laws and regulations.
- South–South PTIAs differ from BITs in terms of the depth and breadth of
  the investment issues covered. Some such South–South treaties are rather
  modest in content because they establish frameworks for promoting FDI
  and mandates for future cooperation, rather than focusing on far-reaching
  liberalization and protection. Other agreements are substantive in nature,
  and this includes development-related provisions on the establishment of
  an institutional framework, the granting of flexibility through provisions
  for special and differential treatment, the provision of technical assistance and capacity-building and the promotion of home country
  measures.

While South–South BITs do not explicitly mention development aspects in
their preambles, some 81% of the PTIAs reviewed by UNCTAD refer in one
way or another to the development objective set forth in the preamble.

Source: South Centre, *South Bulletin* 92, 30 November 2004.

It should also be highlighted that the South Asian region has been
entrapped in a low domestic savings ratio translated into low levels of
investment compared to the developmental need of the region. This
often dampens its growth profile. This can be overcome with investment
from abroad, especially FDI, which has been regarded as one of the major
sources for boosting a region's poor investment situation. However FDI
inflows are negligible in South Asia and this itself builds a strong case for

intra-regional investment cooperation (see Box 3). This is particularly important as intra-regional investment in the region in terms of its magnitude and sectoral coverage still remains meager.

Box 3:   Case for Intra-regional Investments

There is no denying the fact that South Asian countries urgently need huge investment in order to achieve a sustained level of growth. But the region has been entrapped in a low domestic saving low investment situation, which hampered its efforts for attaining the desired level of growth. In this scenario, investment from abroad, especially FDI has been regarded as one of the major source for boosting the region's poor investment situation.

The examples of European Union, ASEAN, and NAFTA can be cited where member countries have received sizeable amounts of investment from within the region. Majority of South Asian countries are still looking for FDI from a limited number of developed countries such as USA, UK, Japan, and some developing countries like Korea, Hong Kong, Malaysia. All this indicates that most of the South Asian countries are targeting the same sources for FDIs and competing with each other to attain maximum possible share of FDI. South Asia's intra-regional FDI in most countries is less than 5% of the total FDI flow, while intra-regional flow of FDI in South East Asia is much higher. Among South Asian countries, India is the major investor within the region but at a very small amount, especially compared to its outsourcing in other regions. India's FDI outflow in 1996–1997 was on average US$96 million, which in 2003 increased up to US$913 million. In 2003, India's investment in Sri Lanka, Nepal, and Bangladesh was only 0.7%, 0.5%, and 0.1%, respectively of its total outward investment. Interestingly, during 1996–2003, India's average investment in USA was 19%, and in Russia 18%, and it is becoming an important investor for the UK and France. However, outward flow of FDI from other South Asian countries is either low or not directed to the region. It is perceived from the recent development of trade and investment agreements that South Asia's importance, as a strategic location for investment will gradually increase, especially when SAFTA will start to operate. A complete elimination of tariffs, as projected, will increase the intra-regional trade by 1.6 times of the existing level of intra-regional trade. This will attract a lot of intra-regional and extra-regional investment

(Continued)

Box 3: (*Continued*)

in South Asian countries, and presumably investment of TNCs as well. Under India–Nepal FTA, Nepalese manufactured goods get duty free access to Indian markets, which already influence Indian investors to invest in Nepal. India and Sri Lanka signed FTA in 1998, which has a positive impact on bilateral investment situation in Sri Lanka. India–Sri Lanka FTA has stimulated new and more Indian FDI in Sri Lanka, mainly in rubber-based products, ceramics, electrical goods and electronics, wood-based products, and consumer goods, which are worth an investment of $145 million. During the past three years, leading Indian companies such as Gujarat Ambuja, Asian Paints and Larsen and Toubro have committed substantial investments in Sri Lanka, while CEAT and Taj Hotels, for example have expanded their operations.

To attract FDI, South Asian countries immediately need to improve business environment in their respective countries. Firstly, South Asian countries should immediately sign BITs and Double Taxation Avoidance Treaties (DTTs) with other member countries. Second, South Asian countries need to improve their infrastructure, such as power, transport, and port, which would substantially improve the region's competitiveness.

Source: Moazzem, KG. Taking the regional route (16 March 2006). *The Daily Star* 15th anniversary Special.

One of the reasons behind poor FDI flow in South Asia has been argued to be the absence of a large market in South Asia, which did not develop due to poor regional integration. The trade-investment nexus is of crucial policy importance in the South Asian context as production and export capabilities of the LDCs are limited. As highlighted earlier, encouraging trade creating joint ventures would thus help in enhancing their supply capabilities (RIS, 1999). Moreover, trade deficits between smaller and bigger countries can be compensated by inflows on the capital account by way of FDI inflows (RIS, 2004 and see also Box 4).

This is only to emphasize with the help of the South Asian case study that investment cooperation in RTAs is also a challenging aspect on which negotiating strategies are yet to evolve especially in the developing world.

Box 4: Indian Investment in Sri Lanka

India is today the fourth largest overall foreign direct investor in Sri Lanka (following Singapore, UK, and Australia). Although historically inflows have been low, there has been a dramatic increase after the FTA. A major attraction for Indian investors has been the ability to re-export to India while benefiting from lower tariffs on raw materials in Sri Lanka. Reversing the erstwhile trend, India became the biggest FDI investor in Sri Lanka in 2002 and 2003. For 2004, India slipped to fourth place behind Switzerland (Holcim cements), Malaysia (Dialog mobile network), and UK (HSBC BPO) which invested in some large projects.

As of August 2004, 147 enterprises/projects have been approved under Board of Investments in Sri Lanka at an investment of US$450 million. Over 50% of Indian investment in SAARC countries is in Sri Lanka. The biggest Indian investment in recent times has been Indian Oil Corporation's investment of US$75 million. Seeing the potential for investments from India, the Sri Lankan Board of Investments opened its first overseas branch in Bangalore on May 23, 2005.

Some of the most visible Indian investments are Lanka Indian Oil Corporation, TATAs (Taj Hotels, VSNL, Watawala tea plantations) Apollo Hospitals, LIC , L&T (now Aditya Birla Group), Ambujas, Rediffusion, Ceat, Nicholas Piramal, Jet Airways, Sahara, Indian Airlines, and Ashok Leyland. Indian Human Resources and Education Companies like ICFAI have also started entering the Sri Lankan market. In the pipeline are Indian banks like ICICI, UTI Bank and education establishments like Manipal Medical Institute.

Source: High Commission of India, Colombo (http://www.hcicolombo.org).

6.4.1. *Investment and services inter-linkages in Regional Trading Agreements*

The linkages between investment and services trade is often not understood except in the case of mode 3 negotiations, despite the fact that investment and services trade are interlinked in other modes as well. Table 6.1 lists the broad categories of disciplines and associated measures that can be found in RTA Investment chapters. They typically include a broad asset-based definition of investment, universal coverage of goods and services, core legal protections, establishment and non-discriminatory

Table 6.1. Assessing investment chapters of RTAs.

Definition	Coverage	Investment Liberalization	Investment Protection	Investment Promotion/ Facilitation	Dispute Settlement	Schedule of Commitments
— Asset Based definition of investment Open/Closed Direct/Indirect	— National measures	**General obligations**	**General obligations**	— Investment Promotion	— State-to-State arbitration	— Negative or positive
	— Sub-national measures	— Transparency	— Payments and transfers	— Cooperation/ Capacity Building Mechanisms	— Investor-State arbitration	
	— State enterprises	— Establishment	— Fair and equitable/ Minimum standard			
— Definition of investor	— Corporate responsibility	— Post- Establishment	— Full protection and security			
		— National treatment	— Expropriation			
		— MFN treatment	— Compensation			
		— Performance requirements				
		— Senior Management/Board of Directors				
		— Temporary Movement of Key Personnel				

(Continued)

Table 6.1.   (*Continued*).

Definition	Coverage	Investment Liberalization	Investment Protection	Investment Promotion/ Facilitation	Dispute Settlement	Schedule of Commitments
		— Standstill/rollback				
		— Country exceptions				
		— Economic integration clause				
		— General exceptions				
		— Monopolies and Concessions				
		— Taxation				
		— Environment				
		— Labor				
		— Origin requirements/ Denial of benefits				

Source: Extracted from OECD (2006).

treatment, investment promotion and facilitation and capacity building, and recourse to investor-state international arbitration (OECD, 2006). These chapters also employ, as a general rule, a negative list of reservations or exceptions with respect to liberalization. Annex 1 provides an overview of how these various provisions are covered in the sampled agreements.

Table 6.2 lists the broad categories of investment disciplines and associated measures that can be found in GATS-based RTA trade in services chapters. Striking differences emerge from a comparison with the investment template provided in Table 6.1. Trade in services is generally defined as the supply of a service through four distinct modes: cross-border trade (Mode 1), consumption abroad (Mode 2), commercial presence (Mode 3), and temporary movement of natural persons (Mode 4). All the measures listed in the chapter apply to these four modes of supply. If the inclusion of Modes 3 and 4 underlines the importance of factor mobility to trade in services, these two Modes are also those that come closest to the activities covered by investment chapters.

This is yet another area where negotiating imperatives in the realms of investment and services trade would have to converge in a more seamless manner.

6.5. Trade Facilitation

Trade facilitation is a concept that considers the simplification, harmonization, standardization, and modernization of trade procedures. Its principle aim is to reduce transaction costs in international trade, especially those between business and government sectors at the national border. Trade facilitation looks at how procedures and controls, governing the movement of goods across national borders, can be improved to reduce associated cost burdens and maximize efficiency while safeguarding legitimate regulatory objectives. Business costs may be a direct function of collecting information and submitting declarations or an indirect consequence of border checks in the form of delays and associated time penalties, forgone business opportunities, and reduced competitiveness.

Table 6.2.   GATS-based investment provisions in RTA services chapters.

Definition	Coverage	Investment Liberalization	Investment Protection	Investment Promotion/ Facilitation Provisions	Dispute Settlement Provisions	Schedule of Commitments
Commercial presence (Mode 3) as one of four modes of supplying Services	All services with carve-outs[18] National measures Sub-national measures State enterprises	**General obligations** — Transparency — MFN treatment — Domestic Regulation — Recognition — Monopolies and Exclusive Service Suppliers — Business practices — BOP Safeguards — General exceptions — Security exceptions — Origin requirements/ denial of benefits	**Specific commitments** — Transfers	— Cooperation/ Capacity Building Mechanisms	State-to-State (separate chapter) Investor-to-state (investment chapter)	Positive list

Source: Extracted from OECD (2006).

Understanding and use of the term "trade facilitation" varies in the literature and amongst practitioners. "Trade facilitation" is largely used by institutions which seek to improve the regulatory interface between government bodies and traders at national borders. The WTO, in an online training package, once defined trade facilitation as: "The simplification and harmonization of international trade procedures" where trade procedures are the "activities, practices, and formalities involved in collecting, presenting, communicating, and processing data required for the movement of goods in international trade."

In defining the term, many trade facilitation proponents will also make reference to trade finance and the procedures applicable for making payments (e.g., via a commercial banks). For example UN/CEFACT defines trade facilitation as "the simplification, standardization, and harmonization of procedures and associated information flows required to move goods from seller to buyer and to make payment."

Occasionally, the term trade facilitation is extended to address a wider agenda in economic development and trade to include: the improvement of transport infrastructure, the removal of government corruption, the modernization of customs administration, the removal of other non-tariff trade barriers, as well as export marketing and promotion.

Trade facilitation has its intellectual roots in the fields of logistics and supply chain management. Trade facilitation looks at operational improvements at the interface between business and government and associated transaction costs. Trade facilitation has become a key feature in supply chain security and customs modernization programs. Within the context of economic development it has also come to prominence in the Doha Development Round. However, it is an equally prominent feature in unilateral and bilateral initiatives that seek to improve the trade environment and enhance business competitiveness. Reference to trade facilitation is sometimes also made in the context of "better regulation." Some organizations promoting trade facilitation will emphasize the cutting of red tape in international trade as their main objective.

Trade facilitation work in the area has been carried out by organizations such as UNCTAD, UN ECE (now through UN/CEFACT) or the WCO for several decades. Steadily growing volumes of trade, together with tariff levels at an all-time low after the conclusion of the Uruguay

Round and modern technology available to significantly improve the management of cross-border trade and distribution of goods have lately created a strong interest from international business in the improvement of the infrastructure for international trade. The losses that businesses suffer through delays at borders, opaque and often redundant documentation requirements, and lack of automation of government, mandated trade procedures are estimated to exceed in many cases the costs of tariffs.

Specific elements connected with the simplification and harmonization of trade procedures are already contained in the WTO legal framework e.g. in Articles V, VII, VIII, and X of the GATT 1994 as well as in the Agreements on Customs Valuation, Import Licensing, Preshipment Inspection, Technical Barriers to Trade, and the Agreement on the Application of Sanitary and Phytosanitary Measures. However, only the Singapore Ministerial gave the mandate to WTO to take a more comprehensive look at trade facilitation.

Regional trade agreements can bring consistency to regulations and procedures between trading countries — something that proponents of trade facilitation tend to support. Annexes to trade agreements can include specification on such practical issues as shared procedures for checking vehicle weights, use of common IT systems, documentation and messaging standards, and mutual recognition of official controls, licences and certificates.

However, many agreements are also annexed by very specific rules and other tariff measures. Governing rules and procedures are often perceived to be poorly or ambiguously drafted, adding cost, and causing confusion. For example, key definitions such as "consignment" and "shipment" in EU veterinary and plant health legislation do not match general commercial practices (see Lacors, 2003, p. 5). Occasionally, rules and procedures may not even be implemented in any practical manner, placing costly obligations on parties who are unable to meet them. For example under the UK's Anti Terrorism Act (2000) and its Information Order (2002) it is theoretically possible for Government executive agencies to ask shipping lines and their agents to provide specific cargo related information to which they have no accession. Similarly, IT systems can place considerable development requirements on businesses, requiring adequate lead-times. Where requirements have been communicated too late or are not clearly defined and documented, implementation and transaction costs are likely to be very high.

Consequently, proponents of trade facilitation will make a strong case for any new proposals, policies and regulations to be pre-notified at the earliest possible stage. There are many variants on this theme, but in principle it hinges on businesses' desire for regulatory controls and procedures to fit their operational requirements. One of the most significant aspects of this theme includes ideas revolving around inland clearance — allowing goods to move outside the port to facilities where checks and controls can be conducted more cost-effectively as, for example, when unloading containers and vehicles at the trader's premises. Other themes look at the use of open information standards for Customs' IT systems that integrate easily with existing commercial software, rather than the *de facto* requirement for using the propriety standards imposed by government system suppliers.

Although consistency in enforcement (a "level-playing field") is desirable for fairness reasons, a degree of operational flexibility is considered necessary by many proponents. Infrastructure and systems can break down or be placed under stress due to unforeseen circumstances (e.g., bad weather, strikes, fires, power-outage, military mobilization, etc.). In such instances traders and operators would call for some degree of leniency, if controls in the prescribed manner are not practical 11. Similarly, operational environments can vary from location to location and rigidly formulated procedures may not always work.

Again, traders and operators may ask for a degree of regulatory flexibility. The worry here is that where rules and procedures are applied inconsistently, it diverts traffic from the most direct route and also distorts competition. Some industries will also make cases for ensuring that regulations do not affect them unfairly. For example, lobbyists working for express parcel carriers frequently lament that national post-office companies, who offer similar services, enjoy significant customs privileges that other parcel operators are unable to take advantage of (e.g., see WCO and UPU, 2004).

Messerlin *et al.* (2000), focuses on the research differently by looking at what can be done at a multilateral level in the vast field of trade facilitation. They concluded, following a qualitative review of trade policy papers on technical regulations, that designing common public norms (e.g., following the example of the EU) may seem the best way to eliminate technical regulations related costs at first glance. However, they argued that such an approach would not be feasible on a multilateral basis. Moreover, they stated that "scientific" evidence 23 has proved to be of poor support during WTO dispute settlements. By contrast, they argued that private initiatives to design standards have been numerous and often successful. Thus, the authors suggest that negotiations may be better focused on supporting Mutual Recognition Agreements (MRAs), possibly under the cover of competition policy.

In sum, this chapter has touched upon several dimensions that are crucial for evolving future negotiating strategies for want of adequate research and understanding especially in the context of RTAs.

CHAPTER 7

Conclusion

In conclusion, it can be stated that regional economic integration could pave way for its members to participate more effectively in the multilateral process of economic change, by providing them with opportunities to experiment with the economic change at a smaller scale and magnitude within the region. This could contribute to their preparedness to the multilateral liberalization process at the larger scale by contributing to their efficiency and competitiveness profiles through cooperation. Thus, the recent attempts of regional integration by India and other Asian countries need to be viewed against this understanding that RTAs are building blocks to the multilateral trading system.

The book takes cognizance of the fact that not only RTAs have proliferated worldwide, they have also deepened in terms of their policy evolution by encompassing trade in goods and services along with investment cooperation.

The book initially documents the major RTA initiatives taken by India in recent times. An overview of India's economic cooperation initiatives and RTA engagements suggests that although being a late entrant, India has embarked upon a multitude of initiatives to harness the dynamics of trade in goods and services cooperation with investment integration with countries of importance. It would be thus crucial to understand the conceptual underpinnings of such initiatives that are often missed out from analysis.

It thus further explores into the economics of RTAs that form the basis for such initiatives. This includes putting forth arguments that balances the conflicting objectives of addressing efficiency concerns on one hand and providing level playing field to domestic stakeholders on the other. It further elaborates the issue of growth convergence possibilities through RTAs among members.

The book in its novel exposition also argues a strong case for converting RTAs as avenues for achieving developmental goals in member countries. To this end, trade creation and diversion are placed in a dynamic setting. The interlinkages between trade in goods and trade in services and their further relationships with investment emerge as the cornerstone of this argument.

A central piece of such an argument is based on proposing a new *developmental* role of Rules of Origin, which is often misunderstood as nontariff barrier in the existing literature. The main argument also rests on the employment generation possibilities of RTAs by relieving the size of market constraints via scale effects.

The book provides new insights from some of the negotiating issues like sensitive lists, substantially all trade, investment cooperation, and trade in services. Some methodologies that cover the spectrum of computable general equilibrium models to trade forecasting and include intra industry trade, trade complementarities, etc. are also used to illustratively bring out the trade and economic gains from some RTA initiatives. To this end, the book strengthens the case for a pan-Asian economic integration.

In summing up it is possible from the analysis of the book to underscore one single point that while the merits of RTAs have been well understood and their potentials estimated empirically, the policy implementation issues leave much to be desired for. It is possible to state that if concerted efforts are made on implementation issues then RTAs may well address the genuine concerns of spaghetti bowl effects. Finally, the book touches upon several dimensions that are crucial for evolving future negotiating policy strategies for want of adequate research and understanding especially in the context of RTAs. These include nontariff barriers, trade in services, rules of origin in services trade, investment cooperation, and trade facilitation.

Bibliography

Agarwala, R (2008). Asia's re-emergence: When can Asia reclaim its place in the world economy. In *Asian Economic Cooperation and Integration: Progress, Prospects and Challenges*, Asian Development Bank (ed.). Manila: ADB.

Ahearn, RJ and WM Morrison (2006). US–Thailand Free Trade Agreement negotiations. CRS Report for Congress. http://www.nationalaglawcenter. org/assets/crs/RL3 2314.pdf.

Ando, M (2008). Economic effects of an ASEAN+6 free trade agreement: A CGE model simulation analysis. Asia Research Report, Japan Center for Economic Research.

Ando, M and T Fujii (2002). The costs of trade protection: Estimating tariff equivalents of non-traiff measures in APEC economics. Paper presented at the Japanese Economic Association Fall Meeting, 13–14 October, Hiroshima.

Applegate, LM, B-S Neo and J King (1993). Singapore tradenet: The tale continues. In Harvard Business School Cases, June 29.

Applegate, LM, B-S Neo and J King (1995). Singapore tradenet: Beyond tradenet to the intelligent island. In *Harvard Business School Cases* Oct, 10.

Baldwin, R (1970). *Non-tariff Distortions of International Trade*. Washington, DC: The Brookings Institution.

Beghin, J and J-C Bureau (2001). Quantitative policy analysis of sanitary, phytosanitary and technical barriers to trade. *Economie Internationale*, 87, 107–130.

Bhagwati, J (1984a). Splintering and disembodiment of services and developing nations. *The World Economy*, 7, 133–144.

Bhagwati, J (1984b). Why are services cheaper in the poor countries? *Economic Journal*, 94(374), 279–286.

Bhagwati, J and TN Srinivasan (1993). *India's Economic Reforms*, Ministry of Finance, Government of India, New Delhi.

Bonapace, T (2005). Regional trade and investment architecture in Asia-Pacific: Emerging trends and imperatives. RIS Discussion Paper No. 92. www.ris.org.in.

Bora, B, A Kuwahara and S Laird (2002). Quantification of non-tariff measures, policy issues in international trade and commodities. UNCTAD StudySeries No. 18 (UNCTAD/ITCD/TAB/19).

Brooks, D, D Roland-Holst and F Zhai (2005). *Growth, Trade and Integration: Long-term Scenarios of Developing Asia*. Manila: ADB.

Budget (2007). Analysis: Reading between the figures (3 March 2007). *Business Standard*.

Cecchini, P (1988). *The European Challenge, 1992: The Benefits of a Single Market*. Aldershot: Wildwood House.

Chandrasekhar, CP and J Ghosh (2010). The Asian Face of the Global Recession. International Development Economics Associates. http:// www.networkideas. org/news/feb2009/Global_Recession.pdf.

COM (2003) 452 Final. European Union customs' modernization programme: Communication from the Commission to the Council, the European Parliament and the European Economic and Social Committee — A simple and paperless environment for customs and trade. http://europa.eu.int/ servlet/portail/RenderServlet?search=DocNumber&lg=en&n_docs=25&do main=Preparatory&in_force=NO&an_doc=2003&nu_doc=452&type_ doc=COMfinal.

Crawford, JA and R Fiorentino (2005). Changing landscape of regional trade agreements. Discussion Paper No. 8. http://www.wto.org/english/res_e/ booksp_e/discussion_papers8_e.pdf.

Das, RU (2004a). Industrial restructuring and export competitiveness of the textiles and clothing sector in SAARC in the context of MFA phase out. RIS Discussion Paper No. 85. New Delhi.

Das, RU (2004b). Rules of origin need proper perspective under trade pacts (10 May 2004). The *Financial Express*.

Das, RU (2006a). Apprehensions need to be set aside for steady progress (11 January 2006). *The Financial Express*.

Das, RU (2006b). Poverty reduction in South Asia through productive employment. SAARC *Regional Poverty Profile 2005*. SAARC Secretariat: UNDP.

Das, RU (2007a). *Feasibility Study of India–Malaysia CECA. Inputs provided to JSG*. New Delhi: RIS.

Das, RU (2007b). Technological advances and industrial characteristics: Some evidence from developed and developing countries. *Economics Bulletin*, 15(4), 1–13.

Das, RU (2008). Draft SAARC Framework Agreement on Trade in Services (SAFAS). Submitted to SAARC Secretariat, Kathmandu.

Das, RU (2009a). Imperatives of regional economic integration in Asia in the context of developmental asymmetries: Some policy suggestions. ADBI Working Paper 172. Tokyo: Asian Development Bank Institute.

Das, RU (2009b). *Regional Economic Integration in South Asia: Prospects and Challenges*. Discussion Paper 157. New Delhi: RIS.

Das, RU (2009c). Regional trade-FDI-poverty alleviation linkages: Some analytical and empirical explorations. Discussion Paper 18/2009. Bonn: DIE.

Das, RU (2010a). Prospects for Economic cooperation under the EAS, mimeo.

Das, RU (2010b). *Rules of Origin under Regional Trade Agreements*. Discussion Paper 163. New Delhi: RIS.

Das, RU and M Kathuria. Non-tariff Barriers: An Analytical Review, mimeo.

Das, RU and RS Ratna. *Rules of Origin: Analysis and Policies*, UK: Palgrave Macmillan.

Das, RU and R Sambamurty (2006). Addressing global growth asymmetries through regional trade integration: Some explorations. RIS Discussion Paper 116.

Das, RU, S Ratanakomut and S Mallikamas (2002). A feasibility study on a free trade agreement between India and Thailand, Prepared for Joint Working Group on India–Thailand Free Trade Agreement (Ministry of Commerce, Govt. of India and Ministry of Commerce, Govt. of Thailand). http://www.depthai.go.th/th/newDep/FTA/India/study/pdf.

Das, RU and M Rishi (2008). Are trade openness and financial development complementary? Paper presented at AEA — ASSA Annual Meeting, New Orleans.

Deardorff, A (1987). Why do governments prefer nontariff barriers? *Carnegie Rochester Conference Series on Public Policy*, 26(1), 191–296.

Deardorff, A and RM Stern (1997). Measurement of non-tariff barriers. OECD Economic Department Working Paper No. 179.

Deardorff, A and RM Stern (1998). *Measurement of Nontariff Barriers: Studies in International Economics*. Ann Arbor, MI: University of Michigan Press. Department of Commerce (2004). Preamble, *Foreign Trade Policy: 2004–2009*. Ministry of Commerce and Industry, Government of India.

Dhar, B (2010). Economics of neighbourhood. *Live Mint & The Wall Street Journal*, 19 July.

Dubey, M (2007). SAARC and South Asian economic integration. *Economic and Political Weekly*, 7 April.

Duttagupta, R and P Arvind (2003). Free trade areas and rules of origin: Economics and politics. IMF Working Paper, WP/03/229.

European Commission (2006). Proposal for a decision of the European Parliament and of the Council establishing an action programme for customs in the Community (Customs 2013) 2006/0075 (COD). COM (2006) 201 final.

Elena, SP, NP Jose Antonio and MN Jose (1999). Endogenous preferential trade agreements. *Journal of Economic Integration*, 14(3), 419–431.

Feenstra, RC and GH Hanson (1994). Foreign direct investment and relative wages: Evidence from Mexico's maquiladoras. *Journal of International Economics*, 42, 397–393

Fink, C and A Mattoo (2002). Regional agreements and trade in services: Policy issues. World Bank Policy Research Working Paper 2852.

Fink, C and M Molinuevo (2007). East Asian free trade agreements in services: Roaring tigers or timid pandas? In *Trade Issues in East Asia: Liberalization of Trade in Services*, Washington, D.C.: East Asia and Pacific Region Poverty Reduction and Economic Management, World Bank.

Fukao, K, G Kataoka and A Kuno (2003). How to measure non-tariff barriers? A critical examination of the price-differential approach. *Hi-Stat Discussion Paper Series* d03-08, Institute of Economic Research, Tokyo: Hitotsubashi University.

Government of India (GOI) (2007). India–Malaysia Joint Study Group (JSG) Report.

GOI (2009a). Annual Report 2008. Ministry of External Affairs. New Delhi: Policy Planning and Research Division.

GOI (2009b). India–New Zealand Joint Study Group (JSG) Report.

Grainger, A (2004). A paperless trade and customs environment in Europe: Turning vision into reality. EUROPRO. www.tradefaciltiation.org.uk/europro.

Griffith-Jones, S, JA Ocampo and JE Stiglitz (eds.) (2010). Time for a Visible Hand: Lessons from the 2008 World Financial Crisis. NY: OUP.

Guilietti, M *et al.* (2005). Testing for stationarity in heterogeneous panel data in the presence of cross section dependence. *Journal of Statistical Computation and Simulation*, 79(2), 195–203.

Hadri, K (2000). Testing for stationarity in heterogenous panel data. *Econometrics Journal*, 3, 148–161.

Hadri, K, C Guermat and J Whittaker (2004). Estimation of technical inefficiency effects using panel data and doubly heteroscedastic stochastic production frontiers. *Empirical Economics, Springer*, 28(1), 203–222.

Hanslow, K, T Phamduc and G Verikios (2000). The structure of the FTAP model (electronic resource): Staff research memorandum. Melbourne: Productivity Commission.

Harrigan, J and R Vanjani (2003). Is Japan's trade (still) different? *Journal of the Japanese and International Economies*, 17(4), 507–519.

Harrison, A and G Hanson (1999). Who gains from trade reform? Some remaining puzzles. *Journal of Development Economics*, 59(1), 125–155.

Haveman, J, UC Nair and JG Thursby (2000). The effects of protection on the pattern of trade: A disaggregated analysis. In *Business and Economics for the 21st Century*, D Kantarelis (ed.). Worcester, MA: Business & Economics Society International.

Hertel, TW (ed.) (1997). *Global Trade Analysis: Modeling and Applications*. NY: Cambridge University Press.

Hindley, B (June 1990). Through a glass darkly: Services in The Uruguay round. Paper prepared for *Conference on the Uruguay Round, Institute for International Economics*.

Hindley, B and A Smith (1984). Comparative advantage & trade in services. *The World Economy*, 7, 369–390.

Hirsch, M (2006). Interactions between investment and non-investment obligations in international investment law. *Trade Dispute Management*, 3(5).

Hoekman, B (1995). Tentative first steps: An assessment of the Uruguay round agreement on services. World Bank Policy Research Working Paper 1455. http://www.ecdpm.org/Web_ECDPM/Web/Content/Navigation.nsf/index2?readform&http://www.ecdpm.org/WebECDPM/Web/Content/Content.n$_s$f/7732def81dddfa7ac1256c240034fe65/5eec2f714800b082c1256eed002c6980?OpenDocument.Information Order (2002).

International Monetary Fund (IMF) (2008). *Direction of Trade Statistics*. International Monetary Fund, Statistics Department.

Japan External Trade Organization (JETRO) (2000). *21-seiki no nikkan kankei waika ni aru beki ka? [How Should the Japan-Korea Economic Relationship in the21st century Be?]*. Tokyo: Japan External Trade Organization.

Jones, RW and SL Engerman (1996). Trade, technology and wages: A tale of two countries. *American Economic Review*, 86, 35–40.

JSG Report (2007). Feasibility Study of India–Malaysia CECA. Government of India and Government of Malaysia.

JSG Report (2009a). Feasibility Study of India–Indonesia CECA. Government of India and Government of Indonesia.

JSG Report (2009b). Feasibility Study of India–New Zealand CECA. Government of India and Government of New Zealand.

Kawai, H and I Tanaka (1996). Measuring the cost of protection in Japan, 1990. IDE-APEC Study Centre, Working Paper Series 95/96-No. 1.

Kawai, M (2004). Prospects for monetary cooperation in Asia: ASEAN+3 and beyond. Presentation at the High-level *Conference on Asian Economic Integration: Vision of a New Asia*. Tokyo: RIS.

Kawai, M and G Wignaraja (2007). ASEAN+3 or ASEAN+6: Which way forward? ADBI Discussion Paper No. 77. Tokyo: Asian Development Bank Institute.

Kemp, S (2000). Trade in education services and the impacts of barriers to trade. In *Impediments to Trade in Services: Measurement and Policy Implications*, C Findlay and T Warren (eds.). London and New York: Routledge, pp. 231–244.

Kesavapany, K (2005). A new regional architecture: Building the Asian community. Public lecture delivered in New Delhi on March 31, 2005. Excerpted in *New Asia Monitor*, April 1, 2005.

Kim, Y-H (2003). *Korea–Japan FTA and Japan's Distribution Barriers*. Seoul: Korean Institute for International Economic Policy.

Konsynski, B and J King (1990). Singapore Tradenet: A Tale of One City. Boston: Harvard Business School Cases. Sept 30 (9-191-009), pp. 1–18.

Korea Institute for International Economic Policy (KIEP) (2000). *Economic Effects of and Policy Directions for a Korea–Japan FTA*. Seoul: Korean Institute for International Economic Policy.

Korea Institute for Industrial Economics and Trade (KIIET) (2002). *Addressing NTB Problems in the Korea–Japan Free Trade Agreement*. Seoul: Korea Institute for Industrial Economics and Trade.

Korea International Trade Association (KITA) (various years). *The Present Status of Japan's Non-tariff Barriers against Korea*. Seoul: Korea International Trade Association.

Krueger, AO (1983). *Trade and Employment in Developing Countries: Synthesis and Conclusions*. Chicago: University of Chicago Press.

Kumar, N (1998). Multinational enterprises, regional economic integration, and export-platform production in the host countries: An empirical analysis for the US and Japanese corporations. *eltwirtschaftliches Archiv*, 134(3), 450–483.

Kumar, N (2001). Flying Geese theory and Japanese foreign direct investment in South Asia: Trends explanations and future prospects. *Journal of International Economic Studies*, 15, 179–192.

Kumar, N (2002). Towards an Asian economic community: Relevance of India. RIS Discussion Paper No. 34. www.ris.org.in.

Kumar, N (ed.) (2004). *Towards an Asian Economic Community: Vision of a New Asia*. New Delhi and Singapore: RIS and ISEAS.

Kumar, N. (2005a). Prosper thy Neighbour in South Asia (15 February 2005). *Financial Express*. http://fecolumnists.expressindia.com/full_column.php?content_id=82602.

Kumar, N (2005b). Towards a Broader Asian Community: Agenda for the East Asia Summit. RIS Discussion Paper 100.

Kumar, N (2007a). Investment provisions in regional trading arrangements in Asia: Relevance, emerging trends, and policy implications. RIS Discussion Paper 125.

Kumar, N (2007b). Towards broader regional cooperation in Asia. Discussion Paper. Colombo: UNDP–RCC.

Kumar, N (2007c). Towards broader regional cooperation in Asia. UNDP-Regional Centre in Colombo Discussion Paper.

Kumar, N, K Kesavapany and Y Chaocheng (eds.) (2008). *Asia's New Regionalism and Global Role: Agenda for the East Asia Summit*. New Delhi and Singapore: RIS and Institute of Southeast Asian Studies (ISEAS).

Lacors (2003). Importation of Goods Subject to Animal or Plant Health Regimes. SITPRO. http://www.sitpro.org.uk/reports/lacors.html.

Laird, S and A Yeats (1990). *Quantitative Methods for Trade-Barrier Analysis*. London: The Macmillan Press Ltd.

Leamer, E (1990a). Latin America as a target of trade barriers erected by the major developed countries in 1983. *Journal of Development Economics*, 32(2), 337–368.

Leamer, E (1990b). The structure and effects of tariff and nontariff barriers in 1983. In *Festschrift*, A Krueger and R Jones (eds.). Robert Baldwin, Basil Blackwell, pp. 224–260.

Lesher, M and S Miroudot (2006). Analysis of the Economic Impact of Investment Provisions in Regional Trade Agreements. OECD Trade Policy Working Paper No. 36, TD/TC/WP(2005)40/FINAL.

Levin, A and CF Lin (1993). Unit root tests in panel data: New results. Discussion Paper No. 93–56, Department of Economics, University of California at San Diego.

Linnemann, H (ed.) (1992). *South-South Trade Preferences: the GSTP and trade in manufactures. Indo-Dutch Studies on Development Alternatives*. New Delhi: Sage.

Lipsey, RG (1970). *The Theory of Customs Union: A General Equilibrium Analysis*. London: Westfield and Nicolson.

Low, P and A Mattoo (2000). Is there a better way?: Alternative approaches to liberalization under the GATS. World Bank.

Madhavan, S (2007). Key changes in customs valuation (7 May 2007). *Business Standard*.

Madison, A (2001). *The World Economy: A Millennial Perspective*. Paris: Organization for Economic Cooperation and Development.

Mattoo, A, RM Stern and G Zannini (eds.) (2008). A *Handbook on International Trade in Services*. Oxford: Oxford University Press.

Mayer, L and A Gevel (1973). Non-tariff distortions in international trade: A methodological review. In *Prospects for Eliminating Non-Tariff Distortions*, Scarlanda, A (ed.). AW Sjithoff/Leiden, p. 316.

MCOT News (2006a). Thailand, January 10. http://etna.mcot.net.

MCOT News (2006b). Thailand, January 12. http://etna.mcot.net.

MEA (2004). www.mea.nic.in. Government of India.

MEA (2009). India foreign relations 2008. Documents, Ministry of External Affairs. Published in corporation with the Public Diplomacy Division, Ministry of External Affairs. Government of India.

Meade, J (1955). *The Theory of Custom Union*. Amsterdam: North Holland.

Mehta, R and S Narayanan (2006). India's Regional Trading Arrangements. RIS-DP 114.

Mei, Z and J Dinwoodie (2005). Electronic shipping documentation in China's international supply chains. *Supply Chain Management: An International Journal*, 10(3), 198–205.

Melvin, JR (1989). Trade in producer services: A Heckscher–Ohilin approach. *Journal of Political Economy*, 97, 1180–1196.

Messerlin, P (2001). *Measuring the Costs of Economic Protection in Europe*. Washington DC: Institute for International Economics.

Messerlin, P. and J. Zarrouk (2000). Trade facilitation: Technical regulations and customs procedures and the role of the WTO. *The World Economy*. Oxford, UK and Boston, MA: Blackwell Publishers.

Michalopoulos, C. (1999). Developing countries in the WTO, World Economy, 22(1).

Milner, C and P Wright (1998). Modelling labour market adjustment to trade liberalisation in an industrialising economy. *The Economic Journal*, 108, 509–528.

Ministry of Foreign Affairs of Japan (MFAJ) (2004). Joint press statement: A Japan–Philippines economic partnership agreement. http://www.mofa.go.jp/region/asia-paci/philippine/joint0411.htm

MFAJ (2005). Joint press statement: Japan–Malaysia economic partnership agreement. http://www.mofa.go.jp/region/asia-paci/malaysia/joint0505.html.

Moazzem, KG (2006). Taking the regional route (16 March 2006). *The Daily Star 15th Anniversary Special*. (www.thedailystar.net/suppliments/2006/15thanniv/investment/invest26.htm).

MoC (2004). Annual Report 2003–2004, Government of India.

MoC (2008). *Handbook of Procedures*, Vol. 1. Ministry of Commerce and Industry, Government of India.

Moenius, J (1999). *The Bilateral Standards Database (BISTAN) — A Technical Reference Manual. mimeo*. San Diego: University of California. Mohanty, SK et al. (2004). Implications of economic cooperation among JACIK economies: A CGE modelling approach. In *Towards an Asian Economic Community: Vision of a New Asia*, N Kumar (ed.). New Delhi and Singapore: RIS and ISEAS.

Mohanty, SK and S Pohit (2007). Welfare gains from regional economic integration in Asia: ASEAN+3 or EAS. RIS Discussion Paper No. 126. www.ris.org.in.

Moreira, MM and S Najberg (2000). Trade liberalisation in Brazil: Creating or exporting jobs?. *Journal of Development Studies*, 36(3), 78–99.

Movchan, V (1999). Welfare costs of certification. *EERC conference proceedings*.

Movchan, V and I Eremenko (2003). Measurement of non-tariff barriers: The case of Ukraine. *Prepared for the Fifth Annual Conference of the European Trade Study Group (ETSG)*, Madrid, Spain.

Mulligan, RM (1998). EDI in foreign trade. *International Journal of Physical Distribution & Logistics Management*, 28(9–10), 794–804.

The Nation (2006a). Bangkok, 12 January. http://www.nationmultimedia.com.

The Nation (2006b). Bangkok, 16 May. http://www.nationmultimedia.com.

OECD (Organisation for Economic Co-Operation and Development) (2001). Trade in Services: Negotiating Issues and Approaches. Paris: OECD.

OECD (2002). The relationship between regional trade agreements and the multilateral trading system — Services, Working Party of the Trade Committee, TD/TC/WP(2002)27/FINAL.

OECD (2003). Regionalism and the ultilateral trading system, http://publications.oecd.org/acrobatebook/2203031E.PDF.

OECD (2005a). International Investment Law: A Changing Landscape. Paris.

OECD (2005b). Novel features in OECD Countries' recent investment agreements: An overview. http://www.oecd.org/dataoecd/42/9/35823420.pdf.OECD (2005c). Relationships between International Investment Agreements. Working Paper 2004/1.

OECD (2006a). Novel features in recent OECD bilateral investment treaties. In *International Investment Perspectives*.

OECD (2006b). Salient features of India's investment agreements. In *Investment for Development*, Annual Report.

Panchamukhi, VR and RU Das (2001). Conceptual and policy issues in rules of origin. *South Asia Economic Journal*, 2(2), 253–279.

Petit, P (1995). Employment and technological change. In *Handbook of the Economics of Innovation and Technological Change*, P Stoneman (ed.). Basil: Blackwell Ltd, pp. 366–408.

Quinn, J and P Slayton (1980). Introduction. In *Non-Tariff Barriers After the Tokyo Round*, Quinn, J and P Slayton (eds.), *Proc. of a conference sponsored by the Canada–United States Law Institute London*, Ontario.

Rajan, R (2006). Monetary and financial cooperation in Asia: Emerging trends and prospects. RIS Discussion Paper No. 107.www.ris.org.in.

Raven, J (2005). A *Trade and Transport Facilitation Toolkit: Audit, Analysis and Remedial Action*. Washington DC: World Bank.

Reade, JJ and U Volz (2009). *Measuring Monetary Policy Independence Across Regions*. Bonn: University of Oxford and DIE.

RIS (1999). SAARC *Survey of Development and Cooperation: 1998–1999*. New Delhi: RIS.

RIS (2002). *South Asia Development and Cooperation Report 2001/02*. New Delhi: RIS. www.ris.org.in.

RIS (2004). *South Asia Development and Cooperation Report 2004*. New Delhi: RIS. www.ris.org.in.

Rodrik, D and A Subramanian (2004). Why India can grow at 7% a year or more: Projections and reflections. IMF Working Papers No. 04/118. Washington: IMF.

Rowley, A. Asian integration needs and overarching framework. (7 January 2004) *The Business Times*, online edition, (6 March 2004) Excerpted in *New Asia Monitor*.

Roy, M (2003). Implications for the GATS of negotiations on a multilateral investment framework: Potential synergies and pitfalls. *Journal of World Investment*, 4(6), 963–986.

Roy, M, J Marchetti and H Lim (2006). Services liberalization in the new generation of preferential trade agreements (PTAs): How much further than the GATS? WTO Staff Working Paper, ERSD 2006–2007.

Rugman MA (1998). The rules for foreign investment in NAFTA. *Latin American Business Review*, 1(1), 77–94.

SAARC Secretariat (1998). SAARC vision beyond the year 2000: Report of the SAARC Group of Eminent Persons, Kathmandu.

Saksena, SC (2005). India's monetary integration with East Asia: A feasibility study. RIS Discussion Paper No. 64-2003. www.ris.org.in.

Sampson, G and R Snape (1985). Identifying the issues in trade in services. *The World Economy*, 8, 171–181.

Sazanami, Y, S Urata and H Kawai (1995). *Measuring the Costs of Protection in Japan*. Washington DC: Institute for International Economics.

Schware, R and P Kimberley (1995). Information technology and national trade facilitation, guide to best practice. World Bank Technical Paper 317. Schedule 7 to the Terrorism Act 2000 (Information) Order 2002.

Sen A (2007). Asian immensities, Keynote Address in commemoration of the 60th Anniversary of UNESCAP, Bangkok.

Sen, S (2008). The Global Financial Crisis: A Classic Ponzi Affair? ISID Working Paper No. 2008/12.

Seth, VK (2006). *Economic of Services*, New Delhi: Ane Books India.

Shankar, V (2004). Towards an Asian economic community: Exploring the past. In *Towards an Asian Economic Community: Vision of a New Asia*, N Kumar (ed.). New Delhi and Singapore: RIS and ISEAS.

Shinawatra, T (2001). Asian cooperation dialogue. Speech delivered in New Delhi on November 28, 2001. Excerpted in RIS Digest, December 2001, 3–5.

Sinha-Roy, S *et al.* (2004). Complementarities and potential of intraregional transfers of investments, technology and skills in Asia. In *Towards an Asian Economic Community: Vision of a New Asia*, N Kumar (ed.). New Delhi and Singapore: RIS and ISEAS.

Sohn, C-H and J Yoon (2001). *Does the Gravity Model Fit Korea's Trade Patterns?* Seoul: Korean Institute for International Economic Policy.

South Centre. The rising tide of South–South investment agreements. (30 November 2004). *South Bulletin 92*.

Stephenson, SM (2002). Regional versus multilateral liberalization of services. *World Trade Review*, 1(2), 187–209.

Stephenson, SM and WE James (1995). Rules of origin and the Asia–Pacific economic cooperation. *Journal of World Trade*, 29(2), 77–103.

Stern, R and B Hoekman (1988). The service sector in economic structure and in international transactions. In *Pacific Trade in Services*, L Castle and C Findlay (eds.). Sydney: Allen & Unwin.

Stiglitz, J, JA Ocampo, S Spiegel, RF French-Davis and D Nayyar (2006). *Stability with Growth: Macroeconomics, Liberalization and Development*. UK: OUP.

Stolper, WF and PA Samuelson (1941). Protection and real wages. *Review of Economic Studies*, 9, 58–73.

Szepesi, S (2004). *Comparing EU Free Trade Agreements: Investment*. Maastricht: ECDPM.

Teo, H-H, BCY Tan and K-K Wei (1997). Organizational transformation using electronic data interchange: The case of tradenet in Singapore. *Journal of Management Information Systems*, 13(4), 139–165.

Terrorism Act (2000). *Terrorism Act, 2000, Chapter 11*. http://www.opsi.gov. uk/acts/acts2000/ukpga_2000001 1_en_1.

Ullrich, H (2004). *Comparing EU Free Trade Agreements: Services*. Maastricht: ECDPM. http://www.ecdpm.org/Web_ECDPM/Web/Content/Navigation. nsf/index2?readform & http://www.ecdpm.org/Web_ECDPM/Web/Content/ Content.nsf/0/DF191BF77F3E50C7C1256F08002B8CFE.

UN/CEFACT (1981). *Recommendation No. 1: United Nations Layout Key for Trade Documents*. Geneva, UN. ECE/TRADE/137: 11.

UN/CEFACT (2004). *Recommendation No. 33: Single Window Recommendation*. CEFACT. Geneva: UN. ECE/TRADE/352: 37.

UNCTAD (United Nations Conference on Trade and Development) (1998). Country-Specific Lists of BITs. http://www.unctad.org/Templates/Page. asp?intItemID=2344&lang= 1.

UNCTAD (2004). *World Investment Report 2004: The Shift Towards Services*. Geneva: United Nations.

UNCTAD (2007). *Trade and Development Report*. United Nations Conference on Trade and Development, Geneva: United Nations.

UNESCAP (2009). RTA Database, Bangkok.

Urata, S and K Kiyota (2003). The impacts of East Asia FTA on foreign trade in East Asia, NBER Working Paper No. 10173.

USDA Foreign Agricultural Service (2005). GAIN Report-E35076. http://www. fas.usda.gov/gainfiles/200504/1 46119474.pdf.

Viner, J (1950). *The Customs Union Issue*. NY: Carnegie Endowment for International Peace.

Walter, I (1972). Non-tariff protection among industrial countries: Some preliminary evidence. *Economia Internazionale*, 25, 335–354.

WCO (1999). *Kyoto Convention. International Convention on the Simplifications and Harmonisation of Customs Procedures*. Brussels: WCO.

WCO and UPU (2004). *Customer Guide: A Joint Publication of the World Customs Organization and the Universal Postal Union*. Bern: UPU.

WTO (2001). Roots: From *Havana to Marrakesh*. www.wto.org. WTO (2006). *World Trade Report 2006: Exploring the Links Between Subsidies, Trade and the WTO*. WTO Publication.

Index

ADBI 165, 166

Anti-dumping (AD) 13, 20, 100, 171, 173, 191, 198

ASEAN Economic Ministers (AEM) 58

ASEAN–India Free Trade Agreement (AIFTA) 59

Asia Pacific Trade Agreement (APTA) 9, 26, 27, 114

Asian Development Bank (ADB) 11, 108, 165, 166

Bilateral investment agreements (BITs) 201–203, 205

Brussels Definition of Value (BVD) 178, 179

CDE 152

change in tariff heading (CTH) 9, 70, 95–98, 197, 198

Comprehensive Economic Cooperation Agreement (CECA) 4, 5, 7, 15–18, 21–25, 59, 96, 162–164

Computable general equilibrium (CGE) 22–24, 145, 147, 150, 153, 154, 157, 161, 162, 164, 168, 216

Constant Elasticity of Substitution (CES) 152, 153

Council for Trade in Goods (CGT) 178

Customs Valuation Rules (CVR) 180

double taxation treaties (DTTs) 201, 202, 205

Early Harvest Scheme (EHS) 4, 14, 15

East Asia Summit (EAS) 29, 30, 59, 60, 164–167

Economic and Social Commission for Asia and the Pacific (ESCAP) 26

Economic Research Institute for ASEAN and East Asia (ERIA) 30, 59, 60

ENT 195

Foreign Direct Investment (FDI) 1, 9, 16, 22, 25, 58, 64–66, 70–73, 79, 80, 101–103, 106, 109, 123, 126, 129, 131, 133, 137, 140, 142, 147–149, 153, 192, 200–206

Free Trade Area (FTA) 4, 7–9, 31, 92, 107, 109, 139, 154

GATT 1, 12, 26, 138, 178, 179, 185, 186, 194, 212

GATT/WTO 1, 2, 186

General Agreement on Trade in Services (GATS) 25, 35, 36, 42,

46, 49, 56, 103, 112, 194, 195, 200, 209, 210
global FDI (GFDI) 64, 65
Global System of Trade Preferences (GSTP) 27, 28, 123, 145
Global Trade Analysis Project (GTAP) 145, 148, 150, 152–154, 156, 162, 166
Government Consumption (GC) 65, 66, 70, 71, 79, 80, 152
gross domestic product (GDP) 20, 22–24, 59, 60, 65, 66, 70–74, 79, 80, 146, 147, 155, 156, 163, 165, 168, 169, 194

Harmonized System (HS) 9, 15, 19, 21, 26, 27, 83, 84, 95–98, 122, 157, 160, 175, 187

information and communication technologies (ICT) 183
intra-industry trade (IIT) 24, 68, 108, 145, 158–160

Joint Study Group (JSG) 21–26
Joint Working Group (JWG) 14

least developed countries (LDC) 9, 27, 32, 50, 53, 94, 114, 120, 123, 139, 205

Most-favored Nation Treatment (MFN) 1, 37, 85, 87, 89, 93, 94, 98, 194, 207, 210
Mutual Recognition Agreements (MRAs) 16, 17, 25, 118, 214

NonAgriculture Market Access (NAMA) 59–61
non-tariff barriers (NTB) 10, 65, 92, 93, 134, 138, 185–189
North American Free Trade Agreement (NAFTA) 71–74, 79, 80, 95, 99, 136, 199, 200, 204

openness of the economy (OP) 66, 70, 79, 80

preferential trade and investment agreements (PTIAs) 201–203
Product-Specific Rules (PSRs) 9, 21, 116
Product-Specific Rules of Origin (PSRs) 21

Qualified Full Banking (QFB) 17
quantitative restriction (QR) 82, 143, 190

regional FDI (RFDI) 65–66, 204
regional trading arrangement (RTA) 1, 30, 31, 66, 67, 96, 97, 111–144, 164, 171, 177, 178, 193, 197, 199, 200, 206, 209, 210, 215, 216
Rules of Origin (ROO) 9, 12–14, 20, 21, 28, 29, 64, 65, 69, 70, 93–100, 111–144, 171, 176, 185, 196–199, 216

Singapore Business Federation (SBF) 17
South Asian Association for Regional Cooperation (SAARC) 9–12, 31, 50, 54, 55, 104, 206

South Asian Free Trade Area
  (SAFTA) Agreement   4, 9–12,
  31, 41, 53–55, 71–74, 79, 80, 104,
  106, 139, 201, 204

Special Economic Zones (SEZs)   17

Tariff Rate Quota (TRQ)   20,
  85–89, 92, 93, 118, 173, 176

About the Authors

Ram Upendra Das is a Senior Fellow at the Research and Information System for Developing Countries (RIS), New Delhi. He obtained his Ph.D. and M.Phil degrees from the Jawaharlal Nehru University, New Delhi. He has conducted a number of studies for various institutions, including the ADB, Commonwealth Secretariat, ILO, EXIM Bank of India, SAARC Secretariat, UNDP and the World Bank. He has also contributed to various studies, including the Joint Study Groups (JSGs), and international negotiating processes on behalf of the Government of India in the context of India's economic engagements with other countries. He has several publications to his credit on issues relating to international economics and development.

Piyadasa Edirisuriya is attached to the Department of Accounting and Finance at Monash University, Australia. He is also a Senior Associate of Financial Services Institute of Australasia (FINSIA). He is the Chief Examiner for a number of undergraduate and post-graduate units at Monash University and has published research work in refereed academic journals articles, books, book chapters and book translations. He has a Master's degree in Economics from the University of New England and a Ph.D. in Economics from La Trobe University, Australia. Before becoming an academic, he served as an Economist to the Ministry of Finance, Sri Lanka, for more than 12 years and has experience in working with the IMF and the World Bank teams in Sri Lanka.

Anoop Swarup is Recipient of the Presidential Award on Republic Day of India in 2003. He joined the Indian Revenue Service (IRS) in 1985 and has been posted in various capacities as Assistant Collector, Deputy Commissioner, Director (Anti-smuggling) and Commissioner of Customs, He has worked as Finance Expert with the UNSC at United Nations (UN) in 2007 and as Vice Chancellor at Shobhit University since 2008. He is the recipient of various prestigious scholarships and fellowships, including UGC scholarship and Fulbright Visitor fellowship to United States in 2005. He holds postgraduate and doctorate degrees in Management, Sciences and also Strategy, as also distinguished by University Gold Medals. He has served on various Panels under UN and those of the Government of India, including the Intergovernmental Panel on Climate Change (IPCC), United Nations Environment Programme (UNEP), International Institute of Strategic Studies, Geneva; National Expert Group on Rules of Origin of the Ministry of Commerce and Industry, Govt of India. He was awarded UNESCAP Hon'ble Mention on HRD for Youth Empowerment (2001). He has represented India in negotiating the Free Trade Agreements with ASEAN, Thailand, Singapore, SAFTA, and MERCOSUR. He has edited several publications including *Nehru Yuva, Yuva Bharat and WCO Asia Pacific Quarterly Journal*; authored books such as *The World of Money Laundering, Financial Crimes and Commercial Frauds*; and has contributed over 200 articles and papers in national and international journals.